MICROCOMPUTERS FOR THE ONLINE SEARCHER

MICROCOMPUTERS FOR THE ONLINE SEARCHER

Ralph Alberico

Meckler Publishing Corporation

Supplement to *Small Computers in Libraries*, no. 3

```
Z
699.3
.A43
1987
```

Library of Congress Cataloging-in-Publication Data

Alberico, Ralph
    Microcomputers for the online searcher.

    Includes bibliographies and index.
    1. On-line bibliographic searching. 2. On-line data processing. 3. Information retrieval. 4. Microcomputers--Library applications. 5. Libraries--Automation. 6. Library science--Data processing.
I. Title.
Z699.3.A43   1986   025.5'24   86-23847
ISBN 0-88736-093-9

Copyright © 1987 Meckler Publishing Corporation.

All rights reserved. No part of this publication may be reproduced in any form without prior written permission from the publisher, except by a reviewer who may quote brief passages in review.

Meckler Publishing Corporation, 11 Ferry Lane West, Westport, CT 06880.
Meckler Publishing, 3 Henrietta Street, London WC2E 8LU, UK.

Printed and bound in the United States of America.

CONTENTS

Introduction	vii
Part One: The Hardware Medium	1
Chapter One: From Dumb Terminal to Memex	3
Chapter Two: Putting It Together	17
Chapter Three: Modems and Telecommunications	41
Chapter Four: Memory	71
Part Two: Software Tools	87
Chapter Five: Operating Systems as Blueprints	89
Chapter Six: Utilities for the Searcher	99
Chapter Seven: Software in General	111
Chapter Eight: General Purpose Communication Tools	117
Chapter Nine: Software for the Search Product	151
Chapter Ten: Specialized Tools for the Searcher	163
Part Three: People and Machines	201
Chapter Eleven: End-users and Gateways	203
Chapter Twelve: Software for Beginners	219
Chapter Thirteen: Expert Systems and the Searcher	235
Chapter Fourteen: Database Products for Micro Users	245
Chapter Fifteen: Value-added Online Searching	261
Glossary	277
Vendor List	287
Index	293

INTRODUCTION

Microcomputers are playing an increasingly important role in the online community. Because rapidly evolving technology has spawned a host of new products for the searcher who uses a micro, librarians and information managers are being confronted with technological, economic, legal, and management questions that were unheard of a few short years ago. Personal computers now function superbly as intelligent communication devices, and that is perhaps where their greatest potential lies.

Hand in hand with this recent technological development has been the increasing sophistication of research techniques. Online databases are becoming more important as sources of information, while the database industry finds itself in a period of upheaval as its members scramble to introduce new products and services directed toward those ultimate information consumers known in the jargon as end-users.

Desktop computers have for the first time placed significant computing power at the searcher's end of the online connection. This development will revolutionize the way in which electronic information is produced, distributed, and consumed. Opportunities exist to change the nature of the search process and the search product.

This book is intended for those people who are in a position to take advantage of personal computing technology as online searchers and information managers. Librarians and professional searchers are certainly among that group. So is anyone who has had experience using online systems and who has the desire to continue gathering information from electronic databases.

This book is not intended for neophyte searchers. It will assume that its readers are already familiar with the basic principles of automated information retrieval as well as the command set of at least one of the online services. It will not simply list and describe available databases. Examples taken from specific databases and search services will be provided to demonstrate how a micro may be used to add something to the search.

Value-added online searching will also be discussed. Micros promise to add value to the search product and the search process. A major emphasis of this book will be the development of small systems that enable researchers to take advantage of the global information network in ways that meet local needs. Micros can be used to custom design solutions to the online research problems of both institutions and individuals who are interested in developing personal information systems.

A basic introduction to hardware, software, and telecommunications will be provided within the context of online searching. Theoretical discussions will be illustrated with examples drawn from situations encountered by searchers. Emphasis will be on selecting hardware and software that can be made to work together for the searcher. Information on types of general purpose software and hardware that are of use to searchers will be provided.

Software designed specifically for the online searcher will be examined in detail and illustrated to show how searching can be made easier and more efficient and how search output can be manipulated for a variety of purposes. Most examples will relate to the IBM PC and its compatibles, which, for a variety of reasons, have become de facto standards in the online industry.

The implications of the use of this technology will also be treated. The widespread use of micros is altering the economics of electronic publishing. Vendors and producers of electronic information are trying to find ways of matching pricing strategies to technological realities. What are searchers paying for--and why? How are micros saving us money and how are they costing us?

Another issue that has its origin in the presence of micros in homes and offices is the end-user phenomenon. This book will examine the issues and look at the ways micros are being used by new searchers. An overview of the approaches taken by libraries and other institutions will be provided. Suggestions will be made for micro-based services that libraries could provide and advice given on adapting off-the-shelf hardware and software to meet the needs of client searchers and the institutions charged with supporting them.

Re-use of machine readable-data is at the center of the downloading controversy. The economic and legal implications of downloading will be examined, but the benefits of downloading will also be discussed. A micro can be used to add value to downloaded data. Personal databases can be created from downloaded records. Numeric and directory data can be manipulated to produce something that is more than the sum of its parts. The search product can be made more attractive, and more useful.

The search process is the subject of intense study. Much of the research centers around the development of front-end and gateway software that mediates between information users and information systems. The principles of artificial intelligence are being used to develop expert systems for searching. Personal computers eventually will play an important role as search intermediaries. Some of the more important experiments will be described and discussed. Trends that are of interest to searchers will also be discussed.

Jargon has long been the bane of those interested in learning about computers. Terms that mean one thing in plain English can mean something entirely different in the language of computer discourse, where simple concepts are often obscured by dense and cryptic terminology. An attempt has been made to keep the use of jargon in this book to a minimum. A glossary that defines terms related to micro-based searching has been included for those who wish to become familiar with the latest buzzwords.

Companies in the computer industry, especially those in the software business, rise and fall like the tides. A list of software vendors has been included. However, readers are advised to consult the trade literature, manufacturers, and yes, even online databases for the latest product developments in an industry not known for its stability.

A list of references/recommended readings has been included at the end of each chapter.

PART ONE
THE HARDWARE MEDIUM

CHAPTER ONE
FROM DUMB TERMINAL TO MEMEX

Antecedents--The World Brain

Let's begin by looking at a couple of classics of the information futurist genre. Both predate personal computing by several decades yet each resonates deeply with the technology of today.

The year is 1937. H.G. Wells travels for the first time to America and delivers a lecture on the "Brain Organization of the Modern World." At the time, Europe is reeling from the effects of the first World War, poised on the brink of the second. Wells proposes a concept he calls the New Encyclopaedism. He hopes it will become a force for world peace and understanding by enabling an international community of learning and cooperation.

Wells speaks of "the abolition of distance," of "an enormous increase of the speed and facility of communications." His vision involves a global network of knowledge and information that "would centralize mentally but perhaps not physically." Compare his description with the "supermarket" online systems of today.

> A World Encyclopaedia no longer presents itself to the modern imagination as a row of volumes printed and published once for all, but as a sort of mental clearing house for the mind, a depot where knowledge and ideas are received, sorted, summarized, digested, clarified and compared.

A global information system, much like the one described by Wells, is emerging. Thousands of databases are now available to inquirers worldwide. The computerization of recorded knowledge has become routine. And Wells, who knew nothing of computers, was able to predict the global information organism which now exists in a nascent form. Ironically, Wells saw microfilm as the driving technology behind his "world brain."

Antecedents--The Memex

Let's move forward in time to the last months of World War II. Vannevar Bush, the man in charge of America's scientific war effort, is turning his thoughts to more peaceful ideas. Bush also is concerned with developing an information system that will contribute to human knowledge and understanding. He wants his ideas to move beyond the boundaries of the scientific community, so he submits his article to the *Atlantic Monthly*, where it receives greater exposure than it would have received had it appeared in a scientific journal. In his classic work, "As We May Think," Bush describes a hypothetical device he calls the memex.

> Consider a future device for individual use, which is a sort of mechanized private file and library. It needs a name, and, to coin one at random, "memex" will do. A memex is a device in which an individual stores his books, records, and communications, and which is mechanized so that it may be consulted with exceeding speed and flexibility. It is an enlarged intimate supplement to his memory.

Bush draws a parallel between his device and the human brain. The memex will not employ the indexing schemes traditionally used to describe and organize recorded knowledge. Nor will it store knowledge as printed pages. The memex will store vast quantities of information in compact spaces just as the brain does. It will allow its users to form dynamic indexes by permitting them to create "associative trails" which connect documents and ideas to one another as they would be connected in the mind. His description of his method for linking records to one another predicts the "windows" that are all the rage among today's computerati. His idea will serve as a model for the most creative minds of the computer era.

The memex is a device that integrates many of the functions performed by the human mind. It is able to store words and pictures and to record both the thoughts and experience of the scientist for whom it is intended. Above all, it makes possible the creation of a complex web of interconnected thoughts, data, images, and documents. Each memex is an extension of its owner's personality. It is a medium which can be made to serve as the extension of a single human mind. It is the epitome of a personal information system.

The World Encyclopaedia, on the other hand is a common store of knowledge, a global civilization comprised of the entire intellectual community and corpus of recorded knowledge. The memex is a city. Its perspective is local, personal, and small scale. The World Encyclopaedia is a civilization. Its perspective is global, social, and large scale.

We are beginning to see something much like the "world brain" as Wells described it. Bush's vision has been more elusive. The memex doesn't exist--not yet. But the formula for the memex is bound to include the personal computer as one ingredient and the existing store of electronically recorded knowledge as another.

Antecedents--Personal Computing

Let's jump forward in time again to the end of the 1960s. During the Vietnam war, a group of brilliant computer scientists have created for the military an electronic, interactive (i.e., online) network called ARPAnet. This technology makes possible a new kind of relationship between person and machine. Interactive online information retrieval systems are now possible. ARPAnet represents a quantum leap toward the world brain. Bush's memex idea influences many of its developers. The members of the ARPAnet team recognize the implications of their invention. One of them, J.C.R. Licklider, has even written a book called *Libraries of the Future*. The computer has become something more than a fast and powerful calculator. It has become a new medium for the exchange of knowledge.

Many of the scientists who develop ARPAnet move on to the Xerox Corporation's Palo Alto Research Center (PARC). Once again, a war is ending and its technology begins to be applied for peaceful purposes. At PARC, the concept of the memex is nourished, and the intellectual and technological foundations of personal computing are laid down. One of the concept's most vocal proponents is Alan Kay, who later goes on to become a scientific consultant to more than one of the big microcomputer manufacturers.

The year is now 1982. IBM startles industry insiders with the introduction of a personal computer to its product line. By 1983, microcomputers have established a strong beachhead. *Time* magazine names the microcomputer its "person of the year" for 1982. People are becoming aware of the micro's potential as a communications medium. Personal computing is entering a new dimension. In 1983 Alan Kay describes the micro as a medium rather than a tool.

> When I say medium, I'm talking about the computer, among other things. The computer is not a tool--that is a very weak characterization of the thing. The tools on the computer are the programs that make it into various kinds of levers and fulcra. The computer itself is a medium like paper--zillions of degrees of freedom, used in many ways that the inventors of it can't and don't need to understand, making a fundamental change in the way people think about the world. Not necessarily a better change, not necessarily boosting intellectual capacities; the book didn't do that--it

simply changed us from one way of doing business to another.

Both the memex and the micro, then, represent modular, integrative technologies. Each system is unique and each is assembled from component parts selected by its builder. The number of possible memexes, and the number of possible microcomputer systems is at least as great as the number of possible structures a child might assemble from a large box of Tinker Toys.

Something More Than a Terminal

Because it is so modular and adaptable, a microcomputer has tremendous potential as an intelligent node on a global information network. Different microcomputer systems can be assembled to interact in different ways with the global system. Each individual and each institution has the capability of designing a tailor-made connection to the universe of electronic information.

Essentially this book is about the quest for the memex. The memex can be designed to meet the needs of a single person, or it can be designed by an institution to meet its own needs as well as the needs of its clients. It is now possible to develop something very much like a memex using easily available hardware and software tools. We will look carefully at the building blocks from which a searcher's workstation can be constructed. First, let's examine some of the reasons a searcher's workstation might be desirable.

The skeptic might say, "Who needs a memex?" Don't we already have a world brain? Won't a simple terminal suffice for connecting us to this pulsating web of information? Isn't a terminal cheaper and easier to use? Why should the person who spends most of the time searching online databases need to learn to use a microcomputer? Wouldn't it be better to concentrate on learning the complexities of the world brain itself--of the online systems where the information resides? After all, terminals have improved. We no longer have to settle for that fading scroll of post-industrial papyrus shed by our trusty Silent 700 terminals. Most terminals nowadays even have a modicum of intelligence.

Data Processing verus Information Retrieval

Yes, but. . . .Terminals and general purpose micros represent two fundamentally different sets of assumptions. Let's begin our analysis by differentiating between data processing and information retrieval.

Data processing is what one does with a terminal. Data (not knowledge) is stored in a central computer (usually in the Data Processing Department) to which are connected terminals. People at the terminals do the same things, ask for the same kinds of information--day after day, week after week, year after year.

Databases are involved but they are qualitatively different from the informational and bibliographic files used in information retrieval. In data processing, databases are highly structured. Records are comprised of clearly defined fields. The contents of each field are unambiguous. The employee's name is either John Smith or it is Jane Doe. A name is a name and when the clerk in Personnel wants to process an employee's record, there is no problem. John Smith's social security number will stay with him for his entire life and his age will always be incremented by one year on his birthday. There is little ambiguity here and little need for deep thought. The routine hardly changes.

Information retrieval is similar on the surface to data processing. Computers are involved, and terminals are connected to them. Beneath the surface however, there are substantial differences. Information retrieval specialists are faced with thousands of possible databases. Record structures vary widely. Most importantly, the contents of the fields that comprise records can be extremely ambiguous. There is no routine. Each search is unique, and outcomes are unpredictable. Deciding which fields to search, which search keys to use and how to put them together requires thought and understanding. Information retrieval is really concerned with ideas, not names, addresses, and social security numbers.

Terminals were invented for the routine, predictable tasks associated with data processing. The terminal is the point of contact between a person and a computer. If the job being done by the person using the computer is straightforward and repetitive, then the terminal needn't be sophisticated. And if it is sophisticated, the sophistication can be wired into the machine and geared to the task being performed. Banks, insurance companies, and airlines have been quite successful at this.

All Terminals Are Divided into Three Parts

All terminals, even microcomputers disguised as terminals, perform at least three basic functions. Terminals enable a person to send information to a computer. Translated into jargon, this is input. The keyboard part of a terminal is the input device. Terminals also

8 Microcomputers for the Online Searcher

enable people to read information that has been sent by a computer. Output is the jargon word for this process. The video monitor is the output device on many terminals. Other terminals require printed output. Online searching requires a printing terminal. Some terminals feature both video and printed output. Print quality generally ranges from terrible to acceptable.

The Texas Instruments Silent 700 is a printing terminal used by many searchers.

The DEC VT100 is one of the most common video display terminals.

The special purpose print/display terminal provided by Mead Data for its LEXIS system has special features not found on most terminals.

10 Microcomputers for the Online Searcher

Microcomputers are often used as terminals. OCLC chose the IBM PC/XT as the terminal for its M300 workstation.

The input device and the output device are easily seen. It would be pretty hard to use a terminal without being able to look at the keyboard and monitor. The third component of all terminals is usuallly hidden from view. It is the device inside the machine to which the cable from the outside world is connected. Its basic function is to translate back and forth between the electrical language of the computer and the language of symbols that people understand. We'll examine it in detail later. In the lingo, it is the communications interface.

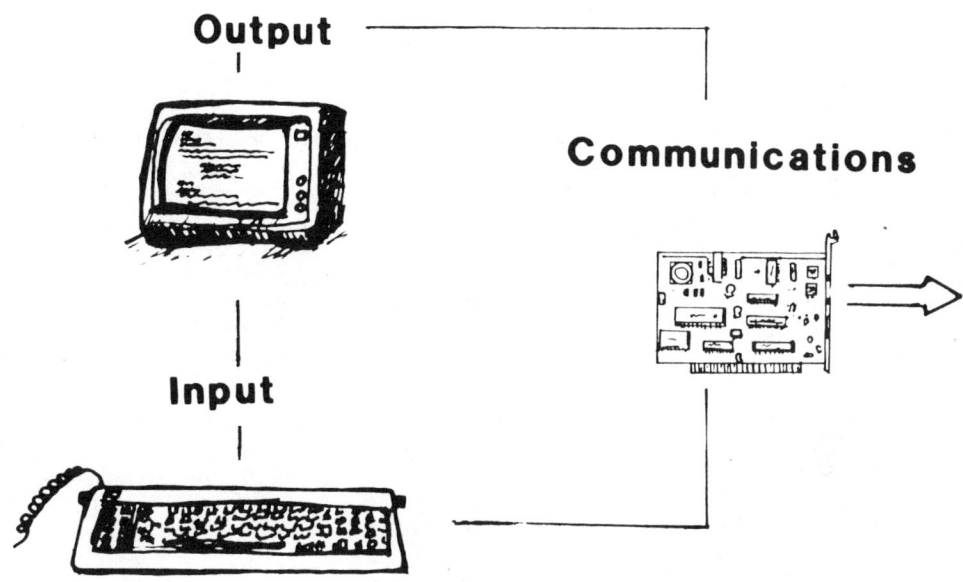

A schematic of simple-terminal components

Intelligent Terminals

Fancier terminals increase the number of basic functional components. Many add a buffer. A buffer is an area of electronic memory that is set aside to temporarily hold information before it is sent or received. A buffer enables the terminal operator to send or receive more than a single character at a time. Some terminals provide buffers that can hold several pages of text. A buffered terminal makes it easier to perform data entry tasks by making keypunching and display independent from the transmission speed of the machinery being used. If information is coming in quickly, it can still be displayed in bite-sized chunks that can be dealt with by the person in front of the terminal. If information is being keyed in slowly, it can be held in the buffer until enough has accumulated to justify transmission.

12 Microcomputers for the Online Searcher

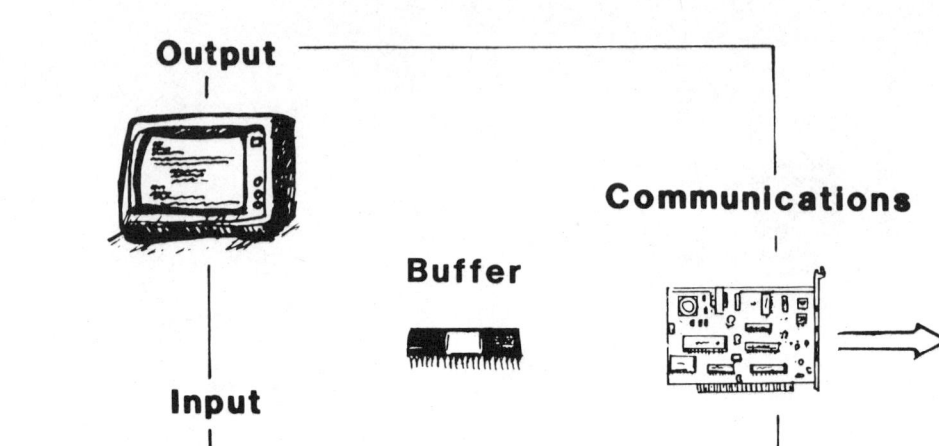

A schematic of a simple terminal with a buffer

Intelligent terminals provide processing capability in addition to buffering. The processor in an intelligent terminal is a chip that is similar to the chip that lies at the heart of every micro. However, the chip in the intelligent terminal can't be as easily instructed to perform the multitude of jobs that can be performed by the processor in a true computer. The "intelligence" of an intelligent terminal is wired into the machine. The instructions that tell the device to function effectively as a specific kind of terminal are part of the hardware.

Among the capabilities of intelligent terminals are greater control of cursor movement, and enhanced display features such as highlighting and reverse video. Some permit the storing of messages and log-on protocols in special keys called function keys. Others are designed for very specific applications and can display forms for data entry. Some begin to cross the dividing line between terminals and computers by permitting programmability and including external storage capabilities.

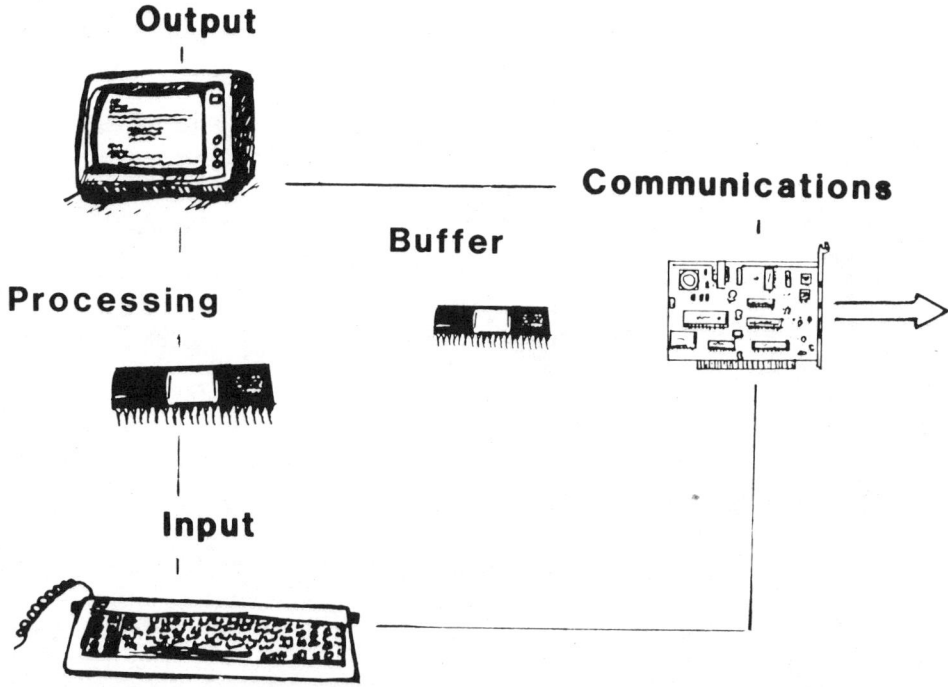

A schematic of intelligent-terminal components

There isn't much difference between a microcomputer and a top-end intelligent terminal. In fact, an intelligent terminal can be quite a bit more expensive than a microcomputer. Many really are microcomputers that have been dedicated to a particular job. Let's not worry about such poseurs. We want to compare microcomputers to garden variety terminals.

What separates a micro from an ordinary terminal? Both allow input and output. Micros don't even usually come equipped with a communications interface. Terminals always do, and many of them have some processing and memory capability. Why is a micro better for information retrieval?

A Medium for Dynamic Communication

A terminal is a device for data processing; a personal computer is a medium of information exchange. As a medium, the computer's uses are infinitely broader. The capabilities of the terminal are fixed by its circuitry. Information retrieval is unpredictable and open-ended. The flexibility of micros suits them ideally for the complexity and ambiguity of information retrieval.

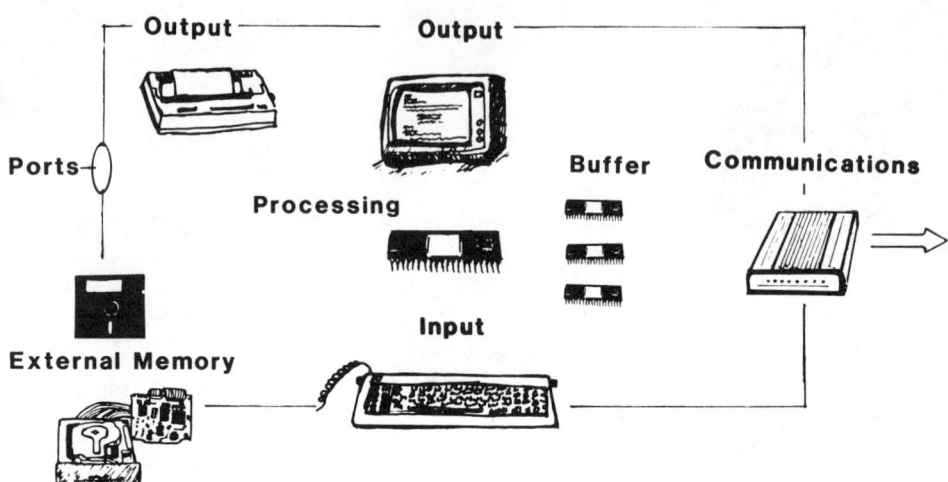

A schematic of the components in a microcomputer with communications capabilities

The activities of an experienced searcher, especially one who is employed by a library or corporate information center, extend far beyond the online session itself. As a specialized tool, the terminal can be of great help to the searcher. But the use of the terminal is limited to the online session. It is not programmable. It can't be taught to do anything other than the task for which it was originally designed.

A communicating micro is as much a medium for the software being used as it is a piece of hardware. And software can be used to help construct a search strategy or suggest a source database. It can be used to handle billing and accounting. It can reformat search results for a nicer finished product. It can sort and rank search results. Local databases can be constructed from online data. Software can be made to control the interaction between the online system and the user. It can help to teach people how to use online systems. Oh yes, it can also establish a communications link with any online system. Programs are tools.

A terminal is complete when you buy it, but a personal computer is never finished. Hardware can be added to accommodate short-, medium-, or long-term storage. Components can be plugged in to improve the quality of display or the printed product. Communication speed can be increased, as can the number of connections with the electronic universe. Hardware components are electronic Tinker Toys.

Hardware and software combined provide the medium and the tools from which information structures can be assembled. The online electronic civilization provides a limitless source of information raw material. Right now, in the academy and in industry, in libraries and offices, people are beginning to build memexes. Each will fit into the larger scene in a different way, each will provide its own conduits to the world beyond, and eventually, as more memexes communicate with one another, a new type of world brain will evolve.

References/Recommended Reading

Bush, Vannevar. "As We May Think." *Atlantic Monthly* 176, no. 1 (July 1945): 101-108.

Kay, Alan. "Learning vs. Teaching With Educational Technologies." *EDUCOM Bulletin* 18, no. 3/4 (Fall/Winter 1983): 16-20.

Licklider, J.C.R. *Libraries of the Future.* Cambridge, MA: MIT Press, 1965.

Rheingold, Howard. *Tools for Thought.* New York: Simon and Schuster, 1985.

Wells, H.G. *World Brain.* Garden City, NY: Doubleday, 1938.

Williams, Martha E. "Electronic Databases." *Science* 228, 26 April 1985, 445-456.

CHAPTER TWO
PUTTING IT TOGETHER

Hardware Basics for Searchers

The post-industrial society is no longer the clairvoyant vision of a few sociologists and economists. Evidence of the information society forecast by Daniel Bell and others is hard to ignore. The predictions concerning the number of "knowledge workers" in the economy have certainly come to pass. Online searching, at one level, is knowledge work of the highest order, for the mastery of system and subject that make a good searcher cannot easily be delegated to the machine. Searchers deal with ideas. The machine is only a medium that makes it possible to move and manipulate information.

However, at another level--a lower level to be sure, but a vital one--the machine is able to outperform the human by many orders of magnitude. Until recently the computing power brought to the search process was concentrated at the host system's end of the search connection. The microcomputer has the potential to add computing power to the other end of the connection--to place it in the hands of the searcher.

Conventional wisdom has it that software is more important than hardware. It probably is, but nothing can happen without certain basic hardware components in place. You don't have to think about what your hardware is doing while you're searching. You can't see the electricity moving around from place to place, representing information. Neither are you aware of the electrochemical transformations taking place in your brain as you write a letter or participate in a conversation. Without that brain, though, intellectual activity would not be possible. And without hardware, the higher level search activities handled by people and software would not be possible.

General Considerations

Your brain came as part of the basic package when you were born. Hardware you have to buy. And choosing a system that meets your needs as a searcher and fits your budget can be quite daunting. Let's begin by examining some of the general considerations upon which purchase decisions might be made.

- We have a limited amount of money to spend and we don't want to spend it all on hardware; we want to save some for software and database connect charges.

- Despite the fact that we don't want to spend a lot of money initially, we do want a machine that can be expanded to take advantage of future developments in hardware and software.

- As searchers we will need a machine whose communications, processing, storage, display, and output characteristics will enable us to deal with the large quantities of information available from online vendors.

- We want it to be cheaper to search with our micro than it was to search with our 300-baud, acoustically coupled terminal, and we want the final product that we supply to our clients to be more attractive and more useful to them.

- We would also like equipment that is durable enough to be used by clients who are interested in performing searches for themselves.

- We want a machine that can be used for other purposes when we're not using it for searching. Let's imagine our machine will be in a library reference department, and that we would also like to be able to use it to produce bibliographies, library guides, and in-house databases.

- Flexibility is one of our primary concerns. Eventually we would like a hardware configuration that is custom-designed to meet the local needs of our staff and clients, but we want to build our custom-designed system from standard components that are widely available and easy to get fixed if they should break.

Of course, the specific hardware choices made will be based on our unique situations. Among the factors to consider are the volume of searching done, the types of searches done, the needs of clients, and whether searching is done by information professionals or the clients themselves. For example, the searcher who does numerous demonstration searches at classrooms scattered around a large campus would probably want to get a portable, while the library that wants to make micros available for client-searchers would probably want a machine that could withstand heavy use and that could easily be secured.

De Facto Standards

Some of the choices have already been made. De facto standards exist. When it comes to hardware for searching, no matter whose product you buy, there are two names you have to reckon with-- IBM and Hayes. Like it or not, those companies have set the standards, and if you want the widest choice of software and to be on the same wavelength as most everyone else, you should buy hardware that is compatible with their products. The arguments in favor of IBM and Hayes compatibility have already been made in many places. Software availability, a large user group, OCLC's choice of IBM for their M300 workstation, and an established performance record are among them. Chances are that if you are employed by a large organization, the choice has already been made for you at the institutional level.

People do search with non-IBM compatible machines. You don't have to have an IBM compatible. Nor does a modem really care about the kind of computer to which it is connected. Almost all communicating micros use the RS-232 electrical standard, one of the few true standards in the industry. There are rumblings about the Macintosh's superior communications abilities and several of the major communications programs are available for the Mac. RACAL-VADIC's communications program *GEORGE* was renamed *MacGEORGE* for that machine. Nevertheless, the IBM PC and its compatibles predominate in the online marketplace.

Things aren't as simple as they seem, though. IBM has set the standard for micros and Hayes has set the standard for modems, but there are dozens of IBM and Hayes clones on the marketplace. And there are printers and other peripherals to buy as well as numerous options regarding what to put inside your micro. Maybe you already have a micro that you're using for something else. If you want to adapt it for searching, most of your decisions will relate to software, but you'll probably still have to buy a modem and maybe some other pieces of hardware as well.

Alternatives

It is unarguable that certain companies dominate in the production of personal computers, but now that some standards have been imposed there is a smorgasbord of basic systems from which to select. Relatively new American companies like Compaq and Kaypro have had great success with PC compatibles. Mainline companies like Zenith, IT&T, and AT&T have changed operating systems and hardware specifications to conform to IBM standards. Foreign manufacturers like Epson and the Korean producer of Leading Edge micros have introduced quality products at low prices. And everyone has attempted to improve in some way upon IBM's basic design while beating its price.

It is also possible to buy build-it-yourself kits. Those in the know say that building a kit is the best way to really understand the hardware. Generic micros are also an alternative. Components are assembled or imported, and marketed via direct mail by companies in every region of the U.S. True, it isn't much fun mailing computers back and forth. Also true that some of the generic machines are real featherweights. But the technology is changing so rapidly and the generics are getting so cheap that it may soon be possible to write off the cost of a generic as a learning experience, a prologemena to buying a sturdier, more expensive, and technologically more advanced machine. Large organizations might consider the cost of providing a cheap generic to each employee as a necessary training expense, required for speedy expansion of staff computing knowledge.

IBM's marketing strategy has always been that of the classy a la carte restaurant that charges separately for each item on the menu. A meal is more expensive that way, but high expectations are usually satisfied. Expensive restaurants that serve bad food quickly go out of business.

Other manufacturers are more similar to restaurants that sell complete, multicourse meals. Most throw in the monitor and communications hardware as part of the package. Others offer an All You Can Eat Buffet that offers most of the major hardware and software entrees. Kaypro and Leading Edge are examples of buffet systems. Some manufacturers, like exotic ethnic restaurants, have focused on a single clientele. Zenith offers impressive discounts to educational institutions and government agencies.

Small is Beautiful

Many of the early entries in the compatible field offered portable computers that nicely filled a niche initially left vacant by IBM. Companies like Compaq, Kaypro, and the ill-fated Osborne made their names in the portable field. The original portables weren't really easy to lug around but it was possible. Most weighed between twenty-five and fifty pounds. Bulk was also a factor.

A new generation of truly lightweight portable micros has sprung into being. Weighing fifteen pounds or less and including everything from monitor to disk drives, they represent an important evolutionary step. Improved display technologies are the basis of such machines as the IBM Laptop, the Zenith Z-171, and the Radio Shack S-100. Flat screens able to display output of acceptable size and sharpness are available on all of the new lightweights. In 1986 Zenith signed a contract with the Internal Revenue Service to supply several thousand of its battery-equipped Z-171s.

In many ways, portables are ideal machines for searchers. Searchers in academic settings will appreciate the ease with which portables can be used for demonstration searches and instruction sessions. Portables enable those who work standard 9-to-5 hours to take the machine home with them and conduct searches after hours when costs are lower. For better or worse, an increasing amount of homework is being done by employees of a variety of organizations. Portable machines have made possible site-independent personal computing.

"Telecommuting" is now a real possibility for many knowledge workers. Self-employed professional searchers can take advantage of the ability to bring their computers to the offices of their clients for training, demonstrations, consultation, and the delivery of online-based products and services. Journalists and other researchers who travel frequently can use a communicating portable to connect to a wealth of online information. For the researcher with a communicating portable, the world brain is only as far away as the closest telephone jack.

The memex idea is evolving in that direction. Alan Kay and the others at Xerox PARC envisioned a small-scale, easily portable version of the memex called the Dynabook. The Dynabook is seen as a new medium merging the potential of the book with the possibilities of the computer. Telecommunication is a vital link in the Dynabook concept, connecting notebook-sized computers to vast quantities of text and graphic information that can be displayed in high resolution on the "pages" of the Dynabook. The Apple Macintosh embodies many of the Dynabook's principles. Unfortunately, easy portability and a self-contained power supply are missing. Future generations of portables may fill in the gaps.

Follow the Electricity

Both the computer and the library literature are replete with advice on buying hardware. Read the reviews. Talk to people. Narrow the field. Try to see it in action and look at the specs. Visit the stores. . . .By all means do those things. But when it comes to searching, it may be ultimately more useful to think of hardware as something that makes it possible to move information--information-cum-electricity--from place to place. So, to paraphrase Deep Throat's advice to Woodward and Bernstein, "Follow the electricity."

The hardware ads always show computers sitting on pedestals in clean, starkly modern environments. You never see the tangled cables, the piles of paper, the manuals spread out on the table top in wild disarray. But the wires and cables come with the rest of the paraphernalia and, when everything's clicking, there is electricity flowing through those wires. So, since the wall outlet is where the electricity comes from, it's as good a place as any to begin.

Surge Protection

A surge protector is one of the least expensive pieces of equipment you can buy. A plug-in surge protector is never part of the package; you have to buy it separately, and you might never need it. But it's the best insurance policy against the electrical demons who are hiding in the wires waiting for the opportunity to erase your computer's memory and shock its circuits into submission.

You can spend as little as ten dollars on a surge protector or as much as several hundred. Expensive models are full of circuitry that is able to clamp down and dissipate power surges and voltage spikes caused by lightning, appliances, or the power company. Good surge protectors are able to respond to electrical irregularities with speeds in the low nanoseconds range. Monitors, printers, modems, and other peripheral devices also require protection, so surge protectors can include several outlets.

The author once had the sobering experience of coming to work on a Monday morning and discovering that power problems caused by electrical work on campus had charred his $15 hardware store surge protector and vaporized the fast blow fuses inside of it. As a surge protector, it wasn't much good anymore; it had a brighter future as a charcoal briquet. But it had sacrificed itself for a good cause. The computer equipment that was plugged into it remained unscathed.

Some models will survive a jolt, others won't; most will protect your equipment nevertheless. The May 27, 1986 issue of *PC Magazine* includes the results of extensive laboratory tests. Some surprises can be found in the reports of the tests. The companies with the largest advertising budgets don't necessarily make the best surge protectors.

PC's technicians made the ironic discovery that circuitry often provided for the suppression of electrical noise sometimes interfered with a device's ability to protect against power surges. In any case, don't count on a noise-filtering surge protector to help you out with line noise, that bane of searchers which comes from the telephone exchange, not the power outlet.

The Power Supply

After it leaves the surge protector, the electricity travels up the cord and into a device known as the power supply. The power supply converts the alternating current that comes out of the wall outlet to direct current that the computer is able to use for representing information. Power supplies are rated according to the number of watts of direct current that they are able to deliver to your computer. IBM's original PC is rated at 60 watts (a small power supply by today's standards) and IBM's XT is rated at 130 watts.

The inside of a PC/XT with one floppy and one hard disk drive. Clockwise from upper right are the power supply unit, the hard disk drive, the floppy drive, and several expansion cards in slots on the system board.

When we buy our computer let's not scrimp on the power supply. An expandable system is one of our goals, and the amount of electricity our power supply is capable of delivering will determine the number of options we will be able to add to our machine. Let's try to get a machine with a power supply that's at least as large as the XT's 130 watts. Remember that all of those nifty add-ons that we can't afford right now will increase the system's demand for electricity once we are able to install them.

Electrical Traffic Control

After it leaves the power supply, the electricity that will ultimately become information (now direct current at much lower voltage levels) flows into a circuit known as the bus. The bus is the main circuit along which information-laden electricity travels. Separate buses handle power, control signals, instructions, and actual data.

To the bus are connected the various chips, circuit boards, and devices that manipulate and transform electrical information. The additional cards and devices that will eventually be connected to the bus make the number of available connection points (called expansion slots) an important consideration. IBM's original PC came with five slots. The XT is equipped with eight. Let's try to get at least as many as the XT provides while remembering that many machines nowadays (unlike IBM) come with quite a few of the slots already occupied by a variety of circuit boards (cards).

Within the computer, electricity travels from place to place along parallel lines in much the same way that vehicles travel in parallel lanes on a freeway. "Architecture" is a term often associated with computer hardware. Think of the parallel pathways within the computer as eight-lane highways within a large city. The city has an architecture that evolved to facilitate human activity. There is a transportation network that enables people to move from place to place. There are places (public and commercial buildings) at which people can congregate and enter into various exchanges with one another. Most people in the city also have a place they call home, and each apartment, house, and building has an address.

The computer also has an architecture. There are pathways along which electricity can travel, points at which electrical exchanges and transformations occur, and addresses where specific pieces of information reside. Traffic signs and signals control the flow of humans within the city. Traffic within the computer is controlled and synchronized by a clock that sets the speed limit and enforces it vigorously.

The Clock

The clock in most microcomputers sets the speed limit according to a frequency of 4.77 megahertz. Some of the newer micros, in additon to having a 4.77 MHz clock speed, are capable of operating at the faster speed limit of 8 MHz. Some software will not operate properly at the higher clock speed, so those machines generally allow their users to toggle back and forth between the different speeds. Such high-speed machines are often referred to as turbos.

Don't confuse the clock that is part of the computer's processing unit with the circuit board component known as a clock/calendar. The clock/calendar-equipped card is similar to the clocks we are all familiar with, the ones that hang on the wall and wrap our wrists. The clock in the processor is an intricate timing device; a clock/calendar is a device for keeping time.

Control is the main purpose of the processor clock. Every computer has one whose crystal works generate steady pulses that control all the action. The clock/calendar isn't as domineering. It can be made to give the signal that sets things in motion, but it is a lot more flexible, like an alarm clock that can be turned off on Saturday. Software is the tool used to set the clock/calendar. Though it is an extra that most can live without, a clock/calendar can add value to the searcher's workstation and serve as a medium for a useful group of software tools.

Some software will make the clock/calendar-equipped computer keep track of all activity on your machine. The electronic log of computer time produced by the software can be quite useful when tax time comes if you're a freelance professional searcher. The clock calendar can also be set to wake up the computer and conduct a prerecorded search at 4 A.M when things ought to happen faster than they would during the work day, or be used to process document delivery or interlibrary loan requests or other tasks that don't require the presence of a person for high-level online interaction. Clock/calendars open up the night for your computer. The machine can work while the person relaxes.

If you're adding a circuit board for some reason, and there are lots of good reasons, by all means add a clock/calendar. You can usually tell if the add-on board you've purchased has a clock/calendar by looking for a little battery. Since the clock and the calendar have to work when the computer's power is turned off, a battery is required.

Parallel versus Serial

A network of eight-lane highways is practical and efficient for intracity traffic. However, it would be prohibitively expensive to build a system of eight-lane highways for traffic between cities. Computer-to-computer exchanges over large distances pose similar problems. A different type of pathway is required for long distance traffic. Once it leaves the computer, electricity--rather than travelling along parallel lines--travels along the equivalent of single-lane highways in what is known as serial transmission. Since online searching is by definition computer-to-computer communication, our machine must be equipped for serial transmission.

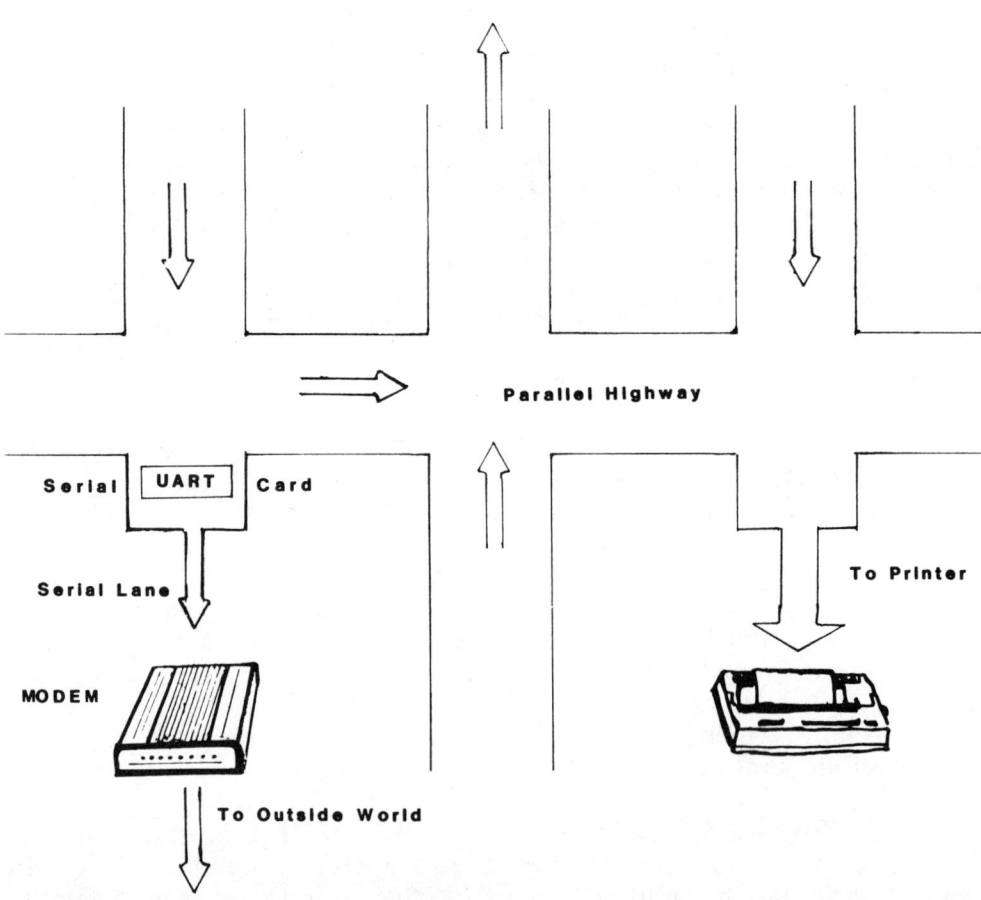

A simple schematic of parallel vs. serial printing

Putting It Together 27

Within the machine, parallel transmission of information works fine. The clock and other chips insure that the flow is synchronized and controlled. The relatively short distances between components keep the expense of wiring everything together to an acceptable level. If the information is to leave the machine, though, some way of channeling those eight lanes of electrical traffic into the single lane that connects to the outside world is required. And it is also necessary to route incoming messages from the outside from the single lane they arrive on to the eight-lane circuitry inside the machine. We're really talking about a sixteen-lane highway system with eight lanes going in each direction. The circuit board that handles this task is known as a serial card because it converts parallel to serial and vice versa.

The Asynchronous Micro

Serial transmission requires that each character transmitted be individually synchronized by the addition of framing bits called start and stop bits. Some forms of computer communication don't require the synchronization of each character. Each computer's operation is precisely synchronized with the other's making it possible to transmit information in large chunks. This form of communication is called synchronous transmission and is hardly ever used with micros.

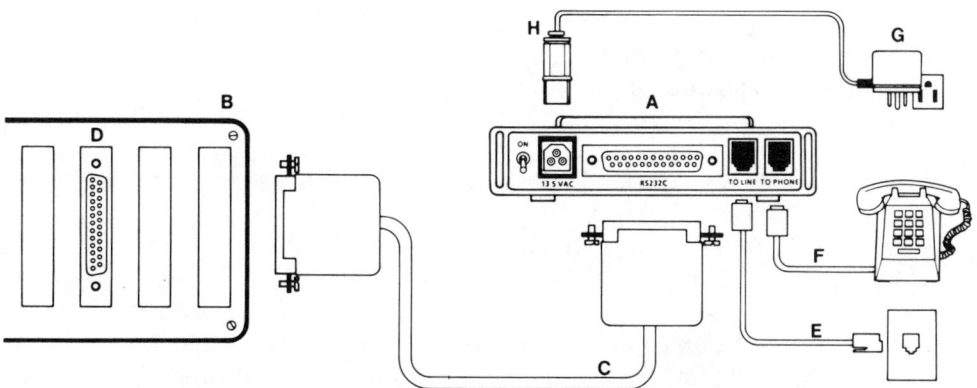

This schematic illustrates how the Hayes Smartmodem (A) is connected to a PC (B). Cable (C) connects the computer's serial port (D) to the RS-232 connection on the modem. Two phone lines (E, F) allow a telephone to be connected to the same line used by a modem. A transformer (G) steps the power down so it won't damage the modem's delicate circuits. (Courtesy: D.C. Hayes, Inc.)

Micros use the form of communication in which each character is individually synchronized. It is known as asynchronous transmission and the serial card is also referred to as an asynchronous communications card. The information entering the card from the bus is travelling along eight parallel lines. The information leaving the serial card through a port at the back of the machine marches single file through a connector known as a DB-25 (because it has twenty-five pins). The chip that actually accomplishes this electrical legerdemain is known as the UART (Universal Asynchronous Receiver Transmitter).

Many machines nowadays come with serial ports built in. If you want to use an external modem and your computer doesn't come equipped with a serial card, you'll have to buy one. Remember that the serial card will occupy one of the expansion slots. It is also possible to buy an internal modem which, in addition to being a modem, contains the parallel-to-serial, serial-to-parallel circuitry needed for asynchronous data communications. We'll talk more about modems later.

So far we've seen how electricity moves around within the machine and how expansion slots are used to route that electricity into devices known as cards, where it can be transformed, manipulated, or simply stored. We know that at the very least, we'll require either an asynchronous card with an external modem or an internal modem on a card. One of the things with which we've been concerned is the flow of information within the machine and the connection points at which electricity is transformed from one type of information to another.

Where the User Meets the Machine

Still focusing on the most basic of systems, let's now examine the flow of information between human and machine. The keyboard/monitor combination more than any of the other circuits or devices in the architecture has come to connote computer. Perhaps this is because within our information traffic system, the human is the link in the loop between keyboard and monitor. When you search with a micro, the monitor becomes your window on the information universe and the keyboard becomes your voice.

The Keyboard

On the top of any keyboard are symbols that people have proven quite capable of understanding and manipulating. Put together in the right ways, those letters, numbers, and symbols express the depth and breadth of human experience. Underneath the keys on which those symbols have been inscribed are--you guessed it-- electrical connections. You choose the symbol. Press the key and it's transformed into light on the screen of your monitor, printing on a piece of paper, an arrangement of electrons on a piece of coated mylar, or an electrical impulse received by a computer on another part of the planet.

How does it happen? It's really more of a software trick than anything else. The keyboard itself is just a collection of eighty or so little switches called keys. What each key means and how the monitor responds when a key is pressed are actually determined by instructions etched onto a ROM chip in the computer's innards. The group of instructions that control the keyboard and monitor are called the BIOS (Basic Input Output System). So the meaning of the keys on the keyboard is determined by software. This fact and the fact that software can be used to redefine key meanings have important implications for searchers.

But we're talking about hardware here so let's get back to the keyboard. What kind of keyboard does a searcher need? Keyboards are pretty similar to one another, especially if you don't want to spend a lot of money on one of the super duper models. The ergonomicist who designed the IBM PC/XT's much-maligned keyboard will probably testify that the size and location of the keys are important factors. With minor variations and a few major exceptions, such as the British-made Maltron (which looks as if it were designed by Henry Moore), most keyboards use the QWERTY key layout that we all know and love.

Searchers will want large, easily identified Return and Shift keys. A Break key would also be nice, but remember the meaning of the key is determined by software. The feel and sound of the keyboard are also important. IBM's keyboard feels substantial. It outweighs most of the clone keyboards by a wide margin. If you need a machine that will be used frequently by a variety of people, a heavy duty keyboard is important. A noisy keyboard does give you lots of feedback, which can be helpful, but there are many situations in which the clickety clack can be a nuisance.

The Monitor

Keyboards always come as part of the basic system so the keyboard decision becomes part of a larger decision. Unless, that is, you happen to like everything about a system but the keyboard, in which case you could buy one for a hundred dollars or more depending upon your taste. Monitors, on the other hand, often don't come as part of the package and a choice must be made. The monitor is your window on the search world, so it is important to get one that you can live with.

You can buy a color monitor for searching (and there are two kinds to choose from, composite and RGB), but you don't really need to. A few of the search assistance packages make use of color but it isn't required, and the searcher's domain is still one of words and numbers. The words and numbers displayed on the screen if they are to be sharp enough to be read easily must be filtered through a graphics or monochrome adaptor card that provides for the high-resolution display of text.

A monochrome monitor is sufficient for searching (in many cases more desirable), but be sure to get one with a card for display of text. Oops, there goes another expansion slot. A composite monochrome monitor just doesn't get it for the searcher, who should be able to concentrate on the content of the information being displayed without having to concentrate on trying to read it.

Monochrome means one color, but there is more than one color from which to choose. The usual colors offered are ethereal green, amber, which is said to be easier on the eye, or electric white. Most monitors provide a standard display of twenty-five lines and eighty columns per screen, a configuration that is often inadequate for searchers.

For those high rollers who can afford $1,395 for a monitor, the MicroDisplay Systems company (800-328-9524) offers the GENIUS VHR monitor. This monitor looks more like a standard sheet of paper than a computer monitor. Its screen display of sixty-six lines by eighty columns makes it more similar to the format we print-oriented types are used to. It's also supposed to be exceptionally sharp. There are those who say it's a throwback to print-on-paper, which isn't supposed to be the searcher's domain, but if it is, it's the kind of throwback that most searchers would appreciate.

One reason for the proliferation of independently produced display devices is the ho hum nature of the display technology being peddled by IBM. Multiple windows and the use of a mouse input device to control icons on a high-resolution, bit-mapped graphics screen were developed by the pioneers at Xerox PARC in the early 70s. IBM, always the last to shed its three-piece suit and jump into the pool with everyone else, is well behind Apple (Macintosh, Lisa) in this area. As displays gain in sharpness and graphic capability,

Putting It Together 31

The image on the GENIUS display monitor from MicroDisplay Systems of Hastings, Minnesota, bears a surprising resemblance to a printed page.

we can expect to see more display-oriented software. Currently, however, most software for searchers is quite businesslike and doesn't take advantage of graphic display capabilities.

Liquid Crystal and Plasma Displays

Encouraging technological advances are being made in nonvideo display technologies. The quality of liquid crystal displays (LCDs) is improving. The LCDs found in the newest generation of portables are far superior to the dim, easily washed away images of a few years ago. Plasma displays hold even greater potential as low-power, lightweight, flat, high-resolution displays. Notebook-size computers will almost certainly incorporate one of these display technologies.

The search process itself is somewhat different when a monitor is used rather than a printout. The limitations of human short-term memory necessitate more frequent requests from the vendor for a display of previously created sets. Scrap paper becomes an important way of keeping track of the sets you've created before they scroll off the top of the screen. The speed with which information travelling at 1200 baud moves across the face of the monitor can also add a rather frenetic edge to the search.

Printers

Anyone who uses a computer knows that the machine is more likely to increase the amount of paper to be dealt with than it is to reduce it. Monitors are fine for conducting a dialog with an online system. A monitor is the preferrable output device for the search process. But when it comes to the search product, the printer still reigns. Despite all the talk about the paperless future, the printed word remains as the most important mode of information exchange, even when it comes to online search results. The printer is a vital part of any online workstation. As emphasis on the search product increases, the role of the printer becomes even more important.

Printers have been called the bad boys of computer systems. They are hard working and tough, but they are likely to be unruly and difficult to control. Printers have one foot in the world of electronics and the other foot in the noisy, messy, realm of mechanical things. Printers require constant attention. Paper has to be loaded, ribbons have to be changed, and, because moving parts are involved, printers break down regularly.

Choosing a printer for an online workstation is not an easy

task. There are literally hundreds of manufacturers from which to choose. The big manufacturers each have four or five different models, which are changed every six months or so. There are at least five or six basically different technologies involved. The advantages presented to the searcher by one technology are hardly ever duplicated by the others. Compromises must be made.

The searcher's financial resources and searching environment will determine which type of printer is best. Is the search product the most important thing, or is the search process? Is speed a consideration? Noise? Cost? Convenience? Let's look at the strengths and weaknesses of different printing technologies from the point of view of the searcher.

Dot Matrix Printers

The most common type of printer is the dot matrix. There are different kinds of dot matrix printers, but most form characters by striking a ribbon with pins that are located in the printhead. The dots formed by the impact of the pins are arranged on a matrix in different configurations to yield a variety of type fonts. The quality of the type produced by these printers can vary from illegible to excellent. The cost of these machines is subject to the same wide variation.

The big advantages of dot matrix printers are low cost and high speed. The big disadvantages are print quality and noise. Those disadvantages are overcome by some of the better dot matrix printers, but the price advantage is sacrificed, and the cost of high quality is usually slow speed. Nevertheless, the dot matrix printer is the best bet for the searcher who is more interested in the contents of search output than its physical appearance.

Print quality can be improved either by increasing the number of pins in the printhead, thus achieving a tighter, higher-resolution arrangement of dots on the matrix, or by making more than one pass for each character, slightly offsetting the printing on subsequent passes to fill in spaces between dots. Users of these printers can switch between draft and near-letter-quality (NLQ) modes. NLQ machines usually have twenty-four pins in the printhead, more than double the usual number, but they often cost more than double the usual price of three- to five-hundred dollars. And printing in the NLQ mode can be much, much slower than usual.

It is easily possible to send several pages of very dense text to the printer during a routine online search. Many printers can't even keep up with information being received from the online service. One solution to that problem is to download and print while in the offline mode. Another solution is to use a buffer. Good printers include a buffer as part of the hardware. Good communications software also will provide buffering capabilities. It is also possible to purchase a circuit board and software known as a print spooler. Print spoolers regulate printing and allow the micro to be used for other purposes while printing is occurring. Another solution is to purchase an in-line print buffer, a small device that is spliced into the cable between computer and printer. No matter which solution is taken, a fast printer is recommended for frequent searchers. It is a waste of resources to occupy most of the micro's time printing voluminous search results when it could be used more productively for other tasks.

```
Normal Printing
12 Pitch
10 Pitch
Bold Printing
Shadow Printing
Underline
                        Letter Quality
                        Pica
                        Elite
                        Compressed
                        Expanded     Letter Quality
                        Emphasized   Pica
                        Double-Strike Proportional
                                     Elite
                                     Compressed
                                     Expanded
                                     Emphasized
                                     super and subscript
                                     Underline
                                     Italics
                                     condensed superscript
                                     condensed subscript
```

Examples of impact, dot matrix, and thermal printing. Because print quality and speed can vary considerably, printer decisions should be made carefully.

Dot matrix printers are quieter than some other types of printers, but the noise that they do make can be annoying. It's not so much the volume as the pitch. Dot matrix printers generate a high-pitched noise that has often been compared to a dentist's drill --not among the most dulcet of tones, and definitely not recommended for public areas, especially in libraries. The music of a dot matrix will not soothe the savage beast. In fact, it will drive any dogs in the neighborhood into a frenzy. Dot matrix printers in the three- to five-hundred dollar price range will produce acceptable print quality, good printing speed, and tolerable noise levels. More expensive dot matrix printers will provide the print quality at a level that is appropriate for a product-oriented search operation.

If searching is to be done by clients in a public area (an increasingly common situation), the dot matrix loses much of its appeal. Noise is a major detriment, as is inconvenience. Changing a ribbon on some dot matrix printers involves navigating through a maze of posts, rollers, and retainers and emerging as an ink-stained wretch once the process is finished. Changing the paper can be almost as much fun, and if the paper gets off the track an expensive online search can end up being printed on a single line. Try telling a client that the eighty-seven records they thought they were going to get are all printed on that dark band across the middle of a single page.

Ink Jets

Ink jet printers solve many of the problems of public online searching. Fewer moving parts are involved. Characters are formed by squirting fine jets of ink onto the surface of the paper. Ink jet printers are fast and come about as close as printers can come to being quiet. Right now they are the preferred printers for situations in which the noise could interfere with others working in the same area. The Information Access Company has chosen the Hewlett Packard ThinkJet printer for its InfoTrac system (more on this later).

Ink jet printers are very easy to use. The printhead and ink cartridge are the same device. A hard plastic cylinder contains a soft plastic bladder that is filled with ink. The part of the cylinder that sits next to the paper contains the ink jets themselves and the circuitry for connecting the jets to the printer's logic circuitry. Replacing an ink cartridge can be done in seconds, and the ink stays in the bladder where it belongs, not on your hands and clothing. Changing the paper is also easy.

Ink jet printers are not without disadvantages. They cost more than low-end dot matrix printers, usually in the five-hundred to a thousand dollar range. Ink jets are also more expensive to operate. Ink cartridges don't last as long as ribbons and are comparably priced or more expensive. Ink cartridges can also be difficult to obtain. Supplies aren't meeting the demand, and third party suppliers have not yet begun to compete with cartridges, which are available from printer manufacturers.

Special, less-absorbent paper is required. Ordinary paper absorbs too much of the ink that is squirted onto it, resulting in blurry print. Specially finished paper is more expensive and often difficult to obtain. The jets themselves tend to clog and have to be cleaned occasionally. Overall the print quality is equivalent to that of the cheaper dot matrix printers but not nearly as good as NLQ or twenty-four-pin dot matrix printers.

Many of us started out as searchers using thermal printers. Thermal printers use heat to place characters on the surface of the paper. Thermal printers have improved and the best are similar to inkjets in just about every area, including print quality and special supplies.

Despite its drawbacks, the ink jet is indispensible for public searching by a library's clients. It is the only type of printer that is quiet, fast, easy to use, and relatively inexpensive. Print quality is more than adequate for those whose primary need is presumably for the information content of online search results, not the production of the finished documents that incorporate search results.

Letter-Quality Printers

If you are a freelance, professional searcher, or if you are a consultant who incorporates online information in your reports, you probably want a letter-quality printer. If you are in a large organization, or if you do other tasks like word processing, you probably already have one available to you. Letter-quality printers, that is printers that work by striking a fully formed character against a ribbon (they are also often called daisy wheel printers--a description that isn't always accurate), are expensive but prices are falling as dot matrix quality improves.

Letter-quality printers are slow. Most are rated as being able to send somewhere in the neighborhood of fifteen to thirty characters per second. Compared with dot matrix printers, which burn the page at over a hundred characters per second, they are icehouses. And printers never really work as fast as they're rated because carriage returns and form feeding, etc., are not calculated into advertised speeds.

Letter-quality printers are noisy. If you're the type who likes to stand in front of the speakers at a Def Leppard concert, then you would probably enjoy working in the same room with a letter-quality printer. Otherwise you might want to buy an acoustic enclosure, which is about the size of a garage (and you'll probably have to lift it to reload paper). This includes a cooling fan, and will set you back a couple of hundred dollars.

But letter-quality printers are closer to Mr. Gutenberg's invention than any other type of printer. And the results look good, good enough to sell, just as books are sold. The best dot matrixes look nice it's true, even better than cheaper letter-quality printers, but the really good letter-quality printers are hard to beat typographically.

Letter-quality printers also often provide more options when it comes to forms handling and being able to accommodate different paper sizes. Regardless of which type of printer you choose, carriage size should be of concern. The more expensive models in each category have wider carriages. Search system software will allow you to control the width of your output. The default value for most systems is between seventy and eighty characters wide. A ten-inch-wide carriage will accommodate standard 8 1/2-inch, eighty-column-wide paper leaving a little room to spare on the margins.

A sixteen-inch-wide, 132-column carriage might be more useful for the searcher who uses numeric databases and search system report software to generate tables and reports. Large printouts on any kind of printer will require some sort of form feeding or tractor mechanism to keep the paper aligned properly. Sometimes the form feeder comes with the printer. Other times it costs extra.

If you are a freelancer, and if you're not in a hurry to get your printouts, and if you've got clients who demand quality typography, and if you have agreements to download, reformat, and resell online data, and if a really substantial proportion of your business involves reports generated from online data, and if you can deal with the noise, then go right out and buy an expensive letter-quality printer. Expect to spend over a thousand dollars.

Otherwise, if you desire a quality search product you might want to consider a dot matrix printer with a good NLQ mode ($500-$1,000). Or you might want to consider a cheap dot matrix printer ($200-$500) for drafts and proofs connected by a T-switch to a cheap letter-quality printer ($250-$500, but don't expect to get too much work out of a cheapie) for final reports. If you're in an institution, you may be on a local area network (LAN) that provides you with access to a variety of printing technologies, or you may have the opportunity to use the T-switch or carry-the-disk-from-room-to-room approach with institutional-quality machines.

Laser Printers

Laser printers generate type that compares with letter-quality machines; superb graphics are an added bonus and type fonts of all sorts and sizes are available. Laser printers are as quiet as ink jet or thermal printers and fast as well. They print a full page at a time and their output is rated as pages per minute. Most laser printers produce eight or so pages per minute, putting them somewhere in the hundred to hundred and fifty characters per second range. If you want a laser printer, expect to pay a few thousand dollars, and add a few hundred for type fonts, printing cartridges, and software to make it work effectively.

Technologically laser printers are more similar to copy machines than they are to other printers. Most are based on a technology developed by Canon (famous for its cameras and photocopiers). Finely focused laser beams are reflected by spinning mirrors that scan the surface of a polished metal drum. Each beam places an electrical charge in an area the size of a tiny dot on the drum. Laser printers are actually extremely high resolution dot matrix printers. But laser printers are not impact printers like most dot matrix printers. There are no moving pins involved. Because the dots are formed by beams of light they can be controlled more precisely and there can be a lot more of them. Millions of electrical charges placed on the drum attract toner that is fused to paper in a process similar to the one employed by photocopiers.

Most searchers and the institutions that employ them can't afford a laser printer. The expense simply can't be justified with searching as the major application. Maybe some equitable means of paying for electronic information will be developed eventually. Maybe a secondary publishing industry that uses local computing power to repackage and custom design online data will spring into being. Printed works would still be the primary medium of information exchange, but the secondary publishing industry wouldn't mass produce them as they are now published. The development of laser printing with sophisticated graphics certainly foreshadows an era of electronic document delivery and on-demand publishing.

The Searcher as Architect

We've looked at some of the components in a basic search system. When selecting hardware try to think of yourself as an urban planner designing a city whose inhabitants are electricity and information. Try to plan an architecture that will foster the easy flow and transformation of information and electricity.

Each individual and each institution has unique requirements for the storage, retrieval, transmission, and manipulation of information. Some will be more interested in devices that optimize the search process. Others are more concerned with the search product. Now the searcher needs to be concerned with the electrical devices used to build the search system in addition to all the other things that make searching such a challenging and complex activity.

One of the major functions of the searcher's micro is to act as a terminal. Hardware for two of the terminal functions, input and output, has been covered. Now let's examine the third component, the communications interface. A great deal of time hasn't been spent on explaining how the input and output components of the hardware system actually work. Those things are explained in many and varied sources. Before discussing communications hardware and, later, storage devices, let's focus on what's actually going on beneath the surface.

References/Recommended Reading

Casbon, Susan. "Online Searching with a Microcomputer: Getting Started." *Online* 7, no. 2 (Nov. 1983): 42-46.

Chen, Ching-chih. "A New Generation of Microcomputers for Information Processing." In *The Application of Mini- and Micro-Computers in Information, Documentation and Libraries*, edited by C. Kern and L. Perlmutter, 25-34. Elsevier, 1983.

Derfler, Frank J. *Microcomputer Data Communications Systems*. Englewood Cliffs, NJ: Prentice-Hall, 1982.

Kay, Alan, and Adele Goldberg. "Personal Dynamic Media." *Computer* 31 (March 1977).

Kolner, Stuart J. "The IBM PC as an Online Search Machine--Part I: Anatomy for Searchers." *Online* 9, no. 1 (Jan. 1985): 37-42.

Morrison, David. "May the Power Be with You." *Computer Decisions* 23 April 1985, 116-133.

"Special Section: The IBM PC as a Terminal" (various authors). *Information Technology and Libraries* 3, no. 1 (March 1984): 47-68.

Wiswell, Phil. "Surge Suppressors: An Ounce of Prevention." *PC Magazine* 5, no. 10, 27 May 27 1986, 115-146.

CHAPTER THREE
MODEMS AND TELECOMMUNICATIONS

The Language of Electronic Discourse

Imagine that our microcomputer is a city of electricity and information. Beyond its boundaries lies a civilization of electronic information--a nation of interconnected cities, some of which are much larger than ours. The cities, both large and small, are engaged in commerce with one another, and the commodity being exchanged is information.

One of the things that marks a civilization is a common language that all of its members can understand. Written language and electronic language are both systems for manipulating symbols. While you're up there in the heady realm of applied epistemology, the search system software is moving around chunks of structured knowledge with an ease that belies the complexity of the task. The communications network is making sure those chunks of knowledge move swiftly and efficiently across thousands of miles. At the local level your computer and the devices attached to it are skillfully slinging electrons around. Symbols are hauled in, moved around, and pulled together to build higher levels of meaning.

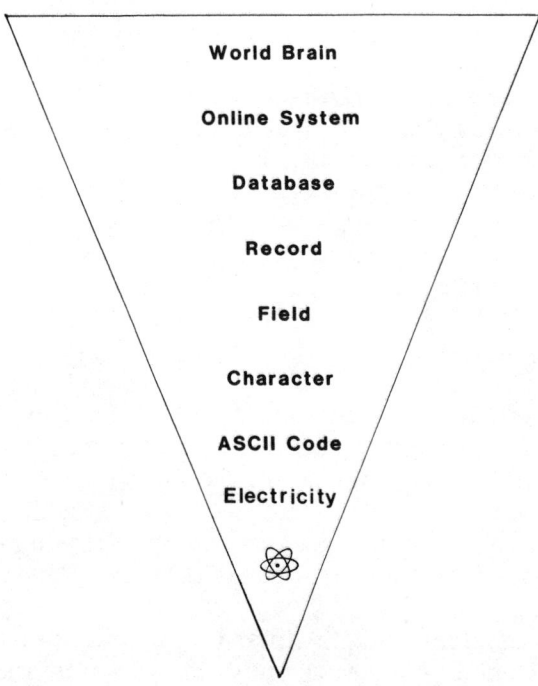

Levels of information

When people communicate with one another, language is just one of the ways in which messages are conveyed. Eye contact, tone of voice, and posture also play an important role. Somehow, unspoken signals are used to determine who should be talking and who should be listening at any given time. Unspoken messages often carry greater meaning than spoken words. For communication to occur, messages must be exchanged simultaneously at many different levels.

Levels of Communication

The civilization of electronic information is also built upon a common language. Communication occurs simultaneously at many levels in much the same way as it does in a conversation. But computer communication must rely upon more formal rules. The language of computer discourse is a language of standards. Each level of meaning is defined by a separate standard. There are standards for codifying the letters of the alphabet in binary form. There are electrical standards that determine which voltage levels are used to represent information, and there are tone signalling standards that enable information to be transmitted over telephone lines.

ASCII Spoken Here

Before we talk about modems (which are essentially translation devices), let's examine some of the standards used in data communications. The first standard we encounter is ASCII, which is universally understood in the world of micros and online services. ASCII (American Standard Code for Information Interchange) is a method of digitally representing the letters, numbers, and symbols that people use to communicate with one another. Put them together and you have words, sentences, books, etc. The permutations are limitless. Computers are capable of dealing with words but must first reduce the letters from which words are formed to a binary language of zeros and ones.

ASCII is a method of putting together the bits (zeros and ones) used by machines to represent the letters, numbers, and symbols used by humans. There are 128 ASCII characters, each formed by a different sequence of seven zeros and ones. All of the familiar keyboard characters are represented as well as some control codes that are understood better by machines than people.

So it takes at least seven bits to represent a single letter of the alphabet. Remember that asynchronous communication calls for a start bit and a stop bit, bringing our total to nine bits per character. Add another bit for parity (a scheme for checking transmission accuracy by specifying that the sum of the bits representing a character always be even or odd; online services that use parity usually specify that the sum be even), and we have a grand total of ten bits per character.

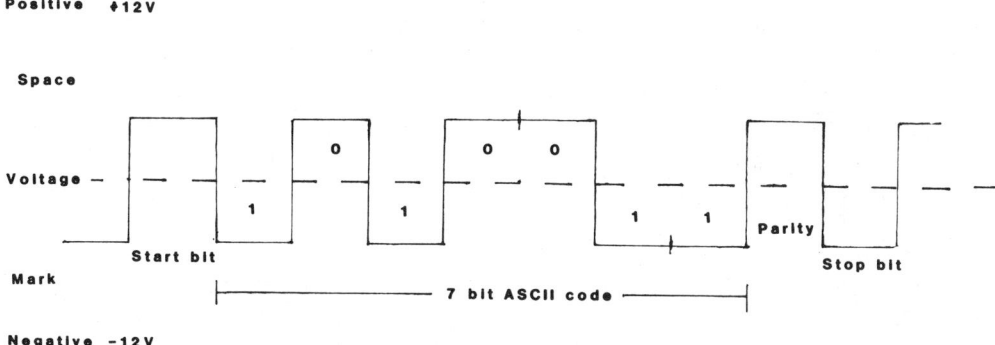

Schematic of ASCII character--capital S with framing bits

ASCII is a tidy, logical way to represent high order symbols as bits (binary digits). But when you plug into the wall socket and power up your computer, a stream of zeros and ones doesn't pour forth from a numerical reservoir at the power company. So the engineers had to come up with a scheme for using electricity for communication. Since a binary language had to be part of the solution, a way had to be found for electrically representing zeros and ones. Two signals had to be devised, one representing a zero, the other, representing a one.

In the lingo of data communications, the signal representing a zero is known as a space and is represented by a positive electrical voltage. The signal representing a one is known as a mark and is represented by a negative voltage. An additional problem was presented by the ASCII characters that included consecutive strings of zeros or ones. The ASCII code for a capital S for example, is 1100101. How could those initial ones be differentiated as two

44   Microcomputers for the Online Searcher

separate bits?   An elaborate synchronization and timing scheme had to be devised.

So one of the possible code elements, a zero, is represented by a positive voltage level.   Ideally the level is + 12 volts, but any positive voltage between + 3 and + 24 volts is acceptable.   The voltage level itself isn't nearly important as whether it is positive or negative.   The other code element, a one, is represented by any negative voltage in the range of -24 to -3 volts.   That's the beauty of a binary system.   The computer only has to worry about changes in state between one condition and another.   The duration of each signal element has to be controlled so the computer can be on the lookout for ASCII codes including consecutive strings of the same character.   And the accuracy of transmission has to be constantly monitored by mathematical algorithms, like parity checking and cyclic redundancy checking.

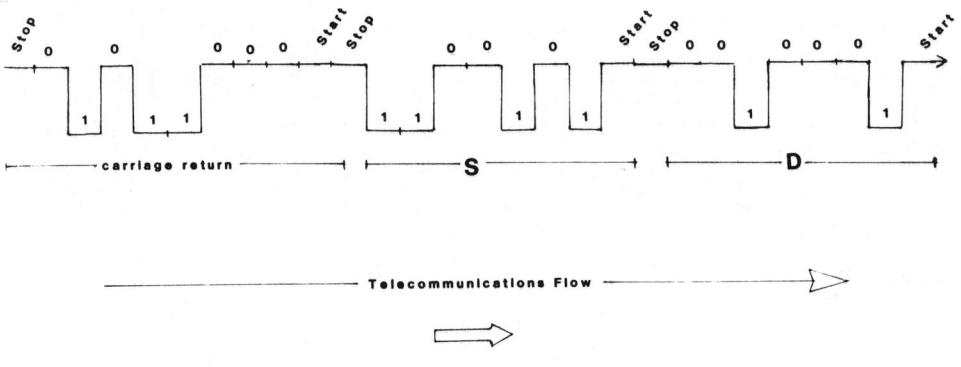

Bit stream for DIALOG display sets command

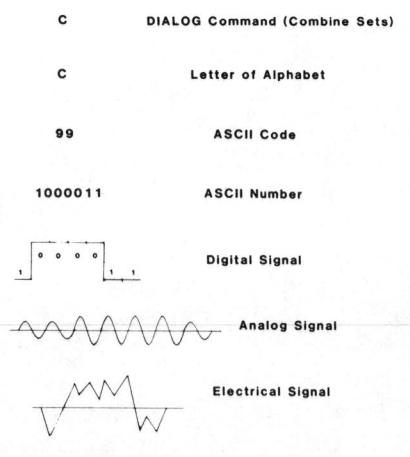

Levels of knowledge representation

The Modem as Translator

ASCII is one of the methods we use for transferring information between electronic databases and our micros. Still, ASCII is a high-level, abstract way of representing information. Modems operate at a more basic level. What we're talking about here is electricity and sound, if it is possible to think of something that can't be heard as sound.

A modem is a vital structure in the searcher's hardware architecture. Let's represent it on our blueprint as a bridge between our little city of electricity and information and the electronic civilization that lies beyond. Think of the modem as a black box. On one side of the box, connecting the modem to the computer, is an electrical cable. Information (in the form of electricity) passes back and forth through that cable. On the other side of the box, connecting the modem to the outside world, is a telephone wire. Information (in the form of sound) travels along that wire between the modem and the world beyond.

In data communications, all pieces of machinery are divided into two classes. A computer component is either Data Terminal Equipment (DTE) or Data Communications Equipment (DCE). Data Terminal Equipment includes more than just terminals. When you are using a communicating micro, your micro itself is a piece of DTE. A printer can also be classified DTE. In the micro community, the designation DCE is most frequently applied to modems. Each end of the communications link must include at least one DCE and one DTE. A channel through which information can flow must also be present. A typical online search can easily involve several DTEs and DCEs. DTEs work with electricity; DCEs use both sound and electricity.

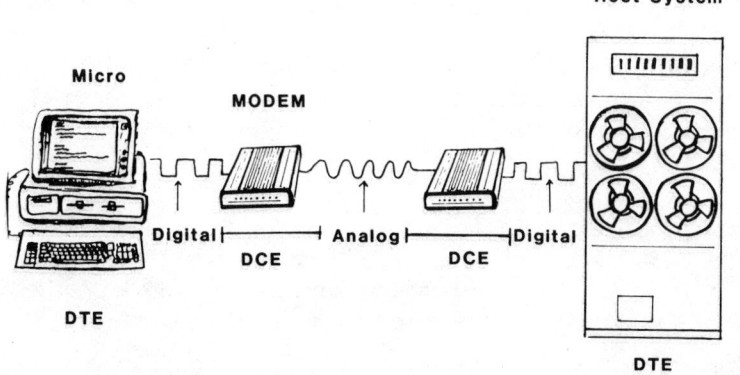

Computer hardware is divided into data terminal equipment (DTE) and data communications equipment (DCE).

Information traffic between DCEs and DTEs can travel along a few different types of channels. For searchers, the type of channel used will be determined by the packet-switching network or online service being used.

Duplex and Echo

Two-way simultaneous communication of the type supported by most online systems is known as duplex or full duplex operation. Duplex communication works like a divided two-way street. Vehicles are permitted to move in both directions at the same time. Four wires are generally required to accomplish this. Two wires are used for each piece of DCE, one wire to carry transmitted signals, and the other wire to carry received signals.

The type of communication known as half duplex is more similar to a single-lane bridge that allows two-way traffic but only permits one vehicle at a time to pass. Information can be both sent and received by each DCE but not simultaneously. Half duplex operation is like a conversation in which only one person at a time is speaking. Half duplex requires two wires, one for each device. Each device both sends and receives on the same wire. The UNINET packet-switching network used to require half duplex operation. Nowadays, half duplex is hardly used for online searching.

Simplex communication is like a one-way street, or a television broadcast. Information is only permitted to move in one direction at a time. For the searcher, simplex would be a dead-end street reminiscent of the early days of batch processing retrieval systems. We'll never see an online search system incorporating simplex. Online and interactive go hand in hand. An attempt was once made by the Mobile, Alabama Public Library to create a half duplex system using simplex technology. Library clients called the library on the telephone with reference questions. The sources containing the answers to the questions were then placed under a TV camera and cablecast on a local cable channel where they could be viewed by inquirers.

There are also channels for the passage of information among the various devices that are part of the searcher's workstation. The keyboard has traditionally been the searcher's way of talking to the outside world. And the monitor has been the searcher's way of hearing the outside world's response. But the monitor also allows the person at the keyboard to see what kind of messages he or she is sending from the keyboard. Information is being sent to the outside, but a channel is also routing information from the keyboard to the monitor.

All of the devices in the workstation are not connected by the same type of channels. If, for example, a message originates from another device, let's say a disk drive, the message itself may not be displayed on the monitor. Chances are the person at the micro will only be able to see the response of the remote system, not the messages being sent from the disk. The message has been sent directly from the disk to the online service, bypassing the monitor. If a searcher wants to see the messages being uploaded from a disk, it might be necessary to first open a channel between the disk drive and the monitor, or tell the remote system to echo every character that is transmitted back to the local system.

Echoplex is the operation in which the remote system echos characters back to the local system as a means of verifying the accuracy of transmission. The term is often used interchangeably with duplex, but the two concepts are different. If both full duplex and echoplex are turned on at the same time, the result may be the same as the double image seen when duplex is set incorrectly.

The duplex switch is a familiar accessory on most simple terminals. Communicating micros can be made to function in one mode or the other by flipping switches on the modem, but this function is usually performed by the communications software being used. Good software can be used to tell your hardware quite precisely what kind of channel you want, what the information travelling along the channel will look like, and how fast it will travel.

Let's follow the electricity. When it reaches the modem, our electricity has already passed through the serial card (though in the case of an internal modem the functions of the serial card are accomplished by circuitry on the modem itself), and the bits representing each character are zipping along single file and asynchronously, framed in such a way that there are ten bits per character. The standard that governs information in its electrical incarnation is known as the RS-232 C (the "C" is optional).

The RS-232 Standard

Unlike many of the so-called standards in the microcomputer industry, RS-232 is a true standard. The caveats relating to RS-232 equipment apply to the cables used to connect different components. There are a number of different receptacles and cables in use, and they aren't mutually compatible. However, once the proper cable has been obtained, any RS-232 computer (99 percent of micros are) can be connected to any modem.

The voltage levels on each of the twenty-five pins of the DB-25 connector are precisely coordinated to control the electrical aspects of the interaction between two computers that are talking to one another. Computer-to-computer communication doesn't always require the use of all twenty-five pins. The searcher who is using the correct cable needn't be concerned with the functions assigned to each pin.

Cable Confusion

RS-232 is indeed a true standard, but the cabling requirements of different pieces of data communications and data terminal equipment (i.e., micros and modems) are anything but standard. Nothing is more frustrating than trying to connect two pieces of equipment with an improperly wired cable. It's impossible to tell which pins are connected by simply looking at a cable that has a male DB-25 connector at one end and a female DB-25 connector at the other end.

A specialized tool called a breakout box can be used to determine which signal leads are connected, but that's something your hardware dealer should be worrying about, not you. When you buy an external modem, buy the cable as well. Don't be surprised at the price of a short cable, which can be around $50. If there are any problems, they can be brought to the store that sold you the cable.

Hardware and software manuals often include pin connection tables and diagrams. There are also reference books that include cabling requirements for a variety of different devices for those who are brave enough to put together their own cables.

Another interesting development is the Smart Cable SC817, priced at $49.95 from IQ Technologies of Bellevue, Washington (800-227-2817). The Smart Cable is advertised as "the first truly universal connector for RS-232 interfaces." Electronic circuitry within the Smart Cable is able to recognize the signals being sent by each piece of equipment and automatically make the proper connection. If you plan to move your modem or serial printer around from one machine to another, the Smart Cable could prove to be a worthwhile investment.

Among the jobs performed by the RS-232 interface are keeping track of which machine is sending and which is receiving at any given moment, determining how fast information is travelling, and monitoring the quality of the signal. Each pin carries a signal related to a different aspect of the communication process. The signals travelling through the pins establish the protocol for communication. Communications protocols, like diplomatic protocols, are highly formal give-and-take encounters.

CROSSTALK, one of the best-selling communications programs, requires that nine of the twenty-five pins be connected when using a Hayes-compatible modem. *Smartcom*, another bestseller from Hayes, requires that a minimum of only five pins be connected.

CROSSTALK PIN CONNECTION REQUIREMENTS

Pin	Signal
1	Protective Ground
2	Transmit Data
3	Receive Data
4	Request to Send
5	Clear to Send
6	Data Set Ready
7	Signal Ground
8	Carrier Detect
20	Data Terminal Ready

SMARTCOM PIN REQUIREMENTS

Pin	Signal
2	Transmit Data
3	Receive Data
7	Signal Ground
8	Carrier Detect
20	Data Terminal Ready

An exchange between two computers involves the establishment of rigid protocols. In a process called "handshaking," modems send signals of acknowledgement to one another to verify the transfer of meaningful signals. Signals are passed back and forth along with actual information. Researchers of nonverbal communication have discovered that much of the information content of human interaction is nonverbal. The control signals exchanged by communicating computers perform many of the same functions that nonverbal cues provide when people are talking to one another. A typical encounter goes something like this:

FIRST COMPUTER:"I'm ready to talk. Are you ready to listen?"

SECOND COMPUTER: "I got your message. Sure I'm ready to listen."

FIRST COMPUTER: "OK, Here it comes."

SECOND COMPUTER: "I'm ready for it. Do youy want me to repeat it to make sure I got it right?"

FIRST COMPUTER: "OK"
SECOND COMPUTER: "Will do."

FIRST COMPUTER: "Blah, Blah, Blah......"

SECOND COMPUTER: "Blah, Blah, Blah......"

Digital versus Analog

Everybody already knows that modem stands for modulator/demodulator, but what does that mean? On one side of the modem is our micro. In the micro information becomes electricity and digital is the language of discourse. Each bit in a digital system is an all or nothing proposition. On the other side of the modem is the telephone network. For the most part, they don't speak digital in telephone territory (though the situation is changing, especially where fiber optic lines are in place).

Analog is the language of the telephone system. There are many shades of grey there. Discrete bits formed by variations in electrical current are replaced by modulated tones that vary in proportion to the information being represented. The modem converts the digital signals produced by the micro to the modulated tones employed by the telephone system (modulation) and translates the modulated tones arriving over the phone line to digital signals with which the micro can deal (demodulation).

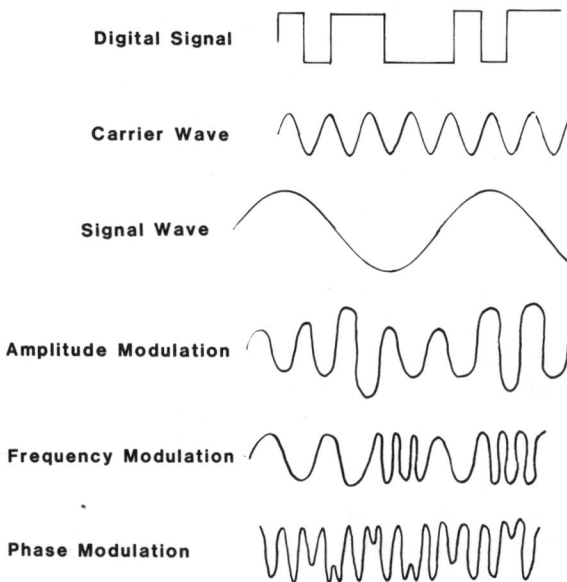

There are several different ways of modulating a carrier wave to transmit digital signals over analog lines.

Tone Signaling Standards

There is a logical standard for representing the letters of the alphabet with zeros and ones (ASCII) and an electrical standard for the serial transmission of information (RS-232). Is there a standard for the tones used by the analog telephone system? This is where things begin to get confusing. Both the ASCII and the RS-232 standards were designed by quasi-official organizations (respectively: the Comite' Consultatif International de Telegraphie et Telephonie (CCITT) and the Electronic Industries Association (EIA)). There are several tone signaling standards, most of which were developed by Ma Bell, which had a monopoly on modems until 1969.

But AT&T, once the sole modem manufacturer and arbiter of signaling standards, is no longer the dominant force it once was-- especially when it comes to 2400-baud modems. Most 2400-baud modems employ a standard developed by CCITT (V.22 bis) and used by AT&T in its 2224 series of modems. However, many of the other manufacturers of 2400-baud modems (most notably Hayes, the Norcross, Georgia company that has set the de facto standard for micro modems) have modified V.22 bis to enable it to deal more effectively with telecommunications practice in the U.S. To be fair, there are also several electrical and coding standards but they aren't as widely used in the micro industry as the different tone signaling standards. And there are some pretty convincing technical reasons for the use of more than a single tone signaling standard.

Standards for the Searcher

Online searching is an interactive process in which information is moving back and forth between searcher and system. Different tones are used for information going in each direction. Some modem signaling standards permit only one party in the transaction to be transmitting at a time (half duplex). Avoid modems using those standards; many online services weren't designed for half duplex. These are the standards that are most important to searchers and the transmission speeds for which they can be used.

Bell 103	Bell 212A	CCITT V.22 bis
300 baud	1200 baud	2400 baud
full duplex	full duplex	full duplex

The number of tones used and the frequency of each tone depend upon the kind of channel being used and the speed with which information is being transferred. The Bell 103 standard used for full duplex 300-baud modems uses four different tones to represent information. The originating modem represents a space with a tone having a frequency of 1,070 Hertz (cycles per second) and a mark with a tone having a frequency of 1,270 Hz. The answering modem uses another set of tone frequencies to represent the two possible signals. It represents a space with a tone of 2,025 Hz and a mark with a tone of 2,225 Hz.

The Bell 212A standard for 1200-baud, full duplex modems uses only two tones to move information back and forth. A different modulation scheme makes it possible to use frequencies of 1200 Hz and 2400 Hz. One modem transmits on one frequency and receives on the other and vice versa.

There are several different modulation schemes used by different modems and the scheme chosen will determine the online speed limit as well as the tone signaling standard used. All of them permit transmission of information over analog telephone lines by superimposing over a steady tone known as a carrier other tones that are modulated in precise ways.

The carrier is a regular frequency tone that is modulated to carry information. The combination of a carrier wave and an information-carrying wave results in an information-carrying analog signal.

Modulation Sets the Speed Limit

Amplitude modulation (AM) is used for low-speed transmission (110 baud). Most searchers use frequency modulation (FM) for higher speeds (300 baud) and phase modulation (PM) for the 1200-baud transmission nowadays. Remember that high-speed modems usually contain the circuitry to commmunicate at lower speeds if the service being used requires a lower baud rate. There have, however, been some problems with the ability of 2400-baud modems to slow down easily to lower speeds. And the signaling standard employed by 2400-baud modems isn't as firmly entrenched as the Bell standards used for 300- and 1200-baud transmission.

The new 1200- and 2400-baud modems often combine different modulation schemes to produce tones that transmit information more efficiently by using four or more signaling levels instead of simply translating two-level digital signals into two-level analog signals. When two bits are packed into one signal, the resulting information unit is known as a dibit.

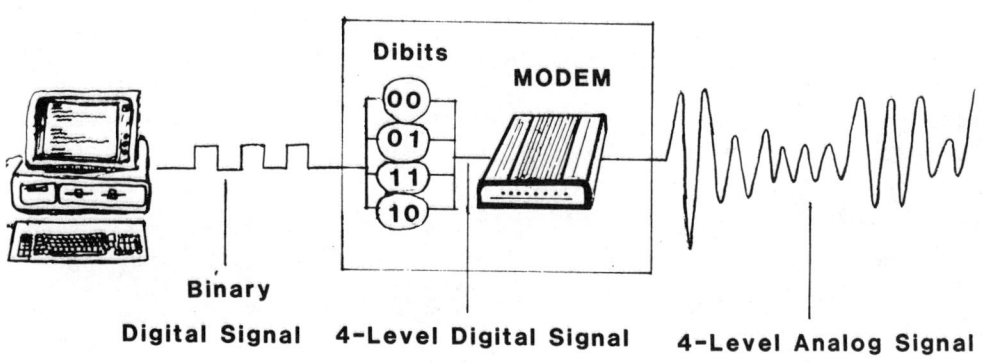

Some modems double the amount of information a baud can carry by using a four-level code instead of the usual two-level binary code.

Noise

Noise is the malady of the postindustrial era. Machines break down, as does communication. Noise can adle the world brain and bother the inhabitants of our city of information. Entropy is on the minds of our writers, our physicists, and our economists. There is hardly a discipline that hasn't embraced the concept. Those who inhabit cities of information and talk to the world brain know about noise.

Random bursts of electricity can interfere with the most logical and elegant schemes for using electricity to represent symbols. Those symbols that make sense to us when put together can be obscured by random tildes and curly brackets. Who hasn't seen authors' names obliterated, titles fractured, abstracts turned into nonsense?

In our electronic civilization, noise assumes the form of electricity. Electricity is mutable and noise takes many forms. All kinds of signals are arrayed against those signals we have loaded with meaning and sent off on the wires. It's bad enough we have to worry about thermal noise. We also have to deal with white noise, cross talk, and jitter.

But the bane of the searcher is most likely to be impulse noise. Fleet, random spikes lasting only milliseconds can make nonsense of our binary language. Representing information with dibits and cramming lots of bits into short lengths of time opens the door for impulse noise. A noise impulse of a couple of milliseconds can wipe out a lot more data at 2400 baud than it can at 300 baud.

Impulse noise can originate on the phone network, or at a PBX or other switching exchange (college campuses are notorious for this), or it can be caused by lightning or phone company repair crews. Todays modems incorporate sophisticated electronic defenses against noise. Networks of circuits known as filters are pitted against every type of noise. Software is also being designed to ferret out noise before it ferrets out your data.

Baud versus BPS

Though modem speed is usually measured in baud, the more proper designation is bits per second (bps). The real baud rate of a modem and the number of characters it is able to send per second often don't correspond. Baud is a measure of the duration of each signal. So baud measures the number of times per second the signal changes; these could be changes in amplitude, frequency, or phase of the tone being generated.

Each signal at 300 baud lasts longer than the corresponding signal at 1200 baud. And, if we figure that it takes ten bits to represent one character, we can calculate the number of characters per second a modem can transmit by dividing the baud rate by ten. A 300-baud modem can transmit thirty characters per second (approximately five average-length words) and a 1200-baud modem can transmit 120 characters per second (approximately twenty words).

Sophisticated modulation schemes make it possible to squeeze two or more bits into the amount of time usually required to send a single bit. So what is billed as a 1200-baud modem could actually be using a four-level dibit modulation scheme to convert a 600-baud signal into a 1200 bps transmission. How it is done is not really important. Nor does it matter that a 1200-baud modem is usually really a 600-baud modem and that most 1200-baud modems also contain separate 300-baud modems. What matters is how much a modem costs, and how well it works. Before looking at modems, let's get back to the electricity.

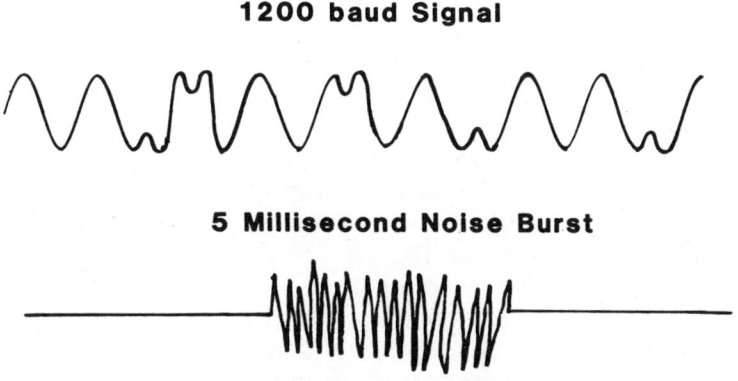

The briefer 1200-baud signal is much more susceptible to line noise than is the relatively long 300-baud signal.

Follow the Electricity: Reprise

What happens to the electricity? We have this machine that allows us to represent information as electricity and move it around from device to device on high-speed, eight-lane highways. When we go online, we pound away on a keyboard, creating messages that we can see on a display screen. Those messages are also detoured to a traffic control center called a UART, where they are funneled into a single lane and shunted onto a long distance highway.

Before our messages can travel along the highway, they must be translated into the language of the country through which they are passing. Our translator is called a modem. Our modem puts us in touch with a labyrinthine network whose tentacles extend to every corner of our civilization. Routes exist to small cities such as ours and to empires of information. As we enter this network we specify the address to which we will send our messages. The address is usually a port on a packet-switching network. Through the port will pass the riches of an empire of information.

Packet Switching

The best analogy to packet-switching comes from the 1957 science fiction classic *The Fly*. Vincent Price plays a brilliant scientist who has developed a method for disassembling all of the molecules in his body, transporting them across a great distance, and reassembling them at the other end of the line. During one of Price's experiments, a fly enters the apparatus and its molecules become hopelessly scrambled with his. At the other end of the line, a human torso with an enormous bug-eyed fly's head emerges. In one of cinema's most tragic moments, the viewer also sees a tiny creature with the winged body of a fly and Vincent Price's head. The creature buzzes around Price's blissfully ignorant colleagues repeating in a tiny, plaintive voice, "Help me. Help me."

A packet-switching network fragments your messages and mixes them with the messages of others just as Vincent Price's molecules were disassembled and mixed with those of the fly. Fortunately, the packet-switching network, unlike Price's device, almost always manages to successfully reassemble the messages at their destination. Packet-switching networks, which are also called value-added networks (VANs), are the direct descendents of ARPAnet. Once you have dialed a local packet-switching number and have been connected, the messages originating at your computer enter a node on a packet-switching network where they are broken into fragments known as packets. Each packet includes a string of characters. Packets can range in length from a few characters to over a thousand.

The size of each packet and the path each travels along the network are determined by the amount of traffic on the network at any given point in time. Located at the nodes of the network are minicomputers called engines that monitor the traffic load on the network and select the most efficient route along which information should travel. Packets that are part of the same message could easily travel to their destination along entirely different routes, avoiding traffic jams by bypassing busy roads. They are travelling at electrical speeds so detours don't matter much. The network has an intelligence of sorts when it comes to moving information efficiently.

The equipment at the nodes is known as DSE, or data-switching equipment. The analog signals that went out on your phone line are reconverted to digital signals on the network and travel most of the way to their destination as synchronous messages along digital lines. The word lines is used loosely here; messages could just as easily be beamed across space on microwaves and bounced off of satellites. Each packet has attached to it information that ensures it will get to the proper destination in the proper sequence with the other packets that are part of the same message. That's why each network uses separate port addresses for different online services. Telenet, for example, specifies the address of the host computer by including its telephone area code.

A packet-switching network establishes what is known as a virtual circuit between the devices at the source and at the destination. Value is added by allowing users of different devices with different electrical and coding standards to communicate with one another. The network is transparent. Sender and receiver are unaware of the ways in which their messages are being manipulated. Value is also added by detecting and eliminating errors. Online searching wouldn't be possible as we know it without these value-added networks. It's amazing when one considers the amount of traffic on these networks that message garbling flies enter the network so infrequently.

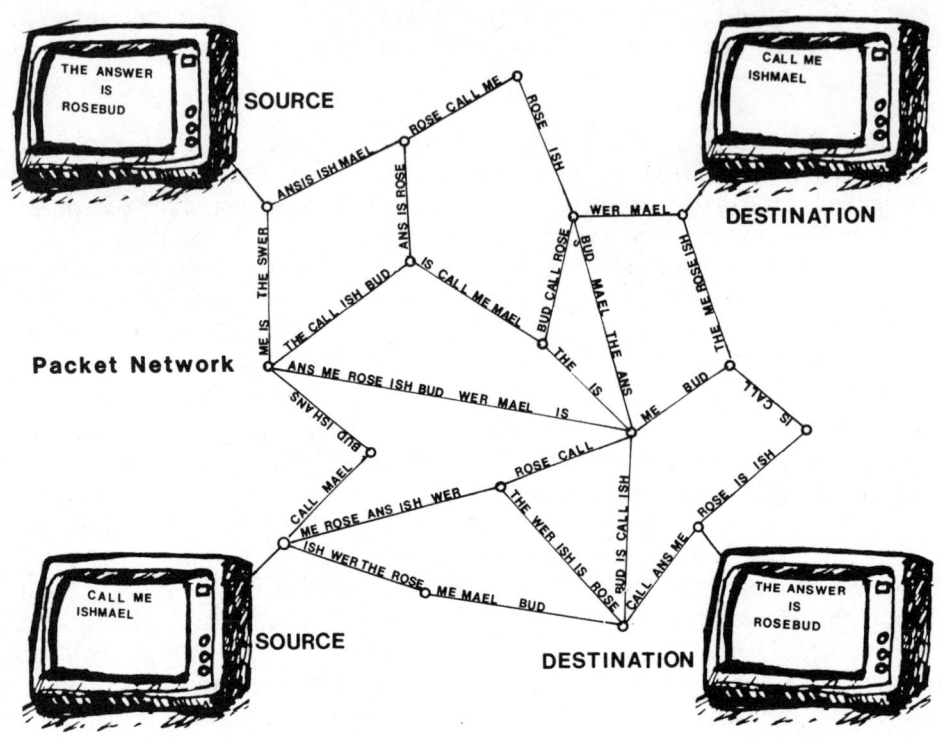

Packet switching

Choosing a Modem

What kind of a modem should the searcher buy? Let's look at cost first. The faster the modem, the more expensive. Higher speeds require more error checking and control circuitry, which drives up the price. The higher speed modem is also usually designed to perform at lower speeds as well, further increasing the sophistication of the circuitry required. A 2400-baud modem is eight times faster than a 300-baud modem and almost as many times as expensive. The price/speed ratio between 300- and 1200-baud modems isn't as disproportionate. A 1200-baud modem that can transmit four times faster than a 300-baud will usually cost only about twice as much. And the prices being fetched by 1200-baud modems have declined dramatically.

The Best Buy: 1200 Baud

The trend in the online industry is shifting from basing charges on connect-time to basing them on units of electronic information consumed. This trend cuts into the amount of money a high-speed modem can save you (another change we can chalk up to our ubiquitous micro). For now most online information vendors don't charge extra for higher speed lines, but that situation seems destined to change. Nevertheless, if you search with any regularity a 1200-baud modem will quickly pay for itself. It would be foolish nowadays to buy anything slower than 1200 baud.

Since 2400-baud modems are the hot new item on the market and since there are fewer manufacturers supplying them, there exists an innovation surcharge that will probably decrease as the novelty wears off and the competition heats up. But for now there are problems. We'll add our voice to the near unanimous chorus in the computer literature and recommend that the searcher wait before purchasing a 2400-baud modem.

The number of cities served by 2400-baud packet switched lines is still relatively small. Even if you do live in an area served by a high-speed line, you will still have to contend with a greater amount of line noise than usual. Susceptibility to noise increases markedly at higher speeds. Compatibility is also something of a problem. Some of the 2400-baud modems are incapable of automatically slowing down to a lower speed when excessive line noise is encountered. No doubt the installation of noise-free optical digital lines and the replacement of electrical computers by optical computers will eventually push the speed limit far beyond its present level.

Hayes: The De Facto Standard

But right now a 1200-baud modem is still the searcher's best bet. There are so many 1200-baud modems on the market right now that it probably would take several pages just to list them. Which one should the searcher buy? As is often the case, the marketplace has already determined to a large extent the type of modem to buy. Hayes compatibility is essential. The command set developed by the Hayes Company for its Smartmodem is supported by all of the major communications and online searching software publishers. If you want the security that comes with a name brand, buy a modem from Hayes.

There are numerous truly Hayes-compatible modems available from other manufacturers. Some are priced at much less than $200 and most have been reviewed in the micro literature. Be aware, however, that the difference between the off brands and the name brands isn't the functionality of the product but the originality of the circuit design and the quality of construction. Many of the cheaper external modems look and feel quite fragile. It is doubtful that some of them could withstand the punishment of institutional use.

The Hayes Command Set

Let's examine the Hayes command set a little more closely, as it is such a perfect example of the symbiotic relationship between hardware and software. The Hayes command set provides programmers with the opportunity to fine tune the hardware, in this case, the modem, to handle the nitty gritty details of moving information from place to place.

It really isn't necessary to know more than two or three of these commands to be able to use your modem effectively as a searcher. It is sufficient to know that your modem supports them because 99 percent of the available communications software uses them to talk to the hardware.

The Hayes commands are also known as AT commands because each command line must begin with the capital letters AT, an abbreviation for ATTENTION. These commands are programmers' tools. They allow the searcher to talk to the modem. They can be used within any program in any programming language, and are used in generic communications programs and in online search assistance programs. You can use them to talk to your modem directly from the level of your computer's operating system. Because the modem is always on the lookout for commands, problems ocasionally arise. If a capital AT ends up in a search statement, it will inadvertently wake up the modem and tell it to wait for a command.

Online/Offline

The Hayes modem has two functional states that correspond roughly to the two phases of an online search. One state is known as the local command state. The command mode is the state the modem is in when you are offline. Instructions may be given to the modem before or after a communications session is initiated. The local command state corresponds to the offline phase of an online search in which tasks like the search interview, identification of terms, and strategy preparation are performed.

The other possible state for the Hayes modem is the online state. This is the mode the device enters once a carrier signal from another modem has been detected and a communications link has been established. The modem's online state corresponds to the online phase of a search when the adrenalin is flowing, the little hairs stand up on the back of your neck, and money is exchanged for a chance to sample the riches of the information empire.

The Modem and Communications Parameters

AT commands may be used to switch the modem back and forth between the two states and to issue instructions to the machine in both the local command and the online state. AT commands are used to control the status of the signals entering and leaving the pins on the DB-25 connector. It is also possible to store values relating to the various aspects of representing and transferring information as signals. Those values can specify things like baud rate, duplex setting, or type of dialling to be used. They are known as communications parameters.

Most Hayes commands can include the command itself (usually a single letter) and a parameter, an argument upon which the command will act. Parameters must fit within an acceptable range. For example, when the modem is set to answer calls, the parameter governing the number of rings the modem will listen to before responding to an incoming call must be a number between 0 and 255. Here is an example of a command that causes the modem to dial a number.

AT DT9,524-4094

The AT tells the modem to wait for a command. The D tells it to dial. The T tells it to use tone rather than pulse dialing. The 9 tells it which number to dial, in this case a PBX exchange. The comma tells it to pause for a predetermined length of time. And 524-4094 is the number it will dial once it has paused long enough to get a dial tone from the branch exchange. It is possible to include more than one command on a single command line, as the example illustrates. Commands are stored in a memory area known as a buffer before they are executed. The size limit of the command buffer is forty characters.

The Hayes modem also includes seventeen storage areas known as registers and numbered S0 to S16. In the registers are stored values associated with communications parameters. The values in the registers are variable and can be changed by using AT commands to reset them. There are default values, that is values which are automatically provided when the modem is turned on. The most common communications settings are usually assumed as default values.

Let's look at our example again.

AT DT9,524-4094

The default value for the amount of time the modem will pause is two seconds, because two seconds is usually a sufficient length of time to receive a dial tone on a branch telephone exchange. The value specifying the pause duration associated with a comma is stored in the register numbered S8. Imagine that our micro is on a campus with bad telephone connections and it usually takes longer than two seconds to get a dial tone, often as long as five or six seconds. If we wanted to avoid having the modem begin dialing the number of a remote system before a dial tone was available, we would have to change the value stored in register number S8. This could be done quite simply with an AT command.

AT S8=7 (translation: ATTENTION SET THE VALUE
         IN REGISTER 8 TO 7 SECONDS)

Authors of communications programs can use these commands to add tremendous flexibility to the communications process. The modem can be intitialized to work in one way and then changed to work on another system. Values in registers can be assigned to meet local conditions. Sets of values for different networks and services can be created with relatively simple commands.

Some communications software takes better advantage of the potential of the modem commands than other software does. If your communications software doesn't do things like let you create your own set of default values, then it isn't taking full advantage of the capabilities of your modem. Even a superficial understanding of the modem commands will result in a greater appreciation of communications software. Communications software will be discussed in greater detail in Part Two.

Here is a description of some of the more accessible AT commands. Remember that any line beginning with AT can contain several different commands.

AT F1--sets duplex to full. This is the default.
AT F0--sets duplex to half.

ATDP524-4371--use pulse dialing to dial a number.
ATDT524-4371--use tone dialing for the same number.
ATH--hang up the phone.

AT ;--return modem to command state.
AT O--return modem to online state.

A/--repeat previous command.

AT S7=60--the value in register 7 determines the length of time the modem will wait before hanging up if it hasn't detected a carrier signal; this command changes the default value of thirty seconds to sixty seconds; the modem receiving this command would wait sixty seconds for a carrier-detect signal before hanging up and displaying the message NO CARRIER.

Internal versus External Modems

If you've already decided that you want to go with a 1200-baud, Hayes-compatible modem, your next choice will be between an internal and an external modem. An internal modem comes on a circuit board that fits into one of the expansion slots on your micro. Internal modems are almost always cheaper than comparable external modems, and an internal modem does not necessitate the purchase of a serial card. Unlike external modems, internal modems do not require a separate power source. Many of the current batch of internal modems come on half cards and will fit into one of your PC's short slots, leaving room for additional peripheral cards. Many internal modems also come bundled with communications software (as we shall see, the reasons for this aren't totally altruistic).

Price is the obvious advantage of an internal modem. Other advantages relate to the internal modem's compact size. A small, relatively expensive piece of hardware like a modem is much less likely to be stolen if it is tucked away inside a micro instead of sitting on a desktop. An internal modem also makes for a less cluttered workspace and won't require the extra electrical outlet that you probably can't afford to spare anyway.

Given these facts, why would anyone want an external modem? One good reason is that an external modem is much more versatile. If you have a micro at work and another at home, you can make an external modem do double duty (as long as each machine is equipped with a serial port). If you ever switch to a different computer, it is much more likely that an external modem will be compatible with your new hardware, since internal modems are often designed to fit under the hood of a specific machine.

An external modem is also advantageous if you need to keep track of the status of your communications sessions. External modems are much more likely to include speakers that will let you hear what is going on than internal modems are. The indicator lights on the front panel of your external modem will let you know the status of your communications link at any point. This is especially useful for troubleshooting if you are having problems with your software. By looking at an indicator light, you will be able to determine such things as whether a carrier-detect signal has been received by your modem. It's pretty easy to forget to plug the phone jack back into your modem after you've used the line for the phone. Without a carrier-detect indicator, some communications software could keep you busy trying to figure out what's wrong.

What the Indicator Lights Mean

The Hayes external modem (Smartmodem 1200) has eight indicator lights on its front panel. If you know what they mean, they will tell you what is going on when you go online.

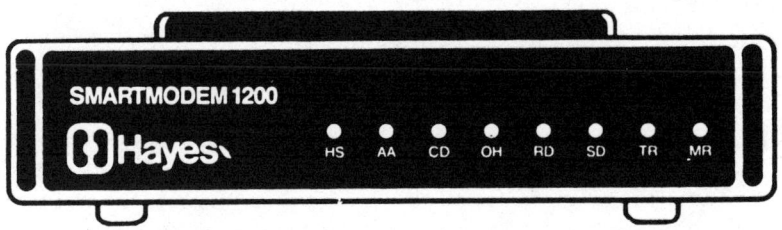

From right to left, the indicator lights are:

MR = Modem Ready
TR = Terminal Ready
SD = Send Data
RD = Receive Data
OH = Off Hook
CD = Carrier Detect
AA = Auto-Answer Mode
HS = High Speed (1200 bps)

Smartmodem indicator lights

Each is labeled with a two-letter code indicating the signal or condition the light is monitoring.

>HS--High Speed
>AA--Auto Answer Mode
>CD--Carrier Detect
>OH--Off Hook
>RD--Receive Data
>SD--Send Data
>TR--Terminal Ready
>MR--Modem Ready

HS--When this light is on you'll know the modem has been set to operate at 1200 rather than 300 baud.

AA--This light indicates whether or not the modem is in autoanswer mode. Since most online services assume that the call will be originating at the local computer, much of the search software require that this light be off.

CD--When you see this light come on, you'll know that the modem at the other end of the line has sent a carrier signal and you're online. If this light goes off during a search, you'll know you've been dropped and are no longer online.

OH--This light tells you that the modem has picked up the phone and is ready to talk.

RD--These lights flicker on and off as you are receiving and sending data.

TR--This light tells you that the power is activated on the micro to which your modem is connected.

MR--This light tells you whether or not the power to your modem is turned on.

DIP Switches

Some software packages require different settings of your modem's DIP switches. Some programs require different settings for different serial ports. Others require that switch number 5, which controls the autoanswer mode, be turned off. Those tiny switches make it possible to enable or disable the signals entering or leaving the DB-25 connector, and in many cases serve the same functions as AT commands. The Hayes modem comes with these switches set on defaults that were determined at the factory. If you regularly use more than a single communications/searching program, you probably won't want to take your computer apart each time you need to change modem switch settings. If you do decide upon an external modem for this reason, make sure the one you select has DIP switches that are easy to get to.

This 1200-baud modem from Hayes has set the industry standard.

Hayes recently introduced a 1200-baud modem on a half-card.

Little Things Mean a Lot

Basic online searching doesn't require a super sophisticated modem. The autoanswer features of Hayes modems aren't really necessary, nor are the dozens of other little extras supplied by modem manufacturers. But some of these features can be very useful in certain search environments. Expect to pay significantly more than usual for some of these capabilities.

Those involved with managing a search workstation that is used by a variety of clients and those allowing clients to make incoming calls to local files will appreciate the security features available on some modems. Some can be assigned passwords that limit their use to authorized people. Other modems can actually be programmed to dial back the numbers from which incoming calls originate. The return call at once creates a record of the attempt to access the computer and verifies that the caller is an authorized user.

Other modems permit remote or unattended operation when used with fancier communications software. A searcher could use a modem at home to print search results at the workstation or use the more powerful computer at work. Some modems provide buffers that can store communications sessions in the modem itself and that don't require the computer to which they are connected to be turned on.

Modems with synchronous capabilities permit more efficient connections to campus or corporate mainframes and minicomputers. There are even wireless modems that use radio signals to transmit information from one location to another within an organization. In this age of local area networks (LANs), it's not hard to imagine an online search workstation functioning as the major external communications and information-gathering node on a campus or corporate network.

Any modem will expand the capabilities of your micro and allow you to use its power to add value to the search process and the search product. A modem is your gateway to the complex and expanding civilization of electronic information. As we have seen in the discussion of the Hayes command set, modems are programmable. A modem is one more medium that can be shaped to meet our needs as information architects.

References/Recommended Reading

Benson, Terry. "Data Communications Today." *Interface Age* (March 1985): 60-81.

Bowers, Dan M. "Origin of the Species" [modems]. *Datamation*, 1 November 1984, 115-119.

Carne, E. Bryan. *Modern Telecommunication.* NY: Plenum Press, 1984.

Daney, Charles. "A Micro-Mainframe Primer." *PC Magazine*, 22 January 1985, 115-130.

Glossbrenner, Alfred. *Complete Handbook of Personal Computer Communications*. NY: St. Martin's Press, 1983.

_____. "2400-bps Modems: He Who Hesitates is Smart." *PC Magazine*, 23 July 1985, 147-149.

Gullo, Karen. "Modem Market Madness." *Datamation*, 1 January 1985, 44-52.

Helliwell, John. "On-Line with Smart Modems and Software." *PC Magazine*, 16 October 1984, 118-125.

Hurwood, Bernhardt J. "Do Your Modems Measure Up?" *Computer Decisions*, 9 April 1985, 134-140.

Lenk, John D. *Handbook of Data Communications*. Englewood Cliffs, NJ: Prentice-Hall, 1984.

Lockwood, Russ. "Modem Magic." *Creative Computing* (May 1985): 14-30.

Loomis, Mary E. *Data Communications*. Englewood Cliffs, NJ: Prentice-Hall, 1983.

Morrison, David. "Fast Modem Slow to Spark." *Computer Decisions*, 17 December 1985, 50-52.

Pepper, Jon. "Eight Modems for a New Standard." *PC Magazine*, 13 May 1986, 229-254.

Sandberg-Diment, Erik. "Modems: How Much Speed Makes Sense?" *New York Times*, 30 April 1985, 18.

_____. "When Computers Need to Chat." *New York Times*, 8 September 1985, F13.

Sandler, Corey. "What's So Standard About RS-232?" *Creative Computing* (June 1985): 24-25.

Sandler, Corey. "Modem Speed: What Does it Mean to You?" *Creative Computing* (Feb. 1985): 30-32.

Seyer, Martin P. *RS-232 Made Easy*. Englewood Cliffs, NJ: Prentice-Hall, 1984.

Stewart, Alan. "The 1200 Baud Experience." *Online* (July 1978): 13-18.

Stone, David. "Choosing and Using Modems." *PC Magazine*, 29 April 1986, 233-238.

_____. "A New Standard in 2400 bps Communications." *PC Magazine*, 23 July 1985, 133-142.

The, Lee. "Data Communications: A Buyer's Guide to Modems and Software." *Personal Computing* (March 1983): 96-128.

Witten, Ian H. "Welcome to the Standards Jungle." *BYTE* (Feb. 1983): 146-178.

CHAPTER FOUR
MEMORY

Memory Makes the Difference

So far we've looked at things that any terminal has. The input/output devices and communications interfaces on terminals may not be quite as flashy as those on talking micros, but they are there. We've seen that micros are modular. You can plug just about anything into one. But so far we've looked at plug-ins with which many terminals are already equipped. What's the real difference between terminals and personal computers?

The thing that micros have in abundance, the thing that even the smartest terminals have only in piddling amounts, is memory. And the amount of memory that can be added to a terminal is ridiculously low, unless the terminal is really a micro in disguise. Memory and modularity combined give personal computers the potential to become memexes. There are at least ten different memory technologies in widespread use in the world of micros. Together they represent the technology that will have the greatest impact on the online community. Terminals with memory are limited to small amounts of short-term memory. Desktop computers can be provided with short-term, medium-term, long-term, or even archival memory.

A Civilization of Memory

Memory can be fleeting and elusive, or it can last for a long, long time. We're not sure yet where electronic memory fits into the scheme of things. It may turn out to be fleeting and elusive, or it may endure among the records we pass on to future generations. Right now, in terms of cost and efficiency, the printed book is still our primary form of recorded thought. And memory, in the form of the printed word, is the fabric of our civilization. Let's find a symbol for memory in the city of information we are trying to build. Memory is the metaphor most often applied to the institution of the library. In our city then, libraries shall function as memories.

Our city, being part of an advanced civilization, will have many other levels and degrees of memory available to its citizens. Memory of a less permanent but more dynamic type than that symbolized by a library might be compared to a newspaper, which is read and then discarded, or an airline reservation office from which information arrives and departs, never to stay for long.

Dynamic memory is also an important aspect of libraries. We could hardly begin to exploit the knowledge locked up in a library without creating less permanent forms of memory to help us. Surely we don't expect our catalogs and indexes to outlast the intellectual artifacts they represent. Let us return for awhile to the computer before we talk about services, syndetic structures, and electronic communication.

Memory as Metaphor

Memory is a metaphor for libraries. Obviously memory is also the dominant metaphor of computing. The terminology overlaps. The same words that we apply to graphic records--libraries, volumes, indexes, records, files--are also part of the computer science vernacular (with meanings somewhat altered). Online databases, offspring of the marriage between library and computer, lie in the same metaphorical bed with their progenitors.

The person who puts the database together provides a structure from which information can (in an ideal world) be easily and efficiently extracted. Archival storage is handled by the gargantuan computers in which the database vendor has invested. The dynamic part of the process is provided at one end of the connection by the search language of the host system and at the other by the actions of the searcher. Increasingly sophisticated search languages, many of them developed with large full-text files in mind, permit highly precise strategies to go along with bigger and more complicated files. An electronic neural network is beginning to emerge. Personal computers, as nodes on the network, place a surprising variety of levels and degrees of memory at the disposal of the researchers who use them.

The Elephant and the Mouse

The memory capabilities of the micro, while puny in comparison to the elephantine machines of the host services, are growing fast. Large amounts of cheap RAM (random access memory) permit the use of ever more powerful software and allow the searcher greater control of the dynamic interaction with the host.

The usefulness of floppy disks is growing along with their storage capacity. The widespread use of hard disks has helped us to organize and store groups of files. It is now possible to develop our own databases and searching toolkits and to use the hard disk and its operating system to organize them for efficient use.

Inventions

Durable, removable, high-density memory devices are now available. Fixed disks are being supplemented by a host of new mass storage technologies. Who knew what a Bernoulli box was a year or two ago, or a hard card? Picture the research scientist or faculty member in the philosophy department, or stockbroker on the fast track, toting to work in a briefcase a dynamic, high-capacity personal information system. Portable databases can be now be had on CD-ROM and videodiscs. People are starting to talk about "electronic jukeboxes." Developments in mass storage technology could eventually turn the entire industry on its ear.

On the hardware front, some of the most impressive announcements relate to our ability to store ever larger volumes of information on smaller pieces of plastic, ceramic, or aluminum. At one level it is now possible to magnetize, etch, or inscribe tinier and tinier areas on the surfaces of storage media formed from the most exotic of materials. In the jargon this translates as increased areal density. On another level, from some of the most abstract corners of mathematics, come coding and error-checking schemes that allow us to use those tiny magnetized areas, etchings, and inscriptions to record thoughts and ideas and to establish webs of connections among them.

While the technology itself is full of fascinating stories, it is not necessary to know what pits and lands are or what sputtering film is all about to understand how different types of memory can be used in our city of information.

Variations

There are at least three major categories of memory employed by micros. And each category is embodied in more than a few technologies. Magnetic memory involves the magnetization and demagnetization of the coated surface of a recording medium, typically a disk or tape. Areas of magnetization known as transitions are used to represent the zeros and ones of our digital language. Optical memory uses irregularities on the surface of a highly polished disk to represent zeros and ones. A laser is used to read information that has been encoded as "pits and lands" on the surface of the disk. CD-ROM is the most commonly used type of optical memory. Finally, semiconductor memory represents digital information as stored electrical charges. RAM and ROM are forms of semiconductor memory.

There are numerous variations on these three basic themes and a number of ingenious schemes for formatting and encoding information on different media. Each category has spawned a batch of inventions. Let's look at the implications for searchers of some of the products whose advertisements fill the pages of most computer magazines.

RAM Chic

Micro enthusiasts talking about RAM have a tendency to sound like high school kids bragging about their cars. Hot rods are measured in terms of the number of cubic inches under the hood. RAM has become the measure of the speed and power a souped-up micro is capable of achieving.

RAM is the dynamic, volatile, and lightning fast short-term memory that lets you take advantage of your micro's raw computing power. The more RAM you have, the more computing power you have. Today's programs, especially spreadsheets and database managers, are notorious for being RAM hungry. Nowadays, programmers assume that there will be lots of RAM available when they are developing software.

Even sloppily written, inefficient software can be made to look good if enough RAM is available. RAM technology is pushing relentlessly forward. Last year's insurmountable barrier is on its way to becoming this year's standard equipment. A micro with 64 kilobytes of RAM used to be considered a respectable machine. Then the standard became 256 kilobytes. Now its not unusual to see standard configurations with 512 or 640 kilobytes of RAM. Conventional wisdom used to be that 640 kilobytes was the ceiling on the amount of RAM one could put into a micro. Recently developed technologies, known as expanded and extended RAM, have raised the limit to ten or more megabytes (million bytes). The research literature now includes references to nonvolatile RAM--fast, dynamic memory that doesn't disappear when the power is turned off. Can products incorporating this technology be far behind?

Do It Yourself

It used to be expensive to add RAM to a micro. You used to have to waste an expansion slot on a memory board. The original PC could only accommodate 64 kilobytes of RAM on its main board; it took a set of several chips to add 16 kilobytes. Then 64 kilobytes became the standard. Now 256-kilobyte chips are common and prices are at bargain basement levels. These 256-kilobyte chips can now be easily added to the main circuit board of many micros, raising the available RAM to 640K, and eliminating the need for an expansion card.

RAM is so cheap and easy to install now that it is hard to justify not having plenty of RAM to spare. Just pop the chips into the sockets, set a few swiches inside the machine, and you're ready to roll. If you do want to add an expansion card you can add an expanded or extended memory board, turning your micro into a multimegabyte RAM powerhouse capable of racing on the same circuit with some of the minis.

Expansion Cards

The XT and more recent generations of the PC can handle up to 256 kilobytes on the main board. If you can't add the maximum of 640 kilobytes on the motherboard, you can add the traditional multifunction expansion card, or you can take advantage of expanded memory technology to really increase the power of your machine. You don't have to be an electrical engineer to add memory chips. Adding an expansion card is even easier. Remove the cover from your PC. Gently press the card into an expansion slot and change any required switch settings per the instructions that come with the card.

The IBM PC is an open system. It's architecture is designed to accommodate circuit boards produced by third-party manufacturers following IBM's specifications. The expansion card market is one of the most active areas for third-party manufacturers. The first generation of expansion cards provided the means to add 384 kilobytes to the 256 kilobytes that the IBM's motherboard can handle. Companies like Quadram, AST, Tecmar, and Tall Tree offer circuit boards that not only will increase a computer's RAM but will add a number of extras.

Products like J-RAM 2 from Tall Tree, Six Pack Plus from AST, and Quadboard from Quadram add clock/calendars, print spoolers, serial and parallel ports, and software as part of the added memory package. Most expansion boards themselves are modular. You can buy them with the full complement of memory and extra features or you can buy a basic unit with no memory to which you can add your own chips.

The Tall Tree J-RAM 2, without memory chips inserted into its slots and minus the clock/calendar and serial and parallel ports, sells for roughly half the price of the model that includes those options. It's usually much more cost-effective to buy the least expensive board and install your own 64-kilobyte chips. The Japanese are now practically giving 64-kilobyte chips away. The boards themselves are heavily discounted by stores and mail order houses. Prices range from $100 to $500 depending upon the brand name and the number of extras included. A mail order purchase is a real option here. Circuit boards are small. If anything goes wrong, they can be easily returned by mail or parcel service. Reputable dealers will repair or replace the defective unit.

Expanded Memory

There used to be a limit of 640 kilobytes on the amount of RAM that was directly addressable by the PC. That limit has been surpassed. Three industry leaders, each with its own reasons for breaking the 640-kilobyte RAM barrier, banded together and came up with a new standard that raises potential RAM in the PC to eight megabytes.

The Intel Corporation (one of the leading chip makers) developed a technology known as expanded RAM. Lotus (producer of the RAM-hungry *Lotus 1-2-3* spreadsheet) and Microsoft (best known for having developed the MS-DOS operating system, which is the standard for PC compatibles) helped Intel by providing specifications that allow best-selling programs to take advantage of Intel's technology. We are starting to see the software tail wagging the hardware dog.

Each of the new expanded memory boards can accommodate as much as two megabytes of additional memory. As many as four of the cards may be added for a maximum of eight megabytes. Tall Tree and other board makers have joined Intel, but the technology is still new and prices haven't fallen yet. Expect to pay between five hundred and a few thousand dollars depending upon how much memory and how many boards are added.

Like most standards in the fast-changing micro industry, the Intel/Lotus/Microsoft expanded memory specification has its competitors. Another "standard" employing a similar approach has been jointly developed by AST, Ashton-Tate (producer of the popular and RAM-hungry *Framework* and *dBase* programs), and Quadram. Which standard is accepted by software producers remains to be seen, but it seems as if future changes in the MS-DOS operating system could tip the scales in favor of Intel's technology.

Clouding the issue further is the development of another memory-increasing technology known as extended memory. Extended memory technology is capable of raising the RAM limit to sixteen megabytes, but it isn't totally compatible with the architecture of the current crop of PCs. Only time and hardware/software producers can determine which technology will ultimately predominate.

RAM for Searchers

How can a lot of RAM under the hood benefit the searcher? Already we are seeing in other application areas the emergence of faster moving, smarter, RAM-intensive software. The better communications programs employ buffers in which search results and search statements are kept. The searcher can scroll through the buffer and print, edit, or save its contents. Since a buffer is really an area of RAM that has been set aside for dynamic storage, its size is dependent upon the amount of RAM available. More RAM means a bigger buffer.

So-called RAM-resident programs (they are loaded into RAM where they sit, waiting until they are summoned) are proliferating. If software developers would agree on standards for these programs, maybe we wouldn't have to worry so much about them bumping into one another with unpredictable results. Caution is advised when using RAM-resident programs together, but the benefits to be gained from these inexpensive programs deserve attention. Some allow the user to create and store sequences of instructions known as macros. As we shall see in the software section, these programs, which are also known as keyboard enhancers, can help the searcher in many ways. Others provide instant outlining, file organization, or thesaurus availability. Ever tried using an online thesaurus like Borland's *Lightning* to generate ideas for search terms? Imagine being able to load the thesauri for specific databases into RAM along with software for moving to and fro among related terms and generating appropriate strategies.

RAM and the Operating System

RAM-resident programs are an example of applications software that takes advantage of large amounts of dynamic memory. RAM has made possible another software trend that is more long-reaching in its implications. As more RAM becomes the norm, the developers of the master control programs known as operating systems will have greater flexibility.

Future generations of operating systems can be expected to make personal computers friendlier. Future operating systems will use RAM to provide high-quality graphics and to shuffle information easily from one application to another. The next generation of operating systems will also accommodate a greater variety of peripherals and increase the searcher's options for input and output.

The tasks performed by a searcher's workstation can extend far beyond simple communications. Higher levels of integration will be required to work with the same data in different applications and to support a wider variety of input and output formats. More powerful, flexible, and friendlier operating systems made possible by more RAM will eliminate the barriers between the tools searchers use. It will become much easier to move from the search process to the finished search product.

RAM Disks

Another benefit of increased RAM is the RAM disk. A RAM disk, or virtual disk, can increase the productivity of most software tools by raising the speed limit for information traffic from mechanical to electronic levels. A virtual disk, like a virtual circuit, only appears to be something it is not. A RAM disk acts like a disk and presents itself to the user and to the machine as a disk. But there is no disk in sight. The RAM disk is sleight of hand, just another clever software trick.

The software that sets aside a portion of RAM to act as a superfast, nonmechanical disk often accompanies memory expansion cards. If your RAM is on your machine's motherboard, or if the expansion card you have didn't come with RAM disk software, there are alternatives. There are RAM disk programs in the public domain, and the latest version of MS-DOS (3.0) includes a program called VDISK.SYS that will trick your computer into thinking part of its RAM is really a disk.

Most personal computers have a minimum of two floppy disk drives. Many replace one of the floppies with a higher capacity fixed disk. Who needs a RAM disk? Speed is the advantage of a RAM disk. Applications programs like *WordStar* and *dBase* move the instructions to perform tasks that are part of the larger application back and forth from disk to RAM as they are required. Anyone who has used a program that keeps running to the disk to fetch information knows how tedious it can become. Placing the complete set of instructions required by such programs into a RAM disk significantly increases effectiveness. Some tasks are optimized by putting entire files in RAM. The searching and sorting associated with database management happen much more quickly when data and index files are placed in RAM. Database programs can complete in seconds tasks that used to take minutes.

RAM and Artificial Intelligence

The information-handling capabilities of high-performance RAM machines are bound to result in the principles of artificial intelligence being incorporated into search software. It is getting easier to store for instant recall the collection of knowledge and rules that comprise the repertoire of a good searcher. Sooner or later someone is going to come up with software that mimics the thought process of a searcher, and that will take an electronic blackboard of enormous size.

Old Floppy--New Tricks

RAM is our short-term memory. Our medium-term memory is the floppy disk. Floppy disks have become almost as commonplace as five-dollar bills and still serve as coin of the realm in our city of micros. When you buy software you usually get it on floppy disk. The word "floppy" conjures up images of a reliable companion, like a familiar old pet that a person can get used to having around. But old floppy is beginning to learn some new tricks.

Floppy disk drives must deal with information as a physical entity. An electromagnetic head senses (reads) and creates (writes) information as magnetized areas on the surface of a disk. Disk drives must also deal with information as a logical entity. Just as the RS-232 standard represents an electrical language and ASCII represents a logical language, there is an electrical language for recording on magnetic disks and a logical scheme for organizing information into tracks, sectors, and blocks. Advances in both areas have steadily increased the capacity of floppy disks.

A highly publicized trend is the move toward 3.5-inch rigid disks. Pioneered by Sony and popularized by Apple's Macintosh, these disks could be perpetuated by that ultimate arbiter of taste, IBM, which announced in April that its new laptop computer (portable as opposed to transportable) would include them. Not only are they more durable and easier to store and transport, they often have more than double the storage capacity of the standard 360-kilobyte floppy. The capacity of old-fashioned, 5 1/4-inch floppies is also increasing. Quad density drives have pushed floppy storage from the kilobyte to the megabyte range.

Database Subsets

Subsets of large databases are beginning to appear on floppy disk. BIOSIS, ERIC, and a few others have all had products on the market for a while now. Larger capacities and more users with the new drives ought to make the subset on disk an attractive marketing medium for database producers. Examples of information products that have migrated from online to disk distribution will be provided in Part Three.

It would seem that easily produced subsets of big databases could establish a volume business among those with specialized needs, shallow pockets, and small computers. The likelihood of large-scale piracy may be deterring database producers from rushing to market disk-based products. A megabyte or so of storage on an inexpensive, easily copied disk has implications for both producers and consumers of electronic information. Depending upon whose point of view is taken, it could exacerbate the downloading problem or serve as a boon to researchers interested in developing their own bibliographic files.

Institutional-Strength Micros

Almost all institutional-sized and a growing number of individual-sized micros now come with 10 or more megabytes of hard disk storage. Hard disks already make it possible to maintain large files at the local level. Most postprocessing software wouldn't be feasible without the mass storage capacity provided by hard disks. The idea of the personal information system containing records from online files, the notes of the individual researcher, and a collection of software tools came into its own with the hard disk. For the first time, individuals were able to store and organize the information and tools required for serious research however they liked.

It is true that the standard 10- or 20-megabyte fixed disk is a commodious information vault. On the other hand, fixed disks are difficult to install, and once installed can't be easily moved. The delicacy of a hard disk belies its name. And the information on the disk is subject to prying eyes and blundering fingers. Valuable information is about as fragile as the mechanism on which it's stored. The potential disasters and the need for back-up have been well documented. The head that reads and writes information is much closer to the surface of a hard disk than it is to the surface of a floppy disk, and the information on a hard disk is crammed in at a much higher density. If the head falls to the surface of a spinning hard disk or encounters a speck of dust . . . crash! It's time to spend a couple of days trying to recover lost files.

Beyond the Hard Disk

Devices that provide the storage of hard disks without being chained to the micro's chassis afford the same type of advantages afforded by paperback books and Volkswagen Bugs. Hard disks on a card, removable hard disks, and Bernoulli Boxes could become the mass media of mass storage.

Bernoulli boxes especially hold great promise as storage media for personal information systems. A flexible disk spins rapidly over a read/write head which projects above a stationary plate. The spinning disk floats on a cushion of air and doesn't wobble like a floppy disk does (permitting higher density storage). The disk is enclosed in a cartridge that only opens when it is inserted in a disk drive. Dirt and dust aren't as big a problem, and head crashes are prevented by the cushion of air on which the disk floats. Disks are economical (approximately $50 for 10 megabytes) and removable, eliminating the data security nightmares associated with hard disks.

Inexpensive, reliable, and removable mass storage media suggest services that a library or information center could provide to its clients. A library could supply its users with disks on which were stored search profiles and downloaded search results as well as software for searching and processing search results. Each disk could be custom designed to meet the needs of a specific individual.

The market researcher's disk would include macros designed to work with numeric files and software for analyzing numeric data. The scholar in the humanities would be given a disk designed to work with textual and bibliographic databases and which included word processing and bibliographic software. Libraries could get into the business of producing custom-designed searchers' toolkits on removable disks. Each client's software could be modified to take advantage of local collections and available online systems and databases.

The same hardware could be shared by different clients with different requirements. The storage medium would no longer be part of the hardware configuration as it is with the hard disk. A variety of people could share the same hardware and still be assured of privacy. The files on a disk would reflect individual idiosyncracies rather than group needs. The ability of this medium to be read from as well as written on would allow its users to edit and modify stored information as required and to merge information obtained from online databases with locally developed material.

Archival Electronic Memory

None of the microcomputer technologies discussed so far come anywhere close to approaching the traditional printed book as a medium of archival memory. Optical storage technology, the most recent addition to the pantheon of micro storage media, provides our best hope of an "electronic book" that can be stored locally instead of deep within the computer of a host service on the other side of the country. Optical technology, particularly CD-ROM, is already the subject of a large and growing body of literature. All indications are that this new storage technology will have a significant impact on the way electronic information is distributed and consumed.

Optical technology could represent the long-term electronic memory we have been awaiting. It is the only microcomputer medium capable of storing database-sized chunks of information. A disk the size of a 5 1/4-inch floppy disk can hold up to 800 megabytes of digital information. An 11-inch disk can store 4 gigabytes. Capacities of that magnitude have made possible the large database on a disk. The *Academic American Encyclopedia* is now available in this format; other reference works are bound to follow.

Digital Equipment Corporation now markets subsets of databases such as COMPENDEX on optical disks.

Optical Hardware

Optical disk drives are similar in many ways to the drives used for magnetic disks. An optical head, which on most current systems is limited to reading information (hence, CD-ROM), replaces the more traditional magnetic read/write head. The optical head also moves back and forth across the surface of a disk, seeking information that has been recorded there.

The disk itself is formed of a polished, highly reflective layer of aluminum sandwiched between a hard plastic substrate and a thin, transparent coating. Most optical disks are single-sided and are inserted in the drive face down. The optical head directs a laser beam onto the disk and senses the quality of the light being reflected back. Etched onto the polished surface of the disk, beneath the the transparent coating (these things are often compared to record albums, but you can't scratch them) are infinitesimal depressions and flat areas known respectively as pits and lands.

Pits and lands represent pieces of digital information laid out on a long, spiral track. Of course, a code is involved and there is a scheme for logically organizing blocks of memory to complement the scheme for its physical layout on the recording medium. And there are error-checking algorithms, as well as standards of the same sort prevalent among other pieces of hardware.

Optical disk drives, like most peripherals, require a circuit board to link them to the rest of the hardware in the machine. Every plug-in needs a plug. Of course, different manufacturers incorporate different interfaces. As is usually the case, technical standards are being developed through a chaotic evolutionary process involving both hardware and software producers. The SCSI (Small Computer Systems Interface) has been suggested as a universal tool for linking computers to peripherals, but its cost presents problems.

Software standards for coding and representing information with this technology have not emerged. Standards as pervasive as those established by IBM and its operating system for magnetic storage are still a ways down the optical road. One encouraging development has been the involvement of Microsoft, developer of the PC's operating system, in a movement to establish definitive standards.

Optical Marketing

Optical disk drives in the online marketplace are generally bundled with a database on an optical disk (more on this later). Prices vary and what you pay for is likely to be a Sony, Phillips, or Hitachi drive with the value-added database vendor's logo slapped onto it. The major impetus for this technology did come from the recording industry, and most information products sell the same 4.75-inch CD-

ROM drives familiar to audiophiles. IAC has bucked the trend by supplying its optical databases on record album-sized videodiscs.

Prices on the drives themselves are in the $1,000 to $2,000 range, although it is hard to tell what part of the cost is for hardware and what part is for information. DEC, the heavyweight among minicomputer makers, is now selling databases on optical disks along with a minicomputer-based, hardware "jukebox."

Optical databases are sold on a subscription basis and prices vary widely. Databases rivaling online products sell for thousands of dollars. Optical publishing may be the first area in which the price of the hardware medium is surpassed by the information it carries. After all, newsprint has been cheaper than news for a long time.

Databases on Disks

Many familiar databases are already available in optical formats. The Silver Platter company now offers several databases on CD-ROM, including ERIC, PsycInfo, and PAIS. H.W. Wilson is experimenting with a CD-ROM version of its files. InfoTrac, IAC's videodisc-based product, was among the first on the market and has received mostly favorable reviews. The InfoTrac software now allows downloading to floppy disks, clearing the way for the electronic re-use of records from the database. Disclosure offers a CD-ROM version of its database of corporate reports at a price that compares favorably to that of its microfiche product. Software accompanying the database allows researchers to manipulate the information contained in the financial records that comprise the file. A detailed discussion of several of these products will be provided in Part Three.

References/Recommended Reading

Desposito, Joe. "Invasion of the Hard Disk Drives." *Creative Computing* (August 1985): 28-35.

Hoagland, Albert S. "Information Storage Technology: A Look at the Future." *Computer* 18, no.7 (July 1985): 60-67.

Laub, Leonard. "The Evolution of Mass Storage." *BYTE* (May 1986): 161-172.

Lewis, Peter H. "Larger Memories Are No Longer a Luxury." *New York Times*, 1 January 1986, 19.

_____. "Adding Memory Boards." *New York Times*, 21 January 1986, 19.

_____. "New Memory Boards Go Beyond the 640K Barrier." *New York Times*, 28 January 1986.

Malloy, Rich. "A Roundup of Optical Disk Drives." *BYTE* (May 1986): 215-224.

Micossi, Anita. "Breaking the RAM Barrier." *Computer Decisions*, 9 April 1985, 16-20.

Moore, Steve. "The Mass Storage Squeeze." *Datamation*, 1 October 1984, 68-79.

O'Malley, Christopher. "RAM Management: Getting More Done Faster." *Personal Computing* (March 1986): 106-121.

Rosch, Winn L. "Plug-ins: The Inside Story." *PC Magazine*, 14 May 1985, 110-113.

_____, ed. "New Frontiers for Add-in Technology." *PC Magazine*, 14 May 1985, 145-158.

Sandberg-Diment, Erik. "Dealing the PC a Bigger Memory." *New York Times*, 13 April 1986, 20F.

Sarisky, Larry. "Will Removable Hard Disks Replace the Floppy?" *BYTE* (March 1983): 110-117.

Shuford, Richard S. "CD-ROMs and Their Kin." *BYTE* (November 1985): 137-146.

Thompson, Lester E. "Floppy Disk Formats." *BYTE* (September 1984): 435-443.

Vaughan, Frank, and Richard Aarons. "The Bernoulli Solution." *PC Magazine*, 18 September 1984, 149-153.

Whieldon, David. "New Lift for Mass Storage." *Computer Decisions* (December 1983): 172-186.

Zoellick, Bill. "CD-ROM Software Development." *BYTE* (May 1986): 177-188.

PART TWO
SOFTWARE TOOLS

CHAPTER FIVE
OPERATING SYSTEMS AS BLUEPRINTS

Hardware provides us with the medium with which to build a city of information and to connect it to an electronic civilization. Software provides us with the tools to work our new medium into a form that meets our needs as collectors and manipulators of symbols. An abundance of hardware building materials and a rich selection of software tools make possible the creation of information structures.

Cities have evolved to take advantage of their environments. A great river, a harsh climate, or the availability of some resource of the earth can shape a city's architecture and determine its fate. The environment shaping our city of information is known as the operating system. Within this environment, it is possible to build structures of functional simplicity or exotic complexity.

Our information metropolis will evolve just as a city does, but before it evolves it must be built, and before it is built plans must be made. The operating system will serve as our blueprint, our building code, and the medium from which we will build the infrastructure of our city. Because part of the operating system lies in the hardware and the other part consists of software, it is at once a medium and a tool.

Part Hardware, Part Software

The operating system (OS) is the bridge between hardware and software, the mediator between electrical activity and human ingenuity. The OS is a collection of programs some of which stay on ROM chips as part of the hardware (often called firmware) and others which start out on a disk and end up in RAM when they are needed. Remember the ROM BIOS? It's part of the operating system. When you turn on (or boot up) your micro, programs sitting in ROM load the most useful part of the operating system into RAM, and the OS presents itself to you by asking for the time and date.

The way the operating system works is of particular interest to the searcher who is charged with moving information around, transforming it, and restructuring it. Searching can easily involve several different types of computing (communications, word processing, database management, calculation, natural language processing) and an assortment of devices (modems, printers, monitors, disk drives). The operating system determines how easily information can be shared by different applications. It can provide the potential for different tools to work together, or it can deny that potential.

The OS is a building code that must be adhered to by all but the most determined hackers. It is the framework within which we are permitted to move information. The OS controls the flow of information between our hardware devices and provides the schema for the way in which software can store and manipulate it.

Operating Systems and Compatibility

The operating system with which a searcher must deal depends upon which machine was purchased. When IBM introduced its PC, the operating system it chose was a dialogue of Microsoft's MS-DOS that it called PC-DOS. Consequently, MS-DOS became the de facto standard operating system for IBM PC/XT compatibles. Before IBM selected MS-DOS, an operating system known as CP/M had been the de facto standard for personal computer operating systems. Apple, which has never worried about upsetting the cart, has always used its own proprietary operating systems on its various machines.

Because the hardware is often different, programs written for one machine's version of an operating system must be modified before they can be run on another machine. Modifying software to run on another machine or OS is known as porting the software from one system to another. The enormous popularity of IBM's PC and XT resulted in the rapid development of a large body of software, which in turn led to the proliferation of IBM-compatible machines that run in the MS-DOS environment. Many of the first applications programs for the PC were ported from CP/M, which was the most heavily supported operating system at the time. Later, programs which were designed to take advantage of the PC's more powerful 16-bit chip began to appear.

Microprocessor chips and the way they are connected to other components determine the design characteristics of operating systems. The fact that IBM uses a 16-bit chip and an 8-bit bus places constraints upon the designers of its operating system.
As the chips at the heart of micro evolve from 8 to 16 to 32 bits, and as buses become able to accommodate more information traffic, operating systems originally developed for minicomputers will become more popular. Already Bell Labs' UNIX system and its derivatives have attracted a substantial following among micro users. Although MS-DOS is the most widely used, there is still no such thing as a standard operating system. Further confusing the matter are the

Operating Systems as Blueprints 91

many programs intended to complement the operating system or mediate between the operating system and the user.

Files and the OS

The part of DOS that is seen by the user is used to deal with higher level information entities. DOS programs are tools that have been designed to handle the information unit known as a file. When using DOS, the searcher is generally not working at the level of the character, the field, or the record but at the level of the file. A file can be a collection of records--a database. A file can be text containing, letters, numbers, and symbols. A plain vanilla text file is also called an ASCII file because it contains ASCII characters. Many of today's word processors generate text files that aren't intelligible within DOS because they add so-called high bits to format and justify text. The result is something other than an ASCII file.

A file can also be a program or part of a program. A file can contain instructions that tell the computer to do something. Some files can be read by people; other files are only intelligible to the machine. In database management, certain types of files are structured so as to point to the pieces of information with which they are associated. There are all kinds of conventions for naming and using different types of files. There are several types of program files alone, and the different file structures used in database management boggle the mind.

The computer will deal with program files in a certain order, knowing by their names the types of instructions they contain. DOS provides the rules for naming files and for manipulating them. DOS file names are limited to eight characters followed by a period and an additional three characters known as the file name extension (e.g., FILENAME.EXT). The convention is to name a file for its contents and to provide the name with an extension indicating the type of file it is. For example, a file containing the text of a document is ordinarily given the extension .DOC or .TXT. Some file name extensions indicate to DOS that the file with which they are associated is a special kind of instruction file or program that must be processed in fixed sequence according to predetermined rules.

The Operating System as Software Tools

DOS also provides the searcher with a useful collection of software tools. The most familiar DOS programs (commands) are those that are loaded into RAM when the computer is booted. Because they stay in RAM until the power is shut off, they are known as DOS-resident commands.

DOS-resident commands are the workhorses with which any micro user will become quickly familiar. Among the resident commands are those that are used to ask for a list of files on a disk (DIR), to copy files (COPY), to remove files from a disk (DEL, ERASE), or to rename files (RENAME).

Less frequently used DOS commands stay on a disk until they are ready to be used. Such commands are known as transient DOS commands because they pass back and forth between RAM and the disk where they reside. Transient commands have to be available on the disk or part of a hard disk currently being used. Transient commands that are important to the searcher can be put on the disks containing the applications programs with which they are associated or in the part of the hard disk reserved for the searcher's applications.

Among frequently used transient commands are those that prepare disks to store information (FORMAT), to edit text files (EDLIN), and to backup hard disks (BACKUP, RESTORE). Many of the transient commands were specifically designed as programmer's tools. The MODE command, for example, can be used within communications software to tell the operating system which communications port is being used and to convey information about the baud rate, number of framing bits, and other communications parameters.

The CHKDSK command is especially useful to searchers because it indicates the amount of space available on a disk. If you are planning to download a file, you'd better have room to spare on your disk or chances are that the information scrolling across your screen as you run out of disk space will be lost forever.

The Operating System as an Organizational Framework

DOS controls the flow and transformation of information within our little city. DOS also provides an organizational schema for storing data and files. The FORMAT command prepares hard or floppy disks to accept data in a way that is consistent with the way the hardware physically records (writes) and retrieves (reads) information on the surface of the storage medium.

FORMAT is one of the most dangerous DOS commands. FORMAT, when used with a disk upon which information has already

Operating Systems as Blueprints 93

been recorded, will wipe the slate clean before the disk is organized for storage. No fail-safe message like "Are you sure? Y/N " is provided. An inadvertent format command or a format command with an incorrect argument (e.g., typing FORMAT C: when you meant to type FORMAT A:) could easily wipe out the contents of a hard disk --programs, files, databases--the whole works.

Earlier versions of MS-DOS did not provide an efficient schema for storing and organizing files. Later versions (2.0 and up) provide a tree structure that can be used to store files hierarchically in logical groupings.

Dividing the Disk

The utility of a hard disk can be increased by partitioning it into directories and subdirectories that reflect the logical or functional relationship of files to one another. File names can include path specifications that describe the route to a file in its subdirectory on the disk. Directories can be used to group programs and/or files together by:

- category of application--for example, all word processing software and files could be kept in one subdirectory.
- function--for example, all of the programs and datafiles used for search tasks could be grouped by function within subdirectories of an online subdirectory; subdirectories could even be created for files relating to specific search systems or databases.
- type of client--for example, all of the accounting records, client profiles, and database-specific files and results associated with a college's psychology department could be stored in a psychology subdirectory.

The Operating System and the User

The operating system is both the user's and the software's primary link to the hardware. Trends in the software industry are moving toward including a more sophisticated user interface and higher levels of integration within the operating system. CP/M was initially directed toward the programmers/hackers, who were the first microcomputer enthusiasts. MS-DOS presented a friendlier face to its users. Its businesslike approach and thorough documentation were favored by the IBM crowd. After all, the original name of Digital Research, the company that developed CP/M, was Intelgalactic Digital Research.

Not surprisingly, the most memex-like of operating systems, Smalltalk, was developed at Xerox PARC. The FINDER operating system employed by the Apple Macintosh is a conceptual descendent of Smalltalk. Smalltalk-influenced operating systems, like the memex, rely upon visual imagery to connect the user to the system. The level of integration between applications is increased by providing a visual shell in which icons are moved around on a high-resolution screen by a mouse that enables the user to move between applications without having to learn complex sequences of commands. Context-sensitive menus pop up on the screen to provide the user with options relating to the task being performed.

The growing popularity of the Macintosh has led to Smalltalk-like programs for the IBM PC and other MS-DOS machines. One problem, however, is the 16-bit chip that lies at the heart of the IBM. The Macintosh includes a 32-bit chip, which makes it easier to process the complex instructions required to implement a high-level user interface.

Failure to take advantage of graphic capabilities and an emphasis on disk storage at the expense of input and output have been major deficiencies of MS-DOS. Microsoft, the developer of MS-DOS, has developed a program called Windows, which was designed to compensate for deficiencies of MS-DOS. Windows provides the visual shell, the icons, and the program integrator associated with the Macintosh.

Unfortunately, Windows was developed without IBM's blessing and hasn't been supported by IBM as MS-DOS has. IBM has developed its own "windowing environment," which it calls TopView. The reviews of Windows have generally been more favorable than those of TopView. Digital Research has entered the fray by introducing Concurrent DOS, an operating system that not only allows easy movement between applications but allows multitasking (working on more than one application at the same time). Operating systems are evolving as hardware evolves and users are becoming more demanding. The operating systems of the 90s are likely to be quite different from those of today.

The Operating System as a Programming Language

DOS is a programming language in its own right, although since its strength is in handling files it is not as flexible as higher level languages such as BASIC and Pascal, which can handle a wider variety of data types. Each DOS command performs as an independent program, but they can be combined to more effectively control the flow of information among the devices and programs that form our city of information. DOS commands can be included in different types of program files to move between applications or to specify where information is located and how to move it among devices, transforming it from electrical charges to print on paper, or records in a structured database.

Files called batch files (they always have the filename extension .BAT) allow the user to group together DOS commands, which will be executed one at a time. Commands in DOS batch files can include commands that load and unload applications programs. After the application program has been run, control of the computer returns to the batch file. A special batch file called AUTOEXEC.BAT specifies which DOS commands will be executed automatically when the machine is booted. Batch files can be used to provided menus for inexperienced users or to display help screens and explanatory messages. It is possible to use batch files to develop a turnkey system.

DOS commands can be used to configure the system to include specific kinds of devices or to specify the type of monitor, communications interface, or printer being used. Other DOS commands will tell the operating system where to look within the maze of directories for specific types of files or programs. DOS commands can be used to request information like the date and time, or to change the prompt.

Most applications programs take advantage of DOS commands by employing system calls. System calls enable applications programs to use already existing DOS commands to move information back and forth between disks, monitors, keyboards, printers, and other peripherals.

The Operating System as File Manager

The OS is a set of hardware, software and firmware (ROM) instructions for handling files. There are several different types of files, ranging from those containing data to programs containing instuctions. Applications programs are the software packages people buy to help them with specific tasks. When people refer to "software," what they are usually referring to are applications programs.

Most applications programs are modular in nature and are themselves comprised of several files. Some of the files contain subprograms which perform a small task that is part of the larger application. Some of the search assistance packages, for example, include separate modules for communications and accounting. Application programs also usually include files that contain help messages and menus for the user.

Some programs include files containing information that is required to meet the needs of specific users and that is placed in the file by those users. For example, an online search program might include files containing passwords, log-on protocols, and so forth that were supplied by individual users. Online search database management applications often include template files that allow the searcher to specify the record structure of the most frequently searched databases.

Modularity is important in designing both hardware and software. Integrated software packages like *Symphony* or *Framework* attempt to include separate modules for functions as different as spreadsheet calculation and telecommunication. There are tradeoffs, however. Thousands of hours of time have already been invested in learning to use stand-alone programs. Stand-alone programs are often superior to the module of an integrated package designed for the same function because the stand-alone product is designed for a single purpose.

Operating systems that permit the integration of functions make it possible to create your own integrated system. In the future, searchers will be faced with the choice of purchasing and learning an integrated system or using the operating system to link stand-alone programs with which they are already familiar. Operating systems are chosen by hardware manufacturers. They have to be, since part of the OS is hardware dependent. Applications programs are chosen by the consumer, and within the MS-DOS environment there are literally thousands of applications programs from which to choose.

Before moving on to applications programs, let's spend a little time examining that category of software known as utilities. Utilities, as the name implies, are general purpose programs that are useful for many applications. The utility programs in which the searcher will be most interested are those that permit the integration of more than one application. Many utilities are designed to overcome limitations of DOS and applications programs. Utilities are especially useful to the searcher who must move from communicating to word processing to database management and back.

References/Recommended Reading

Fertig, Robert T. *The Software Revolution: Trends, Players, Market Dynamics in Personal Computer Software*. NY: Elsevier North-Holland, 1985.

Petzold, Charles. "PC Tutor." *PC Magazine*, 24 June 1986, 293-295.

Sheldon, Tom. "DOS Tips, Tricks, and Techniques." *PC Magazine*, 25 March 1986, 237-267.

Waite, Mitchell, *et al. DOS Primer for the IBM PC and XT*. NY: New American Library, 1984.

CHAPTER SIX
UTILITIES FOR THE SEARCHER

Filling the Toolbox--Utilities for the Searcher

Utilities is a catch-all category for software tools that increase the usefulness of the computer. Most utilities are inexpensive and easy to use. The utilities chosen by the searcher, despite their low cost, will have a major impact on the effectiveness of the machine as a workstation. Different utilities perform tasks like providing type fonts for dot matrix printers, managing the storage space on a hard disk, or simplifying the operating system.

Just about any of the utilities that are of interest to PC users in general will also be of interest to searchers. One category, macro processors, is of special interest to the searcher. Macros are of use to just about anyone who uses a micro; you can't go wrong if you know a little about macros, regardless of whether or not you are a searcher.

Introducing the Macro

Just what is a macro anyway? Test your knowledge by taking this quiz. A macro is:

   A. the opposite of a micro; a computer that is bigger than a mainframe but smaller than a super
   B. a magic key that can unlock the power of your computer
   C. a pasta and Velveeta cheese dish that is very popular in the chic eateries of the Silicon Valley

The correct answer is B, although it's not especially obvious. The term macro must be among the most confusing of terms in the American computerese dialect--a dialect not noted for its clarity. The word macro comes from a Greek word meaning long or large. The computerese use of the term is a shortened form of macroinstruction. A macro is therefore a way of storing a long sequence of instructions in a single key on the keyboard. A special type of program called a macro processor can be used to create macros. Macro processing software gives you the capability to redefine the meaning of the keys on your keyboard.

Let's look at an example. Imagine that you are frequently required to correspond with the Podunk Polytechnic University Library. A macro processor would give you the ability to store the name of that institution in a key on your computer--let's say Ctrl P. Once the macro was created, you could make your computer type the entire phrase by simply holding down the Ctrl key and then pressing P. The macro would make it possible to replace the thirty-seven keystrokes required to type the name of the PPU library with the two keystrokes required to type Ctrl P--a savings of thirty-five keystrokes.

Macros and the Search Process

It may seem that macros would be more useful for word processing than for online searching. It's true, macros can be very useful for word processing. But macros and micros have a similar attraction. Their beauty lies in their general purpose nature--in their flexibility. Both can be adapted to perform an almost limitless variety of tasks. A macro can be as simple as the one just described, or it can set in motion a complex chain of events. The most intricate macros have a quality that brings to mind the fantastic inventions of Rube Goldberg.

Let's think about a typical online search. Let's not concern ourselves with anything as high level as search strategy or inverted files. Let's think about the keystrokes involved in an online search. A search performed on a micro will almost always involve many more keystrokes than the same search done on a dumb terminal. Numerous commands (most of which involve several keystrokes) are required to perform tasks such as:

- loading communications software
- dialing a packet-switching network
- connecting to a system vendor's computer
- selecting a database
- sending search statements
- downloading search results to a file
- loading a word processing program
- editing the search results file
- printing the finished product

You could (although you probably wouldn't want to) store all of the keystrokes required to do all of those things on a single key. Whoever pressed that key--whether or not they knew anything about searching--would initiate a chain reaction that would result in a search being performed and results being printed. It's easy to see how connect-time and cost could be reduced by using prerecorded searches. But searching is an interactive process, and prerecording an entire search to save money might not be the best way to use macros. There are, however, additional benefits to be had by using macros. . .but we're getting ahead of ourselves. Let's look at how macros work and how to put them to work.

Macros and Programs

Macros are sort of like programs. At the most basic level, a macro is simply a stored sequence of keystrokes just as a program is a stored sequence of instructions. However, you don't have to know a programming language to create macros. The thing that makes macros interesting is the fact that those stored keystrokes can be letters, words, commands, or anything else that you can tell the computer by using the keyboard. Unlike a program, a macro doesn't care about the meaning of the instructions being stored. So a single macro can include commands that will load and work with different types of software, such as *WordStar*, *dBase*, or *Lotus 1-2-3*. Remember that the same macro can also include letters, words, or numbers--even the control characters that computers use to talk to one another. Is this starting to sound like a great way to make all of those expensive programs you bought work together as a single entity? Maybe, but is it easy to do and how much will it cost?

Chances are that if you have a micro, you already own some software that will allow you to create your own macros. Many popular spreadsheet, communications, and database management packages feature macros. Those macros will work with the applications programs in which they were created. Unfortunately, they probably can't be used with other software, and many applications programs that allow you to create macros place restrictions on the length of those macros and the ways in which they can be used. If you want to create macros that can include commands from different applications packages, you'll need to buy a macro processor, also known as a keyboard enhancer.

A Software Bargain

A macro processor is one of the best bargains for your software dollar. They are inexpensive ($70 to $130 retail, even cheaper by mail order), incredibly versatile, and surprisingly easy to learn. The thing that makes a macro processor so useful is that it is always there, just sitting in the background waiting to be summoned into service like Aladdin's genie. How is this accomplished? Macro software is turned on by loading it into your computer's RAM memory, where it stays no matter what other program you happen to be using. You can create macros while you are using your spreadsheet, database manager, or word processing software. You can customize your applications programs to do what you want them to do. A macro processor will "remember" the keystrokes required to perform complex tasks that you find yourself repeatedly performing. Once that's done the task can be accomplished by activating the macro rather than typing the original sequence of keystrokes.

Macros are often compared to tape recordings. Once your macro processor is activated, it is very easy to record them and play them back. Keyboard enhancement programs are remarkably similar to one another. In fact, the two leaders, *ProKey* from RoseSoft and *SuperKey* from Borland International, are compatible with one another. The process of creating and using a macro generally involves these simple steps:

1. Choose the key or combination of keys to redefine.
2. Enter the new definition, which can be as long or short as you want and can include just about anything.
3. Press the newly defined key whenever you want to activate the recorded definition.

There are numerous variations on this basic theme and all kinds of tricks you can play with the things you put in your macro. Once a macro has been created it can be saved and used again. An enterprising searcher could build a repertoire of custom-designed macros --some that work with specific software and others that control the action and bounce back and forth between programs. Some macros could even include complex search strategies. In-house SDI, research profiles, the online database as index to a local collection, turnkey systems. . .the possibilities are intriguing. Now that you know a macro from a micro, perhaps you can think of some things you might want to do.

ProKey was the first really popular macro processor on the market. Like much of the best-selling software, *ProKey* is the product of a cottage industry on the West Coast. *ProKey* was the invention of the Seattle-based husband-and-wife team of Eileen and David Rose. When it burst on the scene about three years ago, it was the only software product of its kind. *ProKey* was a good product and it quickly found a niche in the software market--mainly among the crowd that regularly read magazines like *BYTE* and *PC Magazine*. *ProKey* received rave reviews in the micro literature and quickly became a favorite. Although its first customers were experienced computer users, it should be stressed that one doesn't have to be a programmer to use *ProKey* or any of the other macro processors on the market. *ProKey*'s major drawback was a copy protection scheme that required its users to boot it from a floppy disk before it could be used. It wasn't a terrible hassle, but it did make *ProKey* less convenient than it could have been, especially for people with hard disk systems.

Battle of the Macro Processors

In 1985 Borland International, producer of the popular software tools *Sidekick* and *Turbo Pascal*, entered the macro processor market with a program called *SuperKey*. Borland announced its new product with full-page ads in the major micro journals. Borland's advertising was aimed squarely at RoseSoft's customers. *SuperKey* was touted as being able to use macros that had been created with *ProKey*, so that people who had already invested the time and effort required to create libraries of macros with *ProKey* might consider switching to *SuperKey*. *SuperKey* was not copy protected, making it much more useful for those wanting to put together turnkey systems for hard disk users. A turnkey system permits the computer neophyte to use complex software to perform predetermined tasks without learning the commands required by that software. Besides its lack of a protection scheme *SuperKey* offered a sophisticated data encryption capability as well as an assortment of help screens and flashy pull-down menus. Finally, *SuperKey* was listed for $69; *ProKey* was selling for $130.

ProKey responded by introducing an improved version (version 4.0) that lacked the copy protection scheme of previous versions and that included a number of additional capabilities. The clear winner in the escalating battle of the macros is the software consumer. Both programs are sophisticated tools that enable micro users to get a lot more mileage out of their computers. They can be thought of as the capital goods of computer software. *SuperKey* even offers a sixty-day money-back guarantee if it doesn't increase productivity by 50 percent.

Flexibility is a quality that both programs share. For example, both *ProKey* and *SuperKey* permit the creation of macros in any of three different ways:

- Macros can be created by using a special group of commands; both packages make this easier with the extensive use of menus and help screens.
- Macros can be created interactively; a macro can be recorded as the keystrokes it will replace are being typed.
- Macros can be created with a word processor or any editor that will handle standard ASCII files.

Both programs allow macros to be stored in disk files and used as needed. The latest versions of both allow time delays to be included in macros, making it possible for a macro to play back a sequence of keystrokes and then wait a predetermined length of time before continuing. Both programs feature nested macros, or macros within macros. For example, the macros for Tymnet, Telenet, and Uninet log-on protocols could be defined within the macro for logging on to a specific system. The same keys--perhaps the keys labeled F1, F2, and F3--could be used for connecting to those networks no matter which system is chosen. The definition of those keys would vary depending upon whether the macro that defined them is for logging on to DIALOG, BRS, or SDC.

Both programs can also ask for and wait for input from the user. Macros that are defined within other macros can function as variables. One macro can serve as a prompt to the user, and the user's response can be defined as another macro. Macros including variables can specify exactly what type of input will be acceptable. Macros can be written to accept words only or numbers only; they can be allowed to deal with variable-length fields or with fields whose maximum length has been fixed. Such macro variables could be used to query an inexperienced searcher for the terms to be used in the offline preparation of a search strategy or, in a more simple example, to ask someone for their name and then to use the name provided in subsequent prompts.

ProKey and *SuperKey* both come with files of prerecorded macros designed to work with best-selling software like *WordStar*, *dBase*, or *Lotus 1-2-3*. Both also have the capability of producing alternative keyboard layouts by loading macros that change the value of every key on the keyboard and changing a QWERTY keyboard into a Dvorak keyboard or an IBM PC keyboard into an IBM Selectric keyboard.

Neither program is especially difficult to learn, but *ProKey*'s documentation is clearly superior. *ProKey* is accompanied by a quick reference card and its looseleaf manual, besides being more clearly written, can be laid on the desk next to the computer and consulted while the computer is being used. *SuperKey* comes with a paperbound manual that seems destined to fall apart with heavy use and that won't lie flat on a table unless it's weighted down with a book. The online menus and help screens provided by both packages are very easy to understand and use. *SuperKey* makes extensive use of pull-down windows that make the IBM PC look a little like a Macintosh.

Only *ProKey* offers the ability to produce macros that have multicharacter names. *SuperKey* limits macro names to single keys or a single key combined with the Control, Alternate, or Shift key. There is a certain mnemonic advantage to typing LOGON for a log-on macro instead of typing Ctrl L or Alt L. However, both *SuperKey* and *ProKey* do allow descriptive titles and annotations to accompany macros. *SuperKey* is loaded with so many features that it is difficult to remember all of them. Some of them, like the encryption capability, don't seem to have much to do with macro creation but nevertheless can be very useful. Among *SuperKey*'s extras are a cut-and-paste function, an autostart function, and the ability to manipulate the screen display in sophisticated ways.

Macro Processors: Tools for Searchers

There are a few differences between the two packages that will be of interest to searchers. Either package, however, can be used to enhance the search process significantly.

Logging On

Either program will enable a searcher to record the relatively tedious log-on process as it is occurring. Macros can be made to work with the simplest communications software to dial networks, transmit passwords, and even connect to a specific database. The least interesting part of the search process can thus be automated easily. *SuperKey* features an encryption scheme that can be used to secure macro files containing passwords or log-on sequences.

Conducting the Search

Macros provide a great way to prerecord search statements or entire searches in an offline mode. Time and money can be saved by transmitting those prerecorded statements at a high rate of speed after you are online. Searchers who are two-fingered typists wouldn't have to pay for their lack of typing ability with higher connect-time charges. A searcher could use either package to create entire files of related macros that can be loaded and unloaded from the computer's memory at any time during the search process. The ability to change the meaning of a key several times during a search session adds to the dynamic nature of the search process.

Files of macros could be tailored to work with specific databases or search systems. Such files could include macros for frequently used search statements. Database producers are doing something similar by providing "canned" search strategies that, when executed, will create a set that includes references to high demand topics. The PsycInfo database, for example, makes available stored searches including the terms required to search for frequently used concepts, such as children or mental health professionals. Database-specific macro files could also include macros for codes used by many databases. Stored codes, such as the ones used by the Predicasts family of databases, could increase searching efficiency. Finally, local holdings information could be included by storing macros containing CODENs or ISSNs for titles owned by a specific library. Macros representing local holdings could be used to turn a micro in any library into an online subject index to that library's journal holdings. One of the advantages of macro processors over more specialized search assistance software is that they can be adapted to meet the needs of any library and can be made to work with any database or search system.

Macros and End-Users

Without a doubt, "end-user" is the online buzzword of 1986. Macros provide a possible solution to the complex problems of inexperienced end-users. Macros can easily handle the mechanical details of searching from logging on to saving search results in a file. Those responsible for training end-users can concentrate their efforts on the search process itself rather than on the use of communications software. Special groups of macros can be created to meet the needs of specific users. Those macro files can make it possible to develop a turnkey online search system to deal with the problems encountered in any local setting.

SuperKey even permits the creation of display windows that can be superimposed on the screen as a search is being conducted. Such display windows can be designed to be context sensitive. If a searcher is using the Medline database on the DIALOG system, he or she can, at any point, request a window displaying a summary of useful commands that relate to that database on that system. Display macros can also list which keys contain predefined macros for frequently used search strategies or to select local journal holdings. When a searcher switches databases or systems, it is possible to switch macro files as well and to load a group of macros and displays that are designed to work with the new system or database.

Conclusion

Which package should the searcher buy? It is a difficult choice. Copy protection is no longer an issue, and both programs do the same basic thing. *ProKey*'s major advantage is the quality of its documentation and the fact that it is easier to learn to use. *ProKey*'s ability to create multicharacter macros would make it the choice for those wanting to create macros that have some inherent meaning for the user or those wishing to use macros as variables with names that make sense.

On the other hand, *SuperKey* is a more sophisticated program offering more options for its users. Those wishing to create turnkey systems for end-users would certainly want to take advantage of *SuperKey*'s ability to manipulate the screen display. Perhaps *SuperKey*'s greatest advantage is its price. At $69.95 it is $60 cheaper than *ProKey*, which lists for $130. Its price and its additional features make *SuperKey* the better bargain.

Shells

The shell is a software tool specifically designed to overcome the limitations of DOS. Shell programs are most effective on machines with hard disks, but they can be useful on any machine on which a variety of files and programs are stored. The shell program provides a big picture of the DOS environment as well as access to DOS commands for manipulating files within that environment.

When a shell program is operative, it is possible to see on a single display a list of all files and programs, no matter where on the hard disk they are stored. Ordinarily, it is only possible to view a list of files located on the current directory. The shell program allows the searcher to see where on the disk all programs are and to see the memory status of the disk.

The shell provides a way of integrating DOS functions. A single display lists all files and programs in addition to indicating the amount of available memory and the status of keyboard toggles, such as Caps Lock and Num Lock. DOS commands are also displayed and can be easily selected. Files in any directory can be listed, sorted, printed, or copied without entering DOS commands.

Many shell programs also allow the searcher to create DOS batch files, which can be called and executed from within the shell. Programs can be loaded or unloaded from within the shell. Like macro processors, many shell programs provide extra features that go beyond the usual. Some shells include a variation known as a menu generator. Menu generators allow their users to develop menus and prompts to customize the use of the operating system. Menus can be designed to move data between applications or to automate a process involving DOS commands. Just as a macro processor can be used to provide assistance to the inexperienced searcher by changing the meaning of the keys on the keyboard, a menu generator can be used to provide assistance through locally developed menus.

Another type of utility designed to overcome the limitations of DOS is known as a path manager. Version 2.0 of DOS was designed to allow its users to arrange files in a hierarchical tree structure on a hard disk. Files which belonged together--for example, the program and data files for a particular application--could be grouped together in the same subdirectory. It was possible to call up programs stored in one subdirectory to be used in another, but it wasn't possible to move data files back and forth or to use programs like *WordStar,* which relied upon overlay files. For example, the searcher who wanted to use *WordStar* to clean up a search that was done in an online subdirectory would have to copy the file into the *WordStar* subdirectory to process it. It wasn't possible to simply call *WordStar* from within the online subdirectory.

A path manager is a RAM-resident program that allows its users to load and use software residing in a subdirectory other than the currently logged one. A program can be used anywhere on the hard disk without having to copy it or the data its working with onto the same subdirectory. *EasyPath*, at $99 from Polygon Software in New York, is a good example of a path manager. *EasyPath* comes preconfigured to work with several of the most popular applications programs. Batch files included with the program enable software such as *WordStar*, *Lotus 1-2-3*, or *dBase* to be called from anywhere on the hard disk.

Imagine that a search has been conducted and results have been downloaded. Immediately after the search is completed, the results file will be located in the same subdirectory in which the communications program is located. Chances are that the word processor used to clean up results is on another subdirectory. A path manager will allow the searcher to clean up search results without having to leave the subdirectory in which he or she is located, even if the software required for clean-up is on another part of the hard disk. Any program or data file can be immediately accessible, no matter where it's located on the disk. It is not hard to imagine a scholar in the middle of writing a research paper needing to verify something by performing a quick online search. A path management program would permit the scholar to load a communications program, conduct a search, and download results without leaving the current directory.

Path managers also allow their users to specify which directories to read from and write to. A path manager can thus be used to protect a subdirectory or ensure that specific types of files are always placed in appropriate subdirectories.

Programming?

Using operating system utilities properly does require many of the same skills required for computer programming. If you want to get fancy with utilities, it is a good idea to develop an organized plan for the tasks you want them to perform, something like a program. Should the searcher learn to program? It isn't really necessary but it does help. Should the search manager learn to program? It's probably a good idea. The search manager who is already familiar with the structure of the information raw material probably should learn a little more about the instructions for manipulating it. An introductory course emphasizing the principles of structured programming will help even the searcher who never writes a program to understand the problems involved. Programming skills aren't necessary for managing a micro-based search service, but the more you know about programming the greater will be your level of control.

References/Recommended Reading

Dickinson, John. "Stalking the Elusive Subdirectory Path." *PC Magazine*, 28 May 1985, 231-240.

Edwards, Jon R. "Public Domain Utilities." *BYTE* (Fall 1985): 39-54.

Obregon, David. "Power Plays at Your Keyboard." *PC Magazine*, 29 October 1985, 167-175.

Petzold, Charles. "Keyboard Macros and Redefinition." *PC Magazine*, 24 June 1986, 255-265.

Puglia, Vincent. "Extending DOS's Utility." *PC Magazine*, 13 May 1986, 209-225.

_____. "Menu Generators: DOS Made Easier." *PC Magazine*, 10 June 1986, 201-210.

Sall, Steve. "Macros: Powerful Tools for Micro Users." *PC Magazine*, 1 May 1984, 115-119.

Sandberg-Diment, Erik. "The Magnificent Memory Residents." *New York Times*, 15 December 1985, 16F.

Trautman, Rodes, et al. "Uploading and Downloading for Computer-Assisted Reference Service." In *Downloading-Uploading Online Databases and Catalogs*, edited by James A. Benson and Bella H. Weinberg, 13-21. Ann Arbor, MI: Pierian Press, 1985.

CHAPTER SEVEN
SOFTWARE IN GENERAL

Software Tools

There is a memorable scene in the 1967 movie, *The Graduate*. Benjamin, a bright, if somewhat confused young man played by Dustin Hoffman, is enduring a college graduation party he obviously would rather not be attending. He is being showered with platitudes and bombarded with free advice. At one point, a well wisher leans into his face and tells him that there is only one word he needs to know--plastics. If the movie had been made today, the word would have been software.

The most generic definition of software includes both programs (which are instructions to the computer) and data (which is the information those instructions act upon). A multibillion-dollar industry has sprung up around those most nebulous of commodities. But software is the matrix which gives meaning to the technology. In a very real sense, programs are tools.

The "electronic cottage" is term often heard lately. Many of the most successful early programs were the products of an electronic cottage industry. An industry whose major piece of capital equipment was the human mind made instant millionaires of the most unlikely assortment of wunderkinds, ex-hippies, and corporate dropouts. The software industry of today is very different. Teams of specialists start out to provide products intended to capture a segment of an increasingly competitive market. Software has become big business.

Still, it is possible for the determined individual working in his or her living room to come up with a winner. Searching has also become a major enterprise. The searcher can build an electronic log cabin using simple, inexpensive tools and plain materials. Such a structure can be sturdy enough to meet individual needs and can be expanded as needs grow.

At the institutional level, it is possible for a searcher to build a diverse city of information. Of course, it is more expensive to build a city than it is to build a log cabin. More sophisticated tools are required. Plans are more complex and the interrelationships between the parts that make up the whole are more confusing. Building materials are also more costly and a greater variety is required.

Each construction project uses different tools and building materials but each uses tools and materials from a few basic categories. For example, there is a category of tools we might call pounding tools. The builder of the log cabin uses a mallet; the builder of the city uses a pile driver. And within each category are variations and levels of specialization. Think of the different kinds of wrenches there are. Crescent wrenches, open-ended wrenches, and socket wrenches don't even look alike, but they all perform the same basic function.

Structures are built in different environments. A subway built in a city on swampy ground would be constructed quite differently from a subway built in a city that sat on a bed of solid rock. The subway in the swampy city would probably be a tube floating beneath the surface of the ground. The subway in the city built on rock would most likely be a tunnel excavated beneath the surface. Cities of information as well as individual structures must also be built from material and tools that are appropriate for their local environment.

Once tools and building materials have been selected for the jobs that need to be done, it is necessary to organize them in such a way that they are easy to use. A toolbox is required, as is a method for warehousing materials so they are available when needed. The operating system lets us work with files as basic building blocks. Software tools help us work at the nuts-and-bolts level of records, fields, and characters.

Using a computer to query vast stores of electronically recorded information is a relatively recent human endeavor. There have been plenty of predictions but nobody knows for sure what will come of all this. Right now online searching is still a complex task. Using a micro for searching promises to add considerably to the search process, but the decisions to be made, especially the decisions relating to software, add another layer of complexity to the searcher's job. Lately we've seen a spate of articles on searching in the micro and popular literature. Most focus on the technology and trivialize the higher level intellectual aspects of the search process. So, the notion that searching is easy has become common. But we all know that searching isn't easy and that there is a lot more to it than what occurs once the online connection has been made. The searcher has to concentrate on expressing the unknown in terms of the known. Extensive advance preparation is often required. Once online, split-second decisions have to be made, and a single session often involves moving between systems and files that employ totally different search languages and data structures.

At the most fundamental level, the needs of searchers are served by hardware that makes it easy to move electrical information from place to place. At the highest level, sophisticated programs perform many of the functions that were once the purview of the searcher. Front-ends and gateways assist in database selection, query formulation, and search execution. Those programs are among the most exciting developments in the online industry. The problems associated with automating higher-level search activities are the same as the problems faced by anyone attempting to mimic human intelligence with a machine.

General purpose communications software that tends to handle the lower-level aspects of the search process is less ambitious as well as less expensive. Most of it wasn't designed with online searching in mind, but with a little perseverance it can be easily adapted to add a great deal to the searcher's productivity. Communications software isn't the only category in which the searcher will be interested. You may already own other programs that can be used to increase your effectiveness as a searcher.

Many of us have created collection development policies that reflect the needs of our clients. Purchase decisions are based on a carefully thought-out set of goals and guidelines. Yet when it comes to purchasing software, many of us don't have a clear idea of what our goals are. So, before treating specific categories of software, let's outline some of the goals a searcher might have in mind when it comes to software.

The idea here is to get started as quickly and as cheaply as possible. Its corollary is to progressively become more sophisticated and to acquire a collection of programs that can be used in concert with one another to expand our capabilities as searchers. A customized system is our ultimate goal. Eventually we would like to own, and this is important, be able to use, our software to meet our unique needs as individual and institutional consumers of information.

The searcher's software toolbox will contain three basic categories of tools. Each category can include a variety of different tools, some of which are simple and inexpensive, others which are more powerful and more expensive. The three drawers of our toolbox are labelled:

- Process Tools
- Product Tools
- General Purpose Tools

The plan calls for us to acquire our software one piece at a time. Once we have thoroughly mastered one program, we'll move on to another in the next category. Perhaps our software purchases could be scheduled to take advantage of improvements to our hardware. An alternative plan would be to acquire an integrated package or a full-featured search assistance package.

Search assistance packages represent one of the newest product categories in the software marketplace. Products are being introduced and fading from sight as the market evolution which is typical in the industry occurs. Research now being conducted is bound to yield a new generation of products designed specifically for the searcher. Several of the current crop will be described in Chapter Ten.

For now, let's back away from the cutting edge. Let's consider flexible software that can be adapted to meet our needs, software that has withstood the test of the marketplace. It takes time and effort to learn to use any program. There is an argument for choosing "classic" programs. A large user group means that there will be others who understand the lingua franca established by a widely used program and others with whom to share applications.

Downloading has become one of the major legal, ethical, and economic dilemmas in the online community. Software piracy is a problem of equal dimensions. A recent issue (Jan. 14, 1986) of *PC Magazine* included an article on the battle being waged between the developers of copy protection schemes and the producers of software designed to defeat those schemes. An experiment was described. Five lock-breaking programs, most of which sell for much less than $100, were able to copy eight best-selling protected programs, most of which cost much more than $100.

One of our goals is to acquire our software with the least possible expense, but our guidelines will not allow piracy. We are interested in supporting software producers who sell quality programs at reasonable prices. Buying our software from mail order vendors is one way to save money. Using shareware, freeware, and public domain programs is another. The idea is to get maximum use from a few flexible programs. We don't want to own dozens of programs that are incompletely understood and rarely used.

Let's put ourselves in a hypothetical situation and see how these guidelines might be applied to purchase decisions. Imagine that we already have our hardware. Let's say that we have an IBM PC (or true compatible) and a Hayes 1200-baud modem (or true compatible). A limited amount of money is available for software. We are looking for software that will help us as searchers, but we want programs that will serve other functions as well. The rules require that we become completely familiar with each program we buy before moving on to the next. Since online searching is our highest priority, we'll begin with communications software and move on to other categories. These are the generic categories which are of interest to searchers.

1. Communications
2. Word Processing
3. Shell and Utility Software
4. Database Management
5. Spreadsheet

Time and effort are required for this approach to acquiring software. It also requires the kind of enlightened administrator who is willing to allow employees the freedom to learn. The effort can be rewarding. Payoffs include a custom-designed system built around local needs, and the flexibility to change as the environment changes. People involved can achieve a certain amount of satisfaction from having mastered an arcane art--and the knowledge needed to ask the right questions about the coming generation of higher-level search assistance programs.

References/Recommended Reading

Kolner, Stuart J. "The IBM PC as an Online Search Machine--Part 3: Introduction to Software." *Online* (May 1985): 44-50.

Manes, Stephen. "A Computer Course in Classical Appreciation." *PC Magazine*, 9 July 1985, 60.

CHAPTER EIGHT
GENERAL PURPOSE COMMUNICATION TOOLS

Communications Software

Communications software provides us with the ability to move different size chunks of information from one place to another. It allows us to send information from our keyboards to the great beyond. Messages for host systems can be sent from disks (uploading). Messages can also be stored on the keyboard and sent on their way to remote computers with the touch of a finger (macros).

Communications software provides us with a window on the on-line world. It enables us to see displayed before us messages sent from vast electronic warehouses thousands of miles away. It allows us to transform the flickering image on the screen to printed words on a piece of paper.

Flow Control

One of the major functions of communications software is to provide what is known as flow control. This involves coordinating the transfer of messages between two computers. Computers can be told to respond to codes that tell them to start or stop sending or receiving. Those control codes are used to make sure that each machine is keeping up with the other, that neither is talking too fast, or too slow.

In asynchronous communication, the most commonly agreed upon standard is known as the XON/XOFF protocol. When one computer needs a pause to give it time to deal with the information it's just received, it sends a special ASCII control character to the other computer. That control character is known as an XOFF and it's part of the ASCII character set just as a letter is. The XOFF signal may be sent directly from the keyboard by pressing the Control key and S at the same time. Once the computer that needed the rest is ready to receive again, it sends a signal known as an XON, which can be sent from the keyboard by pressing the Control key and Q at the same time. Communications programs keep track of what is going on and send the necessary codes. The person sitting at the keyboard needn't be concerned with pressing the ^S and the ^Q keys.

Communications software also allows us to create files and fill them with information extracted from remote computers (downloading). Files can also be created to hold messages that are used frequently. Communications software takes care of telling the modem, the packet-switching network, and the online service the characteristics of the communications interface. Some communications software can even make decisions based on information obtained from databases or can be made to interact with the user in a predetermined way.

Screens, Keys, and Files

Good communications programs, like good operating systems, include something for everyone. All kinds of hardware drivers must be available. Elements of programming languages are present. Numerous displays are presented for the consideration of the user. Keys are pressed to convey messages. Multiple layers of software are often involved (especially with online searching), and the same eighty or so keys must be used to speak more than a few different languages at the same time. And files are moved from one place to another, across short distances and large, with speeds of the hesitant typist and the lightning bolt.

The way in which communications software communicates with its users is probably as important as the way it talks to parts of the machine and to other machines. The electrical mysteries of just about every possible kind of computer device must be made invisible. The point at which the user comes into contact with the machine must not include a complex jumble of conflicting messages and arcane instructions. Especially in online searching, the person sitting at the machine must be able to focus on the store of knowledge being addressed, not on the mechanics of representing information as electricity and moving it from place to place.

The so-called user interface is especially important for searchers who must deal with an online system and a database. All communications programs must display to the user information that is emanating from a distant source and information about how to control the dialog with that source at the same time. At one time or another, either the remote system or functions of the communications program must be in the foreground; the other must remain in the background, though not too far. Certainly the hardware being used to display messages to the searcher is important. More important is the software that controls the way in which those messages are presented and determines the ease with which they are summoned.

The meaning of the keys on the keyboard must be delineated in such a way that the machine can interpret them correctly as either instructions to one of its devices or as messages to a host. It must also be possible to teach the machine to understand the languages of many hosts. Translations must be made between the language of machines, the language of computer programmers, the language of people, and the language of databases. And keys must be made to convey messages with great economy because the distance between finger and keyboard, in terms of time, is the longest distance involved.

Communications software must be able to handle messages from both the keyboard and the modem. Most software uses one of two different schemes to detect incoming messages. One scheme is called polling. Software that employs polling continuously asks or polls each device (the keyboard, the modem, etc.) to determine if there are any messages that require attention. Polling is not a very efficient use of the computer's processor, which has to spend a great deal of time jumping from one device to another waiting for messages.

Most communications programs use a more efficient scheme for determining if there are any messages that need to be handled. As processing occurs, the CPU is able to detect special conditions known as interrupts. Devices such as modems and keyboards generate interrupts when they need to get the software's attention. When the software receives an interrupt, it sets aside what it's doing and handles the incoming message. Once the interrupt signal is dealt with, processing continues where it left off. When communications software is being used and the person at the micro presses a key, an interrupt signal is generated and the software is able to accept the message that the human wants to send. After the message sent by the human from the keyboard is dealt with, the program can return its attention to the messages coming in from the host.

Files must be changed and moved, just as the smaller units of which they are composed must be changed and moved. Files must be created and destroyed. Files must be able to include fragments of machine language along with text that people can understand. And files that tell the machine what to do must be differentiated from files containing messages for the host. Mechanisms must be provided for storing files and organizing them according to their functions or their contents. Mechanisms must also be provided for sending and receiving files according to rules specified by a variety of online systems and host computers.

The structure of communications programs mirrors the functional states of the modem. The modem is either offline or online, in the local command mode or in the terminal mode. Communications programs must also shift from a command state to a terminal state and back. Rather than looking at communications programs in the abstract, let's use concrete examples. Illustrations drawn from different products can be used to exemplify the variety of approaches which are taken. Remember that the three key concepts are screens, keys, and files. Remember also that much of the search process occurs before and after the searcher actually goes online. Therefore, when looking at communications software, it is a good idea to think in terms of both online and offline capabilities.

There are different classes of communications programs. Terminal programs are designed to mimic any terminal and are usually designed for asynchronous communications. File transfer programs are designed to facilitate the transfer of different types of files. Programs or binary files that are not represented with the ASCII code often require special error-checking and communications protocols to be accurately transmitted and received. Finally, there are terminal emulators designed to mimic or emulate a specific terminal, such as the widely used DEC VT100. File transfer features and terminal emulation are nice extras that come with many microcomputer communications programs, but asynchronous terminal features are the ones that will be of greatest interest to the searcher.

Installation

Communications programs, like many other types of programs, often must be installed or configured. Both processes involve telling the program things like what kind of hardware will be used, and what phone numbers to dial. Installation often involves moving the separate modules of the program into different subdirectories as well as setting up defaults. Often special operating system files like CONFIG.SYS are created or modified to include parameters relating to the way the program functions. Usually there is a special installation program on the software disk that walks the user through the process. Once the program has been installed, the searcher shouldn't be concerned with the hardware configuration being used. All of the proper switches will be set every time it's run.

Levels of Communications Software

There are probably hundreds of different PC-compatible communications packages from which to choose. It's possible to buy a full-featured package that provides a level of programmability and control not found in most applications programs. If you have the time, the ability, and the inclination, it is possible to design a complex communications environment. It is also possible to buy at very little

General Purpose Communication Tools 121

cost programs that will almost immediately add to your productivity as a searcher.

At the lower end of the communications software range are several surprisingly full-featured programs that sell for under $50. The prime example is *PC-Talk*. In the middle range are the best-selling software programs that are often sold as part of the package when you buy a modem. Examples are *Smartcom* and *Crosstalk XVI*. If purchased separately these programs usually cost between $100 and $150. In the most expensive price range are programmable communications packages such as *Crosstalk Mark IV* or *Microsoft Access*, which can cost $200 and up. We are also starting to see low-cost, high-performance, "off brand" communications programs. *BackComm*, a RAM-resident communications program from La Salle Micro, offers multitasking, a script language with a learn mode, and password protection for less than a hundred dollars.

First let's look at three tried and true programs--*PC-Talk*, *Smartcom II*, and *Crosstalk XVI*--each of which illustrates a different emphasis. After examining those standards, we'll look at a newer product. *Microsoft Access* represents another level of communications software, and because it comes from the producers of MS-DOS, it is likely to have as great an impact as *PC-Talk*, *Smartcom*, and *Crosstalk* have already had.

PC-Talk--Simplicity and Low Cost

Let's begin by examining *PC-Talk* ($35 from The Headlands Press, POB 862, Tiburon, CA 94920) and using it as an example of some of the features a searcher will want. *PC-Talk* is the best example of the concept known as freeware. Users of the program are encouraged to copy it and give the copies to friends. The manual accompanying the program is stored as a file on the disk and must be printed to be used. An honor system is used to pay for the program. If you like the program and use it, you are obligated to send to its author some compensation. Users of the program are asked to send the amount they think the program is worth. A contribution of $35 is suggested.

```
                                                  tm
                        F R E E W A R E
                     User-Supported Software

            If you have received this program from another user and
            find it of value, your $35 contribution will be appreciated.

                            MMM Freeware MMM
                            Post Office Box 862
                             Tiburon, CA 94920

              You are encouraged to copy this program as described below.

           ** NOTICE:  Users of this program are granted a limited license to
                    make copies of this program for trial use by others on a private
                    non-commercial basis.  This limited license does not include --
                 1. distributing this program in connection with any other product
                 2. making the program available for any consideration or 'disk fee'
                 3. posting the program for public access via telecommunications or
                 4. distributing the program in modified form.  Please cooperate.

             Copyright (c) 1983 The Headlands Press, Inc.
             Hit any key to continue ...
```

PC-Talk is the most famous of user-supported programs.

The philosophy underlying this idea hearkens to another era. It a perfect example of the hacker ethic that prevailed in the early days of personal computing--programs and information were viewed as things to be shared freely, not marketed as products. Some might call it naive altruism but it is an idea that expresses the potential of technology brought to the personal level.

PC-Talk is the product of a single individual instead of a team of software engineers. You won't see slick advertisements for it in the pages of computer magazines. It's improbable that all of its users sent in the suggested contribution. Nevertheless, it is one of the most popular communications programs ever made. And its capabilities match those of much more expensive programs.

PC-Talk Offline

PC-Talk in its offline mode allows the searcher to set most of the parameters (duplex, baud rate, etc.) that used to be set by toggling switches on a terminal. *PC-Talk*, like many other communications programs, also allows its users to prerecord many of the messages that will be transmitted in the online mode. A dialing directory is capable of storing all of the phone numbers a searcher is likely to use in addition to the communications parameters associated with each number. The dialing directory is an example of a file that contains information telling the computer and its components how to behave.

General Purpose Communication Tools

```
===DIALING DIRECTORY  1 ===    Modem dialing command = ATDT
                               Long distance service +#  =
                                                     -#  =
        Name                      Phone #    Comm Param  Echo Mesg Strip Pace
     1-TYMNET                    8,5221370   1200-E-7-1   N    N    3   p=?
     2-TELENET                   8,5244094   1200-E-7-1   N    N    3   p=?
     3-UNINET                    8,8347113   1200-E-7-1   N    N    3   p=?
     4------------------------   - --- --- ----  300-E-7-1   N    N    N   N
     5------------------------   - --- --- ----  300-E-7-1   N    N    N   N
     6------------------------   - --- --- ----  300-E-7-1   N    N    N   N
     7------------------------   - --- --- ----  300-E-7-1   N    N    N   N
     8------------------------   - --- --- ----  300-E-7-1   N    N    N   N
     9------------------------   - --- --- ----  300-E-7-1   N    N    N   N
    10------------------------   - --- --- ----  300-E-7-1   N    N    N   N
    11------------------------   - --- --- ----  300-E-7-1   N    N    N   N
    12------------------------   - --- --- ----  300-E-7-1   N    N    N   N
    13------------------------   - --- --- ----  300-E-7-1   N    N    N   N
    14------------------------   - --- --- ----  300-E-7-1   N    N    N   N
    15------------------------   - --- --- ----  300-E-7-1   N    N    N   N

    Dial entry #:           I or...   Enter: R to revise or add to directory
                                             M for manual dialing
                                         F / B to page through directory
                                             X to exit to terminal
                           I For long distance service, precede entry # with +/-
```

PC-Talk allows its users to store communications parameters and phone numbers in a dialing directory.

PC-Talk Online

Once online, a status line remains displayed on the screen to describe the nature of the communications link. *PC-Talk* is command driven. A few simple commands are used to instruct the program to tell the modem, the printer, and the disk drives what to do. Pressing the Home key will cause a window containing a summary of all commmands to be displayed on the screen. The summary of commands is available while online or in the command mode.

```
   ===Proceed ...                    MAKE SURE THAT YOUR MODEM IS ON

                                     =====   PC-TALK III   =====

                                      Communications Program for
                                      The IBM Personal Computer

                                 Press: <Home> for command summary
                                        <Alt>-E if you can't see
                                                your keyboard input




   ^PrtSc=prnt  Alt- T=tran R=recv V=view D=dial E=echo M=mesg X exit <Home>=Help
```

PC-Talk requires the user to enter commands.

```
                    ===Proceed ...
                                        ===PC-TALK III   COMMAND SUMMARY===
                                        )PrtSc =   print screen contents
                                        ^PrtSc =   contin. printout (or ^PgUp)
                                         Alt-R =   Receive a file  (or PgDn)
                                         Alt-T =   Transmit a file (or PgUp)
                                        transmit: pacing '=p'  binary '=b'
                                        :ran/recv: XMODEM '=x'
                                         Alt-V =   View file    Alt-Y = delete
                                         Alt-D =   Dialing directory
                                         Alt-Q =   redial last number
                                         Alt-K =   set/clear Func keys (Alt-J)
                                         Alt-= =   set/clear temp Alt keys
                                         Alt-E =   Echo toggle  Alt-M = Message
                                         Alt-S =   Screendump   Alt-C = Clearsc
                                         Alt-P =   communications Parameters
                                         Alt-F =   set program deFaults
                                         Alt-L =   change Logged drive
                                         Alt-W =   set margin Width alarm
                                         Alt-Z =   elapsed time/current call
                                         Alt-X =   eXit to DOS
                                        trl-End =  send sustained Break signal
                    ^PrtSc=prnt  Alt- T=tran R=recv V=view D=dial E=echo M=mesg X=exit <Home>=Help
```

Though the user is required to type in commands, a summary of the key combinations for each command is always at hand.

PC-Talk differentiates between messages the user sends to the program (commands) and messages to be sent to the online service (log-on protocols, search statements, etc.) by specifying that its commands include atypical combinations of keystrokes. Each command involves keystroke combinations of an alphabetic character with the Control key or the Alternate key. Pressing the Alternate key and P, for example, will turn the printer on. It is also possible to change the meaning of keys.

PC-Talk Macros

Stored sequences of instructions called macros can hold log-on protocols, passwords, even search statements. As many as forty of these macros may be stored and can be activated by pressing one of the ten function keys on the left side of the keyboard or by pressing one of the function keys while also pressing the Control, Alternate, or Shift key. Additionally, *PC-Talk*, unlike some other communications programs, will work with either *ProKey* or *SuperKey*.

```
      ===Proceed ...
                                    ===FUNCTION KEY DIRECTORY===
                                              Func F1-10
                                    F-   Input String
                                    1 =  )) D1) C 415 48d)
                                    2 =  PASSWORD)
                                    3 =  S MICROCOMPUTER?/DE,TI)
                                    4 =  S (COMMUNICATION? OR TELECOMMUNIC
                                    5 =  S S1 AND S2)
                                    6 =
                                    7 =
                                    8 =
                                    9 =
                                   10 =
                                   Press:  R to revise Func-F assignments
                                           F / B to page through directory
                                           X to exit to terminal

      ^PrtSc=prnt  Alt- T=tran R=recv V=view D=dial E=echo M=mesg X=exit <Home>=Help
```

Prerecorded statements called macros can be used to log on or send messages to a host. Curly brackets represent carriage returns.

Macros may be prepared immediately before a search session or in advance. When the searcher issues the command to create macros (Alt K), a window containing the values associated with each function key is displayed on the screen. At the bottom of the screen the user is prompted to add or change a macro. Once the searcher is online the prerecorded macros can be easily uploaded to the host system, which reduces connect-time. Unfortunately, the information loaded into macros, including passwords, is not protected and can be viewed by anyone using the program.

Files for Uploading

Files including complex search strategies can also be prepared offline and uploaded. *PC-Talk*, not being a word processor, is of limited use in preparing these upload files, but you can use the line editor in your operating system to do this if you don't own a word processing program. A pacing option allows the searcher to specify the prompt from the remote system. *PC-Talk* will then send files one line (e.g., search statement) at a time, pausing and waiting for a prompt from the host system before the next line is sent. Such files could contain client profiles for SDI. They could be developed by a searcher during peak hours and uploaded by someone else on the staff during off hours when system response time is better. The program cannot be set like an alarm clock to automatically send a file and download search results, a capability provided by some of the more expensive packages.

Downloading with PC-Talk

PC-Talk's online capabilities include the ability to temporarily store information in a memory buffer before it is routed to a printer. It is also possible to open a disk file and record an entire search session on disk. Files may be opened and closed rather easily, permitting the searcher to download only those parts of the session in which he/she is interested. While online *PC-Talk* also permits the searcher to toggle the printer on and off. *PC-Talk* is also capable of transmitting a Break signal to the host computer. *PC-Talk* also supports the XMODEM error-checking protocol, although its use is limited to micro-to-micro communications and shouldn't be of much interest to searchers.

Control Characters and Filtering

There are twenty-six letters in the alphabet. Each has its own ASCII code and ASCII number. Add another seventy or so ASCII codes to accommodate both upper- and lower-case letters and miscellaneous keyboard symbols and we've accounted for about ninety-six ASCII codes. Altogether there are 128 unique 7-bit ASCII codes. Where did the others go? The other ASCII numbers represent control characters. People use the ninety-six symbols on the keyboard to communicate with one another. Control characters (which may be sent from the keyboard by pressing a key while holding down the control key, and which are indicated with one of these two conventions: Ctrl M or ^M) are reserved for machine communication. For example, a control character (Ctrl J) is used to tell the printer when to advance a line (linefeed).

Information being sent from online systems often contains control characters--which can't be seen but can cause problems--embedded among the characters which make up the text. Control characters can even be part of the prompt from a remote system. Printers are especially susceptible to interference from control characters. If your printer switches from normal to compressed or graphics mode during a search, chances are the culprit was a control character that slipped in among the records being sent by the host.

PC-Talk allows it users to selectively filter out unwanted characters by putting their ASCII numbers in something called a character-stripping table. Control characters can be eliminated this way; so can frequently appearing garbage characters such as the notorious tilde. The user can specify which characters to strip and has the option of converting one character to another. However, the number of characters that can be filtered out is limited to three, and the searcher must be careful not to strip out a character that is vital to the functioning of the remote system.

Smartcom--Menus Galore

Smartcom II comes from Hayes, the giant modem manufacturer that has set the industry standard. It would have been hard for this program to lose, especially since it often comes bundled with the purchase of a Hayes modem. The Smartmodem has established a standard command set, which communications programs use to talk to modems. *Smartcom*, like most PC communications programs, represents a higher-level way of telling the modem what to do. Of course, like other good communications programs, it does many other things besides pushing modems around.

General Purpose Communication Tools

Smartcom represents an approach fundamentally different from that of *PC-Talk*. It is a more complex program for one thing. But the thing that really makes it different is the manner in which it presents itself to the user. *PC-Talk* is command driven; the user tells the program what to do. *Smartcom* is menu driven; more mediation is provided. *Smartcom* asks the user how it should proceed. The major problem with this approach is that sometimes it takes longer to get *Smartcom* to ask the questions whose answers will get the job done than it would take to simply tell a program like *PC-Talk* what to do.

```
       Smartcom II            Hayes Microcomputer Products, Inc.

1. Begin Communication    *. Receive File      7. Change Printer Status  (OFF)
2. Edit Set               *. Send File         *. Select Remote Access   (OFF)
3. Select File Command    6. Change Configuration 9. Display Disk Directory (OFF)
A,B - Change Drive                             0. End Communication/Program
                          Press F2 For Help
Enter Selection: 1        Press F1 To Return On-Line

                          Dials or answers phone with Smartmodem




    12:02 am                    Friday June 27, 1986
```

Smartcom is a good example of menu-driven software.

One of the reasons *Smartcom* uses a menu approach is because it is a complex program; it can do a lot more than *PC-Talk* is capable of doing. *Smartcom* is especially flexible when it comes to setting up rules for dealing with a large number of different remote systems. In the online mode *Smartcom* offers a superior buffering capability, allowing the searcher to move back and forth through the buffer viewing information already received from the host.

Smartcom presents itself to the user via six screens:

- the menu screen
- the configuration screen
- the parameters screen
- the create screen
- the online screen

All *Smartcom* functions are accessible from the main menu screen, which is the major controller of the action. On the menu screen are displayed a list of options, a prompt to the user, a status line specifying the current settings and status of the communications link, and a prompt to the user. The options provided on the menu will vary depending upon the mode the program is in when the menu is being displayed.

Menus and Screens

Commands are always entered by filling in a response to a prompt that is displayed at the bottom of the screen once a selection has been made from the menu. Help screens are context sensitive, that is, they display messages relating to the part of the program the user is in when they are requested. The function key labeled F2 is designated the Help Key and may be used while offline or online.

Each menu controls a different aspect of the communications process. The configuration menu prompts the user to specify the hardware devices being used. The parameters menu allows the user to define the duplex, baud rate, and so forth for any online system. *Smartcom* also provides the searcher with the ability to define macros, which are stored in a macro directory rather than on function keys. Because it is menu rather than command driven, *Smartcom* tends to emphasize screens instead of keys.

Smartcom stores the messages from an online session in a buffer as the session is occurring. It is possible to display the contents of the buffer on the screen and to scroll back and forth through the buffer, visually inspecting its contents while still receiving data from the remote system. *PC-Talk* does not provide that capability.

Communications Sets

Smartcom organizes all of the different types of values associated with different online services in files called communications sets. The searcher may define and save up to twenty-six communications sets labeled A to Z. Communications sets include parameters, such as baud rate and duplex, and macros associated with the service they are designed to work with (including an automatic log-on macro).

Typically, there are two or more communications sets associated with each online service, one for each packet-switching network. It's easy to conceive of situations where as many as five separate sets would be required for a single service. For example, a set for each of the following would be required to cover all of the DIALOG connect possibilities in many cities:

- DIALOG via Telenet
- DIALOG via Tymnet
- DIALOG via Uninet
- DIALOG via Dialnet
- DIALOG via direct dial

The Parameters Directory

Some of the parameters associated with online communication, things like local phone numbers, must always be determined by the user. Other parameters, like duplex, baud rate, and bits per character, depend upon the online service and the searcher's hardware. *Smartcom* uses function keys to control the program's actions. The values associated with each function key are also stored as parameters in the parameters directory. If you want to change the way *Smartcom* works (at least the meaning of the keys it uses), you have the option of changing the function key definitions.

```
                              PARAMETERS
Name of Set: Q - DIALOG TELENET              Press F2 For Help

        TRANSMISSION PARAMETERS                 KEYBOARD DEFINITIONS
               Duplex: FULL                   Escape Key: 128 (F1)
      Connection Type: Bell 1200                Help Key: 129 (F2)
  Character Processing: FORMATTED             Printer Key: 130 (F3)
    Show Control Codes: NO                    Capture Key: 131 (F4)
           Page Pause: NO                 Macro Prefix Key: 132 (F5)
     Show Status Lines: YES                    Break Key: 133 (F6)
          Confidential: NO                   Break Length: 35 (0.01 sec.)
   Include Line Feeds: NO                    Protect Key: 134 (F7)
       Character Delay: 0 (0.001 sec.)
            Line Delay: 0 (0.01 sec.)          PROTOCOL PARAMETERS
     Character Format: 8 DATA + NONE + 1 STOP Receive Time-out: 60 (sec.)
             Emulator: TTY                    Send Time-out: 10 (sec.)
                                          Error-Free Protocol: HAYES
      TELEPHONE PARAMETERS              Stop/Start- Stop Char: 19 (DC3)
       Answer On Ring: 1                           Start Char: 17 (DC1)
       Remote Access: NONE  Password:    Send Lines- EOL Char: 10 (LF )
        Phone Number: 8,5244094                  Prompt Char: 63 ("?")

12:14 am              Friday June 27, 1986                       CAPS
```

Smartcom allows the user to create and store values for all of the parameters associated with telecommunications.

Other parameters relate to the ways in which *Smartcom* is able to control the flow of messages. The user has the option of filtering all control characters except the ones that are usually necessary for the machine to work properly--things like linefeed (^J) and carriage return (^M)--which are represented within the machine as control characters. The searcher can also specify whether or not control codes coming from the remote system are displayed. This can be useful when fine tuning your computer to work with the host's by doing things like getting rid of redundant linefeed codes (which cause double spacing) or adding linefeeds to prevent everything from being printed on a single line. As we shall see later, it can also be useful to know whether or not prompts from the host include control codes.

Many of the Hayes-specific as well as more general parameters will be used with just about every online service. Default values are contained in the communications set labeled Z, which is defined as the standard communications set and which can't be changed.

Smartcom Macros

Each communications set has a macro directory associated with it. The macro directory can include up to twenty-six macros, once again labelled A to Z. For any communications set, the macro labeled Z is reserved for automatic log-on. It includes everything needed to log on but the phone number, which is stored in the parameters directory. When a call is initiated from a communication set, the log-on procedure defined within the macro labeled Z is automatically sent to the host.

```
        Smartcom II               Hayes Microcomputer Products, Inc.

1. Begin Communication     *. Receive File          7. Change Printer Status  (OFF)
2. Edit Set                *. Send File             *. Select Remote Access   (OFF)
3. Select File Command     6. Change Configuration  9. Display Disk Directory (OFF)
A,B - Change Drive                                  0. End Communication/Program
                           Press F2 For Help
Enter Selection: 2         P(arameters, M(acros, R(eports, C(opy, S(et, B(atch: M
Enter Label: X

Macro Directory of: B - DIALOG TELENET

  A - MEDLINE HEDGES         J - ABI MKTG JLS         S - PAT DORAN SDI
  B - ABI HEDGES             K - ABI MGT JLS          T - ELIZABETH MENSAH SDI
  C - ERIC HEDGES            L - ABI ACCTG JLS        U - MAX SNOW SDI
  D - PSYC HEDGES            M - MEDLINE CORE JLS     V - CLAY DIXON SDI
  E - BIOSIS HEDGES          N - PSYC CORE JLS        W - UPDATE BIBLIOG 247
  F - PREDICASTS HEDGES      O - ERIC CORE JLS        X -
  G - INSPEC HEDGES          P - INSPEC CORE JLS      Y - Telephone Access No.
  H - HISTORICAL ABS HDGS    Q - BIOSIS CORE JLS      Z - Automatic Log-On
  I - MGT CONTENTS HEDGES    R - HIST ABS CORE JLS
_____

     12:34 am                Saturday June 28, 1986                      CAPS
```

Each communications set can have up to 26 macro files associated with it. Macros can be used for a variety of purposes.

Other macros may be designed for use after you have connected to a host. Macros can consist of one or more lines which will be sent to the host. It is possible to "protect" a macro; a protected macro will be sent to the remote system but its contents will be hidden from the user. Protected macros are one approach to concealing passwords from those who have been authorized to connect to a service but not to have a password.

```
                         MACRO DEFINITION        Press F2 For Help
Name Of Macro: S - PAT DORAN SDI          Set: B - DIALOG TELENET
Time-out  Prompt     Data                                  Send CR
--------  ---------  ------------------------------------  -------
    0     63 ("?")   BEGIN 154                               YES
    0     63 ("?")   S LATERALITY/DE,TI                      YES
    0     63 ("?")   S AUTOIMMUNE(W)DISEASE? ?               YES
    0     63 ("?")   S S1 AND S2                             YES
    0     63 ("?")   T S3/7/1-10                             YES
    0     63 ("?")   LOGOFF                                  YES
```

```
12:49 am              Saturday June 28, 1986                  CAPS
```

A macro can include a locally created search profile as well as statements to print results and log off.

```
                         MACRO DEFINITION        Press F2 For Help
Name Of Macro: Z - Automatic Log-On       Set: B - DIALOG TELENET
Time-out  Prompt     Data                                  Send CR
--------  ---------  ------------------------------------  -------
    0      0 (off)                                           YES
    0     32 (" ")                                           YES
   10     61 ("=")   D1                                      YES
   10     64 ("@")   C 41548D                                YES
   60     58 (":")   ROSEBUD                                 YES
   60     63 ("?")   SET H 65                                YES
   60     63 ("?")   B 154                                   YES
```

```
12:45 am              Saturday June 28, 1986                  CAPS
```

The macro labelled Z is always reserved for the instructions required to log on automatically. This macro connects to DIALOG via Telenet.

It is also possible to specify the prompt for which *Smartcom* should wait for before sending the next line within a macro. *Smartcom* will delay a half second before sending a line after it has recognized a designated prompt character, to ensure that characters embedded within the data being received from the host aren't misinterpreted as prompts. A question mark in an abstract won't be interpreted in the same way as a question mark in a prompt.

Preconfigured Communications

There is a limit on the size of each line within a macro. There is also a limit on the number of lines within a macro. *Smartcom* comes with a number of communications sets already included for popular online services. The emphasis seems to be on general purpose utilities like The Source and CompuServe. None of the full-fledged "supermarket" vendors are supported by a communications set although Knowledge Index--DIALOG's after-hours, end-user product-- is included. The other major information services for which communications sets have been included are the Dow Jones News Retrieval service and the Official Airline Guide. If you want communications sets for DIALOG, BRS, SDC, NLM, Wilsonline, or any of the other biggies, you'll have to create your own.

Using Smartcom Macros

Let's look at some of the things a searcher could do with macros from a *Smartcom* communications set. Imagine a communications set designed to work with the DIALOG version of the Medline database. The communications parameters and automatic log-on macro could be set up with the preferred route to the online system. In this case, let's say it is Tymnet.

There is a good reason for choosing to use only one packet network. If you wanted to accommodate each of the value-added networks, you might have to triple or quadruple the number of communications sets you created. If you had to use a separate communications set for each online system and each network, you would quickly reach the twenty-six-set limit. You'd also be occupying valuable disk space with a lot of redundant information. It's unfortunate that *Smartcom* doesn't provide a mechanism for allowing the phone numbers and log-on protocols of packet-switching networks to be addressed and auto-dialed independently of a communications set.

Back to the macros. One macro could be set up to select the latest Medline file, set the screen width, and use the DIALOG Limitall command to limit search output to English materials. Another macro could be used to make Medline function as an index to a selected group of core journals in a subfield of medicine. This could be done by sending search statements to create a set representing titles included in the selected journals. It would also be possible to send an entire strategy, including output and log-off commands, or to conduct an exploratory search to determine how much material is available and identify some subject terms. It would even be possible to prerecord a fragment of a search representing all of the terms that are part of a larger concept, to do your own pre-exploring.

Smartcom does provide an editing facility that makes it easy to create and modify communications sets and macros. Unfortunately it is not possible to interactively record a macro, that is, to record keystrokes as they are being transmitted and received. When designing macros, it is necessary to work from a printout, specifying each message that will be sent in response to each host prompt.

Batch Sets

Smartcom provides for one other type of instruction file called a batch set. A batch set makes it possible to string together and record a group of commands and macros. If a program is defined as a stored sequence of instructions, then a batch set is certainly a program. However, a batch set is a rather primitive program when compared to the more sophisticated programs made possible by other software.

Once again, the letters of the alphabet are used as labels, and once again, the set labeled Z is reserved for a special function. The batch set labeled Z functions in a manner similar to the MS-DOS Autoexec.bat file. It is automatically executed when *Smartcom* is run and regulates the initial actions of the program.

Other batch sets may be recorded as the user issues commands and executes macros. A batch set can include several communications sets and macros. A batch set could cause *Smartcom* to connect to one service, select a database, perform a search and then connect to another service, select another database, and perform another search. The maximum number of keystrokes that can be incorporated in a batch set is 500. However, batch sets may be chained, or connected to one another.

Batch sets can also be set up to start and stop at a predetermined time. The searcher can begin one batch set which is linked to another. A starting time provided in the first batch set executed can be used to determine the playback time of the second. The searcher who wants to take advantage of cheaper night rates could use a batch set to load a communications set, make a connection, and send one or more macros at a predetermined time.

Although its menus can get in the way once you've learned to use the program (e.g., to send a macro requires eight times the number of keystrokes required by *PC-Talk*), *Smartcom* is still relatively easy to use for a program of its complexity. Its manual is clearly written; the troubleshooting section is especially useful. Just about every possible communications pitfall is described along with possible causes for the problem and a recommended solution.

Crosstalk--Programmable Communications

Crosstalk was the first of the successful, programmable communications programs. *Crosstalk XVI* was given its name because it was designed to take advantage of the processing power of computers equipped with 16-bit chips. *Crosstalk* allows the user to control the communications session in ways that are not possible with *Smartcom* or *PC-Talk*. Besides including its own programming language, *Crosstalk XVI* performs well in all of the more traditional communications tasks.

The Command Screen

Crosstalk uses a combination of commands and menus to interact with the user. A status screen is always available to the user, and if a prompt isn't understood, pressing the "?" key will yield an explanation. Once again, a group of different screens is presented to the user. The start-up screen displays a little joke or high-tech aphorism. Anyone who goes online frequently will have memorized all of them in a week or so.

The status screen displays the values of all parameters and a menu of commands. Each command is a word describing the action the command will perform. Entering the first two letters of a command in response to a prompt at the bottom of the screen will cause a command to be executed. If additional information is required before a command can be executed, the user will be prompted.

The Terminal Screen

In addition to the command screen, *Crosstalk* uses a terminal screen. The terminal screen is used to display a session in progress and to send messages to a host system. The status screen is used to view program settings and to send commands to the communications software. Each screen corresponds to a different communications mode. Once a call has been completed from the status screen, the program automatically switches to the terminal mode. The user can toggle back and forth between the status and the terminal screens by pressing the Home key. Commands can be issued via the status screen while remaining online. Data is stored in a buffer if it arrives while the user is viewing a status screen.

Talking to the Program

While online with the terminal screen displayed, certain keys are reserved for talking to the communications program rather than the remote system. The Esc key tells *Crosstalk* that the user wants to be prompted to enter a command. The Home key switches screens, providing the user with access to all settings, and the End key causes a break signal to be sent.

Crosstalk is well equipped to deal with files of a variety of types. Part of the status screen can contain a display window that provides a directory of parameter settings and available command files. *Crosstalk* command files correspond to *Smartcom* communications sets and can include log-on protocols and macros. Special commands can be used to determine the size of each file and to calculate an estimated transmission time at the current baud rate. DOS file-handling commands like ERASE and TYPE can even be used from within *Crosstalk*.

Function key macros are also possible. Function keys can serve any of three different purposes. A function key can store a message for a host system. A function key can store a *Crosstalk* command. Or a function key can store a variable called a script to be used in a communications program.

Like the other two programs, *Crosstalk* will also filter out unwanted control characters. *Crosstalk*'s filter, by default, removes all control characters except those representing printer controls, such as carriage return, form feed, and linefeed. The debug command causes *Crosstalk* to display incoming control characters and corresponds to *Smartcom*'s direct character processing.

Capturing Data

As with the other programs, incoming data may be routed to a printer or captured in a file. *Crosstalk* enables the searcher to scroll back through a search and examine the contents of the buffer. Of the three programs, only *PC-Talk* does not allow viewing of the buffer contents. *PC-Talk* also requires its users to close a capture file after it's been opened. If the searcher opens a file and forgets to close it with *PC-Talk*, the file becomes a "chain of lost clusters" on the disk, which may or may not be recoverable. *Crosstalk* and *Smartcom* are less likely to let the searcher lose the results of a search through simple oversight.

Crosstalk will also warn the user when the buffer or the disk is approaching its capacity. If a disk fills up while capturing data, a warning is issued and data is routed to the buffer. If data is streaming into the buffer and its limit is reached, the capture feature will be turned off, but data won't be dumped automatically into a temporary or overflow file. *Smartcom* does provide that capability.

Command Files

Command files in *Crosstalk* correspond roughly to *Smartcom* communications sets and the *PC-Talk* dialing directory. Command files contain names, numbers, parameters, and macros relating to a particular system. Unfortunately, passwords contained in *Crosstalk* command files can't be easily concealed like they they can be as *Smartcom*-protected macros. All command files have the extension .XTK. A default command file called STD.XTK establishes the settings most frequently used for asynchronous communication.

When *Crosstalk* is first loaded, the user sees a list of available command files. If a particular command file is chosen by the user, all of the settings associated with it will become active and it will initiate the dialing process. If the command file includes instructions to open a capture file or to upload a file from a disk to the remote system, those instructions will be carried out as well. Any *Crosstalk* command may be included in a command file. Command files may be linked to higher-level instruction files called script files.

```
NAme      TELENET (Hayes 1200)
NUmber    8,5244094
ANswback  On
APrefix   ATS0=1|
ATten     Esc
BReak     End
DEbug     Off
DPrefix   ATV0X1|~ATDT
DSuffix   |
EMulate   None
EPath     ""
FIlter    -------+++-++------------------
POrt      1
PWord     ""
RDials    10
SWitch    Home
TImer     On
TUrnarnd  Enter
VIdeo     EGA/Mono
ACcept    Everything
CWait     None
DNames    200
INfilter  On
LFauto    Off
LWait     None
MOde      Call
BKsize    1
BLankex   Off
CApture   Off
COmmand   ETX (^C)
DAta      8
DUplex    Full
FLow      ^S/^Q
HAndshak  Off
LBreak    200
OUtfiltr  On
PArity    None
PMode     2 (DOS)
PRinter   Off
SPeed     1200
STop      1
TAbex     Off
UConly    Off
FK 1      ""
FK 2      ""
FK 3      ""
FK 4      CROSSTALK - XVI
FK 5      @CApture /|
```

Crosstalk stores communications parameters for each service in a file called a command file.

Script Files

Script files are more specialized and flexible than command files. Like *Smartcom*, *Crosstalk* comes preconfigured with files designed to work with popular online services. *Crosstalk* adds LEXIS, VU/TEXT, and NewsNet to the online services supported by *Smartcom* but does not support the big "supermarket" vendors. System-specific files in *Crosstalk* are script files.

Command files are used to set parameters and establish an on-line connection. Script files control the action once the searcher is online. Script files are programs in the true sense of the word. The qualitative difference between *Crosstalk* and *Smartcom* is *Crosstalk*'s ability to handle script files. Script files may include lists of instructions to be executed in sequence just as command files, and *Smartcom* batch sets do. But scripts may also include programming constructs that enable instructions to be executed out of sequence according to specified conditions. *Crosstalk* recognizes script files by looking for the filename extension .XTS.

Script files can ask the user for information and make decisions based upon the response. Script files can look for specified strings among the messages sent from the host and respond appropriately. Parts of the script can be skipped when certain conditions are met. One script file can even transfer control to another script file. Programming constructs like conditional statements, branching, transfer of control, and pausing for input can be very useful for those who want to establish some measure of control over the online session between a searcher and a host. Script files provide a vehicle for mediating between an online system and a client searcher.

Crosstalk can be made to recognize prompts from remote computers. There is even a feature that will cause *Crosstalk* to automatically "learn" the number of characters in a prompt. The length of the prompt can then be used as a way of determining whether a string of characters from a remote system is really a prompt. Delays may also be incorporated in scripts to account for delayed responses from the host. Like *Smartcom*, *Crosstalk* is not capable of interactively recording the messages and responses in a communications session.

If a command file and a script file are given the same name, the script file will be called automatically from the command file. For example, a search manager could set up a command file that logged on to the BRS version of the ABI/Inform database and link it to a script file that controlled the action once a connection had been established. The script file could be designed to ask the user if he or she wanted to limit the search results to English-language materials or to a single industry, such as telecommunications, or to an aspect of business, such as advertising or accounting. Depending upon the user's responses, appropriate prerecorded statements would be transmitted.

Any frequently used tactic could be accommodated within the script. The search statements uploaded from the script file to the host would depend on the client/searcher's responses to the script's requests for input. Here is one possible scenario. A client has selected an ABI/Inform script and is asked if she is interested in articles dealing with companies. She responds affirmatively by

General Purpose Communication Tools 139

entering a Y. The script jumps to a group of prompts designed to elicit the names of specific companies in which the client is interested. The script also prepares to send a group of terms known to yield documents relating to companies in general.

After the client has finished entering the names of specific companies, she is asked if she is interested in a particular industry. If she says, yes, the terms for the industries she indicates will be combined with terms relating to companies in general. The script can cover requests for data on specific companies as well as data on companies within an industry. The script could also be made to add references to marketing, finance, or production, once again depending on the client's preference. Since a script can include any *Crosstalk* command, prompts allowing the client to print references or review the contents of the buffer, or even to search the buffer for a particular term can also be included. Contrast this approach with the batch set approach that fixes the specific statements sent and the sequence in which they are sent.

```
;         DIALOG at 300 or 1200 baud, via TELENET

;         Set up a WHen statement so whenever TELENET wakes up, we'll be read
when "TELENET" jump WE_ARE_IN
;         Send TELENET a CR every second until it wakes up.
label START
wait delay 10
reply |
jump START
;         Once it wakes up, get on with the show.
label WE_ARE_IN

; Connect to DIALOG port
wait string "TERMINAL"
reply D1|
wait char "@"
reply C 41548D|
wait string "CONNECTED"
wait delay 10
reply |

; Logon to DIALOG, set screen width to 65
wait string "LOGON:"
wait delay 10
reply PASSWORD|
wait delay 50
wait string   "1:ERIC"
wait char "?"
reply SET H 65|
wait string "65"

; Conduct search on communications software, print 1st 10 in format 8
wait char "?"
reply S MICROCOMPUTER?/DE,TI|
wait string "s1"
wait char "?"
reply S (COMMUNICATION? OR TELECOMMUNICATION?)(W)SOFTWARE|
wait string "s2"
wait char "?"
reply S S1 AND S2|
wait string "s3"
wait char "?"
reply T S3/8/1-10|
wait char "?"
reply LOGOFF|
end
```

The log-on portion of this script was taken from a prerecorded script that came with Crosstalk.

Script files are programs. They can be as complicated and kludgy or as simple and elegant as any program. And like any program, if they are to work well, they must be carefully planned. Script files enable the searcher to control higher-level aspects of the search process. When creating a script file, it is as important to be aware of good search techniques as it is to be aware of good programming techniques. You must have a very clear idea of what you want to accomplish, exactly how the script should mediate between the searcher and the online system.

Crosstalk provides the means to develop scripts but doesn't make it easy, especially for the nonprogrammer. All of the commands that can be used in script files are listed and described in the *Crosstalk* manual, but no real tutorial is provided to show the searcher how they might be put together in meaningful ways. Nor does *Crosstalk* provide a facility for editing script or command files. A word processor or line editor has to be used.

The experienced programmer will find some of the capabilities associated with full-blown programming languages lacking in *Crosstalk*'s script language. Searchers will be disappointed by the lack of sophisticated string-handling capabilities since so much of searching involves the manipulation of text strings. Nevertheless, *Crosstalk* represents a fundamentally different approach to communications software. The searcher who expends the effort required to learn to create *Crosstalk* scripts will be able to extend control of the search process from the lower levels associated with setting parameters and logging on to the higher levels associated with extracting information from a database.

Microsoft Access--A Communications Language

Microsoft Access (not to be confused with *PFS Access*, a popular no-frills package) is one of the heavyweights among communications programs. *Access* was developed by the Gregg Corporation--a Massachusetts company specializing in financial and securities information systems--for Microsoft, the software giant that was rather late in introducing a communications product. *Access* was designed for a business environment rather than an academic one. It bills itself as a "business information access program." The first version of *Access* was copy protected, making the program less convenient for hard disk users. The current version is no longer copy protected.

The example usually given to illustrate the program's power involves a script that calls a quote service on one line while simul-

General Purpose Communication Tools   141

taneously dialing a broker on another. Financial information is requested from the quote service. Buy or sell orders are immediately placed with the broker depending on the prices supplied by the quote service, and maybe a formula included in the script. Of course, this requires two serial ports, two modems, and two phone lines. Remember, if you have to ask what the price is you probably can't afford it. You may not be able to afford two modems and phone lines, but for $250, if you need absolute control over your communications environment, *Access* is a good buy.

Access and its competitor *Crosstalk Mark IV* ($245 from Microstuf), a fuller-featured, more expensive cousin of *Crosstalk*, are as much programming languages as they are communications programs. Because *Access* is a programming language designed for communications, it can be used for other than strictly business applications. Several of its features will allow the searcher to develop a set of customized search tools.

Of course *Access* will perform the usual communications functions previously described, and it's surprisingly easy to use for such a complex program. You don't have to know how to blow all of its whistles or ring all of its bells to use it as a searcher. However, *Access* provides some whistles and bells which, in the hands of a programmer/searcher, have a potential far beyond that offered by other communications programs.

All of the programs described provide the user with control of the keys. *Access* permits the user to redefine screens as well. All of the programs described let you talk to another computer. *Access* lets you talk to as many as eight other computers at the same time. All of the programs described let you create files containing instructions. Only *Access* will remember the keystrokes in a communications session and create a script file for you. And the *Access* script language is far more flexible than the one offered by *Crosstalk*.

Access owes a lot to *Crosstalk*. *Access* utilizes a similar combination of menus and commands in addition to incorporating its own programming language. *Access* uses four types of menus: the session menu, the phonebook menu, the editor menu, and custom menus. The first menu seen is the session menu. Displayed on the screen are a command line listing available commands, a status line, and a message line prompting the user to enter commands. The space bar is used to highlight the desired option. Pressing the space bar causes the highlighting to move from one to another of the available commands. When the Return key is pressed, the selected command is executed.

Many of the choices on the menu are likely to have subchoices associated with them. Commands and menus are organized hierarchically. Options at the level below the command level are known as command fields. Once a command has been chosen, the user will often be prompted to fill in command fields. The Tab key enables the user to move the highlighter from one command field to another. For example, if the connect command is selected from the session menu, the user is given the option of filling in command fields indicating the name of the service to connect to, its phone number, the baud rate, and so forth.

Phone numbers and communications parameters are stored in a "phonebook." When the user specifies the name of a service for which a phonebook entry exists, the phonebook is displayed and a call may be initiated. The phonebook menu is designed to enable the user to add to and edit the entries in the phonebook.

In addition to commands selected from menus, *Access* makes use of function keys. Function keys are used to select menus, pause communications, toggle capture-to-disk or file-on and -off, and control the printer. Pressing the funtion key labeled F2 will cause a list of function key definitions to be displayed. It is also possible to create keyboard macros called Quickeys. Quickeys can be linked to specific hosts listed in the phone book.

Custom Menus

Custom menus are provided for use with a variety of information services. Emphasis is on business and financial databanks. Once again, preconfigured instruction files have not been provided for "supermarket" online vendors. If the user opts to connect to a service for which a custom menu is available, that menu will replace the session menu on the screen. Each custom menu prompts the user for input relating to the content, structure, and function of a specific information service.

Custom menus move one step beyond the dial-up and log-on features provided by other software including preconfigured files for specific services. Custom menus concentrate on controlling the content of the interaction with the host. A script is used to allow the user to query the host interactively rather than in a batch mode. Users of custom menus need not be familiar with the commands and syntax of the host system. Each service supported has its own help options which are called from its custom menu.

For example, *Access* includes a portfolio option in the custom menu associated with the Dow Jones News Retrieval Service. The menu is set up to allow the user to develop a strategy to use the Dow Jones quote service to track the performance of a selected group of stocks, bonds, and other investments. Because the emphasis of *Access* is on business information, many of the specialized options available within custom menus can be used with more than a single service. Several of the custom menus offer a quotes option that will retrieve quotes from the source for which they were designed. The read command allows researchers to read news provided on a variety of the services supported, and the travel command permits the use of the Official Airline Guide from within the many information services that make it available.

The MASC Language

Access also makes it possible to create one's own custom menus by offering a powerful script language called the Microsoft Access Script Command (MASC) language. *Access* makes script development easier by featuring a learn mode. When learn is selected as an option, *Access* will remember all of the keystrokes sent to and received from an online service and record them as a script, which may later be modified.

A variant of the learn command called the learn log-in command is avaialble from the session menu and allows the searcher to record a log-on protocol. Unfortunately, no way of providing password protection is provided by learn log-in. The contents of log-on scripts that have the extension .LGN are accessible to anyone who knows the rudiments of using DOS.

Scripts can be developed to log-on or to perform complex search tasks. Branching, looping, and a number of different conditional statements may be used. A variety of different string-handling functions are available. The script programmer also has control over the screen display, which can be divided up into a number of windows. Scripts may also include a variety of different types of variables.

This is an outline of a script fragment that analyzes the results of a BRS search and then makes decisions based on the number of hits obtained. It illustrates some of the advanced features of MASC.

Script with Conditions

This script determines number of hits yielded by a previously sent search and takes action depending upon the number of items in the target set; it is assumed that the target set number is known in advance; in this case the number of the target set is assumed to be 1.

```
MATCH "RESULT"              recognizes RESULT prompt from BRS
READCOM TARGET$,30,12       stores max of 12 characters coming in
                            over line after RESULT msg received
                            in a variable called TARGET$; waits
                            max of 30 sec before timeout

HITS = VAL(TARGET$)         converts string variable TARGET$ to
                            an integer, HITS


TEST:                                       tests for number of hits
IF HITS < 10 THEN GOTO PRINTOUT             takes action based on test
IF HITS > 10 AND HITS <100 THEN GOTO EXPLORE
IF HITS > 100 THEN GOTO REFINE
GOTO END


PRINTOUT:
    ..P 1 F5/DOC=ALL ^M     prints full record for all if less than
    GOTO END                10


EXPLORE:                            prints 1st 20 w /au,ti,de
    ..P 1 AU,TI,DE/DOC=1-20 ^M      if more than 10, less than 100
    GOTO END


REFINE:                         qualifies search to de,ti fields
    1.DE,TI.                    if too many hits
    MATCH "RESULTS"             repeats process if required
    READCOM NEWSET$,?,?
    HITS=VAL(NEWSET$)
      IF HITS > 10 THEN GOTO EXPLORE  see what we've got
      ELSE GOTO PRINTOUT
      GOTO END
END:
    BRS-OFF                     calls script for logoff
```

The *Access* manual is clearly written and includes numerous examples of scripts as well as entire chapters on custom menus (which are also scripts). An editor is provided to create and edit scripts. Some knowledge of programming would be essential to take full advantage of MASC. However, the learn option, makes it possible for the novice programmer to develop scripts by performing searches. Once the searcher has edited a few scripts created with the learn option, he or she will have a better idea of how a script is constructed.

A good searcher shouldn't have too much difficulty learning to work with scripts. After all, you probably have some sort of a script in mind before you sit down at the terminal. Your mental script includes the statements you will be sending and the types of responses you are expecting from the host service. You probably have contingency plans if the host's response is something other than what you expected. And your overall strategy, just like a program, most likely involves getting what you are after with a step-by-step approach in which decisions are made based on the results of each step.

In summary, *Access* represents a qualitatively different kind of communications program. *Access* also costs $250, rather steep as communications programs go. At seven times the cost of *PC-Talk*, you really have to take advantage of either the custom menus or the programmability of *Access* to get your money's worth. Time is another thing you'll have to invest. But in the long run, scripts could save you hours of work.

A good script, a script similar to the custom menus that come with the program, could even offer a financial return. Microsoft seems to be betting that there will be a market for scripts and custom menus. It's possible to order from Microsoft something called the Microsoft Access Script Developer's Kit (suggested price: $25). The kit gives you everything you need to create a custom menu system that includes help messages, windows, and scripts. A compiler is included to produce a machine-readable version of a custom-designed menu. Does anybody want to buy a custom menu for ABI/Inform on BRS, or maybe for the Electronic Yellow Pages on DIALOG, or Medline on NLM? Does anybody want to create one, and sell it---or give it away?

Let's go back to our toolbox, and put all of the communications programs in their section of the drawer labeled Process Tools. On the other side of that same drawer are some funny looking tools labeled Search Assistance. Intriguing. But let's save our curiosity

146 Microcomputers for the Online Searcher

for later, close the Process Tools drawer, and open the one labeled Product Tools.

Communications Software Checklist

Offline Mode (AKA Command mode)

    Parameter setting

        baud rate _____ 300 _____ 1200 _____ 2400 _____

        duplex _____ echowait _____ parity _____

        word length _____ start/stop bits _____ screen size _____

    Programmability

        number of macros _____ offline preparation of search files _____

        maximum length _____ scripting capability _____

        stored protocols _____ clock interface _____

Online Mode (AKA Terminal Mode)

    Downloading capability _____

        download to buffer _____ overflow buffer _____

        download to disk _____ overflow file _____

    Uploading capability _____

        macros _____ respond to prompt from host _____

        files _____ ability to create scripts _____

        Menu driven _____ Command driven _____

        ability to override menus _____

ability to toggle between modes while online _____

Special features

    automatic dialing _____   character stripping _____

    host systems directory _____   scrolling while online _____

    password security _____   keyboard type ahead _____

    user defined defaults _____

    preconfigured for specific systems _____

Display characteristics

    screen width _____   screen height _____

    status line _____   windows _____

    online command summary _____   color/monochrome _____

Documentation

  Online documentation _____

    description of commands _____   help screens _____

    error messages _____   online tutorial _____

    description of available files _____

  Printed documentation _____

    clarity _____   indexed _____

    ease of use _____   tutorial included _____

    quick reference card included _____

Compatability

    Computer required _____ Modem required _____

    Operating system required _____ Memory requirements _____

    Other peripheral devices required _____

    Compatability with other software

        word processing _____

        database mgt. _____

        utilities _____

    Compatability with online systems/databases

        single system _____ multisystem _____

        DIALOG ___ BRS ___ SDC ___ NLM ___ Other _____

        single file or file family _____ all files _____

        automatic query translation within system(s): _____

References/Recommended Reading

Derfler, Frank J. "Crosstalk Mark 4 and Access: Redefining the State of the Art." *PC Magazine*, 3 September 1985, 116-127.

Holland, Maurita Peterson. "Communications Software: Experiences with Perfect Link and Crosstalk XVI." *Online* (July 1984): 75-80.

Keating, Barry. "Choosing and Using Telecommunications Software." *Creative Computing* (February 1985): 101-113.

Kolner, Stuart J. "The IBM PC as an Online Search Machine--Part 5: Searching Through Crosstalk." *Online* (November 1985): 42-50.

Lane, Malcolm G. *Data Communications Software Design*. Boston: Boyd & Fraser, 1985.

Saffady, William. "Communications Software Packages for the IBM Personal Computer and Compatibles." *Library Technology Reports* 21, no.4 (July/August 1985): 355-456.

CHAPTER NINE
SOFTWARE FOR THE SEARCH PRODUCT

Postprocessing Software--The Search Product

The raw material from which the search product is formed is information, that most nebulous of commodities. Fritz Machlup, the late economist whose last years were spent on a monumental study of the information trade, described information as the only commodity that increases as it is consumed. When you think of information as a commodity, you think of services rather than products. But there are clearly defined information products as well. And there are tools for creating and using those products. Information products are most often associated with the form they assume, with their format. Tools for working with raw information may also be categorized according to the format assumed by the final product.

Reformatting covers a lot of territory. It could mean something as simple as removing line noise from search results for a more attractive finished product or something as complex as performing statistical analyses on data downloaded from a numeric database. Most communications programs are of limited use for reformatting. Most allow character stripping. Unwanted characters may be filtered out, but that is about the best a communications program can do.

Traditionally, the online search product has taken the form of print on paper. Any ability to rearrange the words or numbers on the page has traditionally resided with software in the host computer. It has long been possible to sort search results, to print records in different formats (often predefined), or to rearrange records on the page. More recently, report generation software has provided us with the ability to recombine and display numeric and directory data at the level of the field instead of at the level of the record.

We can still take advantage of those search system capabilities to add value to the search product. Those of us with micros can also take advantage of tools which enable us to reformat records delivered by online services resulting in a high-quality printed product which would have been unavailable a few years ago. Personal computers have also opened the possibility of using information products which are transformed to meet our needs, but which remain in machine-readable form. The database is no longer the exclusive domain of the host system.

Communications is the major category into which most process tools may be placed. Product tools encompass several software categories. Among the sections in our product tools drawer are those containing word processors, database managers, and number crunchers. Each broad category of tool yields a different type of end product. Sometimes creating a finished product involves the use of a few different kinds of tools to work the information raw material into shape. It is beyond the scope of this book to include more than the briefest of discussions of word processors, database managers, and spreadsheets. They will be looked at in terms of their use to searchers, but specific products won't be treated in any detail.

The Printed Word as Search Product

Reformatting generally requires that the data to be reformatted be in machine-readable form. Downloading to a disk is the way in which this is accomplished. We all know about the legal problems associated with downloading. Let's imagine that we're dealing with a file that permits downloading (Medline, for example; note: the abstracts are copyrighted). Imagine that a Medline search has been done. The results, minus abstracts, have been safely ensconced on a disk by our trusty communications program.

Chances are good that what we now have is an ASCII text file from which control codes may or may not have been removed. We have a roughly drawn image of the thing we'll eventually put together. Maybe we weren't all that discriminating about what we downloaded. Chances also are that our file contains the entire search session, all of the messages between information central and our little city--every prompt, help message, error message, and flubbed up line is there, even if there is no noise present. What do we do with this odd assortment of electromagnetic charges? The wonderfully alliterative neologism "postprocessing" has been coined to cover all of the possibilities. Let us first consider the search product as printed word.

Where Are the Pages?

This ASCII file that we have, when viewed on the screen, is a series of lines, many of uniform width. Pictured as a printed work, it is a long scroll (if it is a big file). We can only see twenty-five lines of it at a time because that's all our screen will display. The host that delivered our file probably had a default value for the width of each line it sent. Let's say that value was seventy-five. The host probably added a linefeed control code to the end of each line. Most likely all of those linefeeds are still in our file and each line is seventy-five characters long.

Inside of our machine we have a long, rough scroll full of symbols. The symbols on it are arranged in lines the maximum length of which cannot exceed seventy-five characters (also expressed as columns). The page is is an unfamiliar concept at this stage of the production process. Our product, now, is more analogous to an ancient papyrus. One of the first things we might want to do is add pages. We'll probably use a word processor of some sort to add the form feed signals required to keep the information we've paid for from printing on the perforations between pages. The word processor will make it easy enough to add page breaks. They're probably already there by default, but solving the problem of dividing our information into pages introduces other possible problems.

Most word processing programs, and a lot of printers, have a left margin default. *WordStar*, for example, automatically indents eight columns on the left margin. A computer screen which has been set up to deal with standard 8 1/2-inch wide paper is eighty columns wide. A printer with a narrow carriage width is also about eighty columns wide. If a word processor is used to print a file which is seventy-five columns wide in many places, and the word processor is already indenting eight columns, the file will be eighty-three-characters wide in many places. When the word processor comes to its right margin default, it will think it's hit the end of the line and cause the paper to advance a line. When the linefeed from the host is encountered at the eighty-third column, it also will cause the paper to advance.

What happens when you try to print an eighty-three-column wide record on an eighty-column wide printer? The printer can only print eighty characters on a single line, and it does. Having nowhere else to go, it moves to the next line and begins printing the rest of the logical line it began on the previous physical line. After printing eighty-three characters, only three characters into that next line, it encounters the linefeed which was provided by the online service and moves to the next line as it was told to do. The result looks like the printout depicted on the next page.

154 Microcomputers for the Online Searcher

DIALOG Medline Search on Narrow Printer

```
           1/3/1
           2002311    86219311
              Handedness is not a unidimensional trait.
              Healey JM; Liederman J; Geschwind N
              Department  of  Psychiatry, Mount Sinai School of Medicine, New York,
   New
           York 10029.
              Cortex (ITALY)      ,Mar 1986,    22 (1) p33-53,    ISSN 0010-9452
           Journal Code: DSP

           1/3/2
           1941415    86158415
              Reproductive endocrine disorders in men with partial seizures of tempc
   ral
           lobe origin.
              Herzog AG; Seibel MM; Schomer DL; Vaitukaitis JL; Geschwind N
   ael        Department  of Neurology, Charles A. Dana Research Institute, Beth Isr
           Hospital, Boston, MA 02215.
              Arch Neurol (UNITED STATES)     ,Apr 1986,    43 (4) p347-50,
           ISSN 0003-9942    Journal Code: 8OK

           1/3/3
           1941414    86158414
              Reproductive    endocrine    disorders    in    women    with    partial    seizures
   of
           temporal lobe origin.
              Herzog AG; Seibel MM; Schomer DL; Vaitukaitis JL; Geschwind N
   ael        Department  of Neurology, Charles A. Dana Research Institute, Beth Isr
           Hospital, Boston, MA 02215.
   942        Arch Neurol (UNITED STATES)     ,Apr 1986,    43 (4) p341-6,    ISSN 0003-9
           Journal Code: 8OK

           1/3/4
           1940252    86157252
              Dyslexia,  congenital   anomalies,   and   immune disorders: the role of
   the
           fetal environment.
              Behan P; Geschwind N
              Department of Neurology, University of Glasgow, Scotland.
              Ann NY Acad Sci (UNITED STATES)    ,1985,    457 p13-8,    ISSN 0077-8923
           Journal Code: 5NM
              Contract/Grant No.: 06209; NS 17018

           1/3/5
           1940248    86157248
              Mechanisms of change after brain lesions.
              Geschwind N
              Department   of   Neurology,   Harvard Medical School, Beth Israel Hospit
   al,
           Boston, Massachusetts 02215.
              Ann NY Acad Sci (UNITED STATES)    ,1985,    457 p1-11,    ISSN 0077-8923
           Journal Code: 5NM

           1/3/6
           1851043    86068043
              Cortical anomalies in brains of New Zealand mice: a neuropathologic mo
   del
```

If you have a narrow printer, this may be one of the first reformatting problems you'll encounter. If your printer has a wide carriage, this problem could still occur, causing your search results to bleed over the right margin of your paper. There is more than one approach to solving this problem.

Host systems usually permit searchers to change the default values for screen width and screen height. Often it's possible to record a profile with the host that automatically sets the screen size when you log on with the password for which the profile was created. Changing a profile to specify a narrower width (maybe the default width of your word processor) would solve this problem. So would sending the command for a narrower width each time you connected. Commands to tell different systems or even different databases to set different widths could even be built into scripts.

Another approach would be to use commands within the word processor to change the page offset on the left margin. Someone with a modicum of programming knowledge could bypass the word processor altogether and write a simple program to tell the printer to print fifty or so lines on a page before advancing to the next page.

Cleaning It Up

Now we have a file that has been divided up into pages and lines of roughly the same length. There are many levels at which reformatting can continue. The simplest level involves cleaning up and editing search results. Any of the classic word processing programs will make this easy to do. The most basic word processing package will allow the searcher to delete unwanted material from search results and to insert titles, field labels, or other explanatory material for clients. The individual researcher could use a word processor with a strong indexing module to add notes and cross-references to search results. Remember the memex?

A package with a find-and-replace capability will permit the searcher to automatically locate and change or remove unwanted characters. The searcher can specify that words and phrases such as SHOW COST, or any of the messages sent by either computer, be removed or moved. A mark-and-move capability allows the searcher to rearrange search data and will make it possible to create standard bibliographies from downloaded search results. General purpose word processors at the high end of the market can include special commands designed for those involved in scholarly research and publishing.

A word processor that can create standard ASCII files (only 128 codes, no high bits allowed) has the added benefit of being able to create and edit files for uploading and scripts as well. Be aware that using a word processor to clean up and manipulate search results can be time consuming and labor intensive. Remember that the material we are extracting from the host is mined from deep veins. At high speeds, it's easily possible to download unwieldy amounts of information. One of the best uses of a word processor for the searcher is to prepare and edit messages to be sent to the host system and to clients. Messages that can be structured for the searcher's convenience are easier to deal with than boxcar loads of bibliographic records.

It is possible to automate the process to a certain degree. Any sequence of commands used to perform an editing task within the word processor can be placed into a macro, similar to the macros described in the last chapter. Full-featured word processors often come with a macro-creation facility. It is also possible to buy low-cost, sophisticated macro processor programs. Any task that is repetitive and involves a lot of keystrokes lends itself to this approach. With a single keystroke it would be possible, for example, to find and remove all occurrences of certain messages from the host. Prompts, error messages, and help messages could be eliminated more easily this way. Of course, if we had downloaded more selectively with our communications program, there would have been a lot less to clean up.

Even though we are still dealing with the printed word, we'll eventually need to concern ourselves with the way our data are structured. The search process itself has already given us a chance to extract a small, unique, finely crafted set of meaningful records. Our records are further subdivided into information entities we call fields. The host has allowed us to sort our records on different fields such as author, journal title, or publication date to arrange them in a more useful or meaningful sequence.

So far we've been unable to sort and rearrange the fields within a single record, to produce a list of references conforming to a specific bibliographic style, for example. If the thing we're trying to build is a scholarly paper, then we'll need such a capability. Bibliographic standards share many qualities with computer standards. There are as many ways to organize the elements of a bibliographic citation as there are to represent information with electricity. Anyone who has ever written a scholarly paper for one journal and then had to totally reorganize the references for another knows all about bibliographic standards.

Is there a way to get our computer to help us deal with these human standards in addition to the electrical ones with which it deals so well? And wouldn't it be nice to have a systematic way to add our own information to the records delivered to us by the online service? There are specialized tools for that purpose. On the surface they may seem like word processors because they shuffle words around. Beneath the surface, there is something different.

What those tools do is restructure the files we've downloaded. The products of those tools are local databases with many of the attributes of the remote databases we talk to so often. The end result may be a highly organized printed page; it's almost cetain that one of the intermediate stages was a highly organized file or group of files on a disk. Once machine-readable files have been organized, alternatives to the printed word present themselves.

The same discovery that was made in the early online days is being made today. Online systems evolved from applying the computer to solve the problems of producing the printed word. It's not surprising that the ELHILL/NLM search system, originally designed to produce Index Medicus, bears many of the vestiges of a printing and publishing system. There is a difference between software developed to generate printed words and software designed to manage machine-readable data.

The Database as a Search Product

Most database management software was designed for business rather than bibliographic applications. Creating in-house databases from downloaded data presents technical as well as legal problems, especially when a database manager designed for another purpose is used. There are on the market programs designed for this purpose. Biblio-Link from Personal Bibliographic Software and FINDERlink from FINDER Information Tools are two examples. One of the modules of Sci-Mate will also manage downloaded data. Specialized tools for searchers will be discussed in the next chapter.

Flexible database management programming languages like *dBase* may also be used but require time and effort to learn. Before *dBase II*, most database management packages were locked into a certain set of applications and way of doing things. *dBase* added to database management the same kind of flexibility *Crosstalk* introduced to communications. General purpose programming languages such as BASIC or Pascal may also be used. Public domain programs for this purpose are also occasionally listed in various online publications.

Surprisingly, records from online databases often do not lend themselves to being incorporated in local databases. Online services have only recently, that is until a lot of people began using micros for searching, begun to consider the information they deliver as raw material for (perish the thought) local databases. Consequently, online information was not formatted to be easily used by file and database management software on personal computers, nor were such niceties as field labels always provided. Now most of the online services have come around and are at least including field labels. Still there are obstacles to overcome if the searcher wants to avoid having to manually input information that was originally delivered in machine-readable form.

Part of the problem has to do with the fact that the way records are structured varies from one database to another. Field labels and delimiters are often not included, and a single database can include several different record types. It is first necessary to understand the structure of the file you are dealing with before restructuring it to meet your own needs.

Database management tools require that the fields of a record and the type of information each field will contain be specified before a database can be created. It's hard to specify the fields records in a local database will contain if the source from which the raw material was extracted includes several different types of records. Most database managers also require that the length of each field be determined in advance--something which has to do with bibliographic records. Lots of disk space can be wasted by overestimating the length of a field; the contents of a field can be arbitrarily truncated and meaningful information lost by underestimating. Perhaps the number and variety of available files has contributed to the sparsity of programs for developing in-house databases from downloaded records. Of course, the legal and economic situation is also a factor.

After legal and economic hurdles have been cleared and online raw material has been squeezed into a structure acceptable to a database program at the local level, the problems move to a higher level. The framework for our city has been built and it becomes necessary to fill in the details and let each edifice take on its own architectural character.

A local database can certainly be used to generate a variety of printed products. Bibliographies representing subsets of a search that was done on a larger topic can be easily produced. Records can be sorted in different ways to reflect different needs. The individual researcher might want to arrange references by topic or article, while the library might want to organize records by journal title or call number to reflect a shelving arrangement. The database probably already includes index files that accompany the information itself and those indexes can be used to produce printed indexes to records from one or more online files. The ability to impose one's own indexing scheme upon the schemes developed by a diverse group of database producers is a big plus. A local database linked to a word processor could form the core of a "scholar's workstation."

A local database can also be used as an online resource for offline/online searching at the local level. Individuals or clients can extract selected pieces of information using the same Boolean operators used by online services. Full-text search capabilities involving the use of proximity operators and truncation are also available from many database managers, especially those designed for bibliographic applications.

If a database language program like *dBase* is used, it is possible to design a user interface. Clients can be presented with a search system developed for their needs. Menus and help screens can be provided and a library of report formats can be developed. Database languages may be used to implement many of the features provided by online services, although speeds really aren't comparable. It's one thing to get a program that will perform and another to get it to perform with acceptable response times. Compilers that translate the language of the DBMS to the language of the machine and which speed up the programs substantially are available for many of the more popular database programs.

Related databases may also be linked together with one another at the local level. A local database can be a conglomeration of records from more than one public database and can include locally created records as well. Imagine a database used to support researchers in an academic film studies programs. One database, let's call it REVIEWS, could include references to all reviews of frequently shown films. Online searches could be performed on databases that included references to film reviews. Files such as Magazine Index, Reader's Guide, and MLA Bibliography could be searched. Once clearance had been given by database producers, those online records could be merged with locally created records derived from periodical indexes and film review bibliographies.

An attempt could be made to include references to locally available sources. The database could inlude references to movie reviews in critics' anthologies and other books as well as journal sources. The entire gamut of possible sources could be used to compile the database, which could be made to cover the retrospective literature better than public online files do.

A companion database, let's call it AUTEUR, could include material relating to the entire corpus of selected directors. This database would be linked to the REVIEWS database by the director's name which would be a searchable, indexed field in each file. It would be possible to use the two databases together to compile a list of reviews of all of Alfred Hitchcock's films, for example, and to append references to studies of Alfred Hitchcock's life and career in general. It's not hard to imagine other locally produced files being linked to the two described. Why not have a database called GENRE as well?

Crunching Numbers

Creating databases from downloaded numeric data can be intimidating. The files that lend themselves to this kind of manipulation are usually expensive and impose severe restrictions on the electronic re-use of the data they contain. Dizzying technical gyrations are often required to export downloaded files into spreadsheets. The records recognizable to a spreadsheet or database management program aren't delimited in the same high-level way as records originating with an online system. In delimited files like the ones used by BASIC and *dBase*, commas are often used to separate fields and text is indicated with quotation marks. Records are separated from one another by carriage returns. Online records, even those from numeric files, contain commas and carriage returns that were never intended to delimit records. Spreadsheets organize data into columns and rows called domains and tuples. Spreadsheet file structures often have difficulty accommodating downloaded numeric data.

Consequently, we are seeing an increase in the number of numeric files that are accompanied by micro software specifically designed to manipulate those files. The software and the data are being sold as a single package. One advantage to this approach is that the software is produced by the same people who put together the database and is designed to work within the structure of the database. Right now, this is largely limited to costly financial databases that aren't often used in libraries. End-users are the obvious market for this type of software.

Perhaps spreadsheets are of greater value in tracking the activities of a search center. Certainly such an application would be easier to implement. Nor would legal clearances be required.

Specialized Tools for the Searcher

Let's put the generic product tools back into their drawer, each category in its own section. What's this at the back of the drawer? It looks like something we've seen in another drawer. In the product tools drawer is a section labeled Search Assistance.

Searching involves a process and a product. Good search assistance software is modular enough to address both. It has a place in each drawer. Search assistance software usually emphasizes the search process. A search assistance package will almost always include a communications program. However, the search product hasn't been neglected. Search software is likely to include elements of word processing and database management. We are also beginning to see accounting and spreadsheet functions incorporated in search packages. Another development, one which current research in the field suggests will become increasingly important, is language processing capability. Language processing, which will be described later, is something quite different from word processing.

Once again we will approach a category of tools by pulling some specific programs from our drawer and examining them in detail. Before we start describing search assistance programs though, let's take a closer look at a typical search.

References/Recommended Reading

Brewer, James. "Printed Bibliographies: Production from an Online Database Using Techniques of Uploading/Downloading." In *Downloading/Uploading Online Databases and Catalogs*, edited by James A. Benson and Bella H. Weinberg, 30-39. Ann Arbor, MI: Pierian Press, 1985.

Burnam, Judy K. "Users' Needs for Repackaging and Re-use of Information." *Information Services & Use* 1 (1982): 359-366.

Burton, Hilary D. "The Changing Environment of Personal Information Systems," *Journal of the American Society for Information Science* 36, no.1 (January 1985): 48-52.

Clark, Philip M. *Spreadsheet Models for Libraries: Preparing Documents, Budgets, and Statistical Reports*. Chicago: American Library Association, 1985.

Goldstein, Charles M., and Maureen Prettyman. "Processing Downloaded Citations." In *Downloading/Uploading Online*

Databases and Catalogs, edited by James A. Benson and Bella H. Weinberg, 40-49. Ann Arbor, MI: Pierian Press, 1985.

Huleatt, Richard S. "Finishing the Online Search." *Online* (April 1979): 24-31.

Machlup, Fritz. *Information Through the Printed Word: The Dissemination of Scholarly, Scientific, and Intellectual Knowledge.* 3 vols. NY: Praeger, 1978.

Tenopir, Carol. "Identification and Evaluation of Software for Microcomputer-Based In-House Databases." *Information Technology and Libraries* 3, no.1 (March 1984): 21-34.

CHAPTER TEN
SPECIALIZED TOOLS FOR THE SEARCHER

Anatomy of a Search

It's debatable whether there is any such thing as a typical online search. Nevertheless, authorities in the field have largely agreed upon the sequence of higher-level activities that have come to be defined as a "search." Let us back away for awhile from the electrical subsurface where the mechanical details are handled and focus on searching as a human activity.

At the human level, the typical search usually begins with one person approaching another with a request for information. Most likely part of the request involves one person interceding on the other's behalf with a machine. Almost always a form is filled in by the person in need of information and intercession. Thereafter follows a working encounter called "the search interview."

The rules for the search interview haven't been codified as they have for the dialog that transpires with the machine. The search interview is a more subtle, open-ended process. Both parties must agree on the subject of the search. Both must also arrive at limits on things like the cost of the search, the types of documents it will include, and the amount of information it is likely to yield. The search interview is not a simple script to learn.

Next, a database has to be selected. Even the institution that subscribes to a single online service will probably have over a hundred files from which to choose. The entire universe of possibilities includes several thousand files from hundreds of services. Cost, ease of use, and adaptability to the local environment have to be considered. Decisions are based on past experience as is the ability to effectively use a database.

Once a file has been selected, terms have to be identified. It may be necessary to use a thesaurus or to consult a print or electronic reference work to identify special search terms like Chemical Abstracts registry numbers. Terms have to be combined with the intention of creating facets of the larger problem that can be represented as sets. Sets have to combined with Boolean operators to yield more precise sets. A strategy can be convoluted or elegant. Parentheses make it possible to convey complex logical arguments to the host as single statements.

Online services generally don't permit the weighting of search terms to indicate which facet or facets are more important. The good searcher uses a variety of tricks to give more weight to one concept than to others. Proximity operators are used to create precise, full-text search terms. Field qualification will limit the search to high-relevance fields. Sets can be narrowed by further qualifying their contents.

Connecting to a database used to be one of the more involved parts of the process. That is no longer the case. The electricity is being taken care of. Once online, the searcher has to be familiar enough with both the online system and the database to make split-second decisions without having to refer to a manual, often with someone looking over their shoulder and offering contradictory advice. The searcher has to be able to tell the search system to select and combine terms, to delimit a set, to examine an index, or to ask for results.

A good searcher is always ready to react, to respond to good information or bad information, to deal with line noise--too much or too little. And the pressure is always on, the clock is always ticking. Decisions must be made about how much information to purchase, and one doesn't know until after it has been paid for whether it was worth the price. Information is one of the few things which have to be paid for before they can be examined. Since it is paid for on the basis of how much is delivered over the wire, the searcher never can see exactly what she's buying until after it has been purchased. It's like trying to buy a car and being charged to look under the hood first.

After the target set or sets have been created and purchased, they probably need to be put into a format that's acceptable to the client for whom they were purchased. Better turn on the printer. After it has been edited and reformatted, the final product has to be transferred to the ultimate consumer. Maybe the process will need to be reiterated with several databases and the strategy refined before the search is finished and a complete product has been developed. Maybe the topic, despite initial impressions, doesn't lend itself to the online process or to any of the available files. It may be impossible to deliver a final product.

Chances are good that the person who acts as an information intermediary also acts as a financial intermediary between the information consumer and the online service. More forms have to be filled out. Accounting has to be handled. Invoices must be sent, and funds must be collected and transferred between accounts.

And that's only a typical search. A search manager has other concerns. It may be necessary to maintain profiles of different clients and to keep detailed accounting records involving several clients and online services. Records will probably be kept on which services are being used and by whom. Databases and search systems probably need to be evaluated. Staff members may also need to be evaluated. Policies have to be established regarding which databases and services are used and who uses them. Nowadays more search centers are assuming responsibility for training clients and making online products and services directly available.

So there we have a few of the things a professional searcher does. Which of those things lend themselves to being automated? And which will always be the domain of the person? If something can be delegated to the machine, what are the costs and the benefits? Will a program add value to the search process? Will it add value to the search product? Can a program make searching easier, cheaper, or more effective? We know it's possible to make qualitative changes to the search process. Is it possible to change things qualitatively? First let's look at software which focuses on the search process.

Front-End Game

Less than a decade ago the online world was tightly circumscribed by a small group of database producers, an even smaller group of system vendors, and an elite cadre of experienced searchers. It was a world immersed in the rarefied atmosphere of corporate, government, and academic research. The language of searching was only understood by those few who had mastered the arcane rules of a rarely played game.

Times have changed. A diverse crowd of players are anxious to join what has become a fast-moving, high stakes game. Thousands of databases are now being searched by multitudes of searchers using scores of search languages. The online world is now a place of bewildering complexity--a fascinating and labyrinthine information bazaar. A Babel of search languages are spoken there. Technology has changed the nature of the game, pushed in a host of new players, and raised the stakes considerably.

Our ubiquitous micro has been a major factor in changing the rules. Hordes of those newcomers somewhat derisively labelled end-users are lined up at the door, ante in pocket, waiting for a turn at the table. An expanding coterie of databases, systems, and information consumers combined with the growing importance of micros as communications devices has attracted to the game a new player--the front-end. Search assistance software has become the latest competetive arena in the online industry.

In a period of less than three years, front-ends have entered the fray in a big way. Keeping track of them is getting to be nearly as confusing as keeping track of the systems, files, languages, and searchers that prompted front-ends to appear on the scene in the first place. Front-ends employ a surprising number of dissimilar strategies for dealing with an increasingly complex online industry and community of searchers. Let us define a front-end as computer software that mediates between the searcher in Podunk and the system in Palo Alto.

The form this mediation takes is subject to more than a few variations. At one end of the spectrum is the front-end that doesn't do a whole lot more than automate the log-on process. At the other end are products that automatically translate commands from one search language to another. As the name implies, a front-end is something that sits between the consumer of information and the information to be consumed. A front-end acts as a sort of interpreter who stands in front of the retrieval system and assists the researcher who wants to talk to it. Front-ends are computer software and while software is barely there in a physical sense, it has to be loaded into a computer somewhere. A front-end can reside in the searcher's micro in Podunk, in the system computer in Palo Alto, or in a third computer somewhere in between the two places, let's say in Pennsylvania for example.

Many software arenas are occupied by competitors whose products do the same fundamental thing with minor variations. Contestestants in the front-end arena have taken atypically divergent approaches and represent basic differences in philosophy. How did this come about? One reason is that front-end software can reside in the searcher's micro in Podunk, in an intermediary's computer in Pennsylvania, and even in a system vendor's computer in Palo Alto. Remember also that potential customers range from absolute novices to those who spend most of their workday plugged into the memory banks. Most of the serious contenders add modules to their software package that are designed to work with the search product as well as the search process. One easy way to divide the field is to differentiate between microcomputer products and subscription front-end services.

Products versus Services

There is, right now in the industry, a battle being waged on the front-end front. In one camp are programs that were designed to be used by the searcher with a micro in Podunk. In the other camp are those programs that reside in larger, more powerful computers in places like Pennsylvania and that are being marketed as a service to searchers in Podunks throughout the land. The front-end services claim the advantage of being able to adapt to changing circumstances and of being able to attack the problems of searchers with the greater capabilities of larger computers. The micro-based systems approach the problems of searchers with that small scale, personal touch that we've all grown so fond of. The micro front-ends represent a variety of different approaches to the problems of a heterogenous group of information consumers.

When you use a large system front-end you are using a service, a service which you pay for each time you use, a service over which you have very little personal control. On the other hand, when you buy a micro-based front-end, you are purchasing a product, a product which is yours to keep and use as many times as you want to. The micro product, while not as powerful as the front-end service, can be more adaptable. The user maintains greater control with the micro-based product.

The front-end service that chooses a database for you and translates your queries into the language of the system it has chosen may not always choose the system or database you would have chosen. Its translation of your query may also leave something to be desired. The kind of machine intelligence required to perform such tasks consistently and well has not yet appeared and is unlikely to appear in the near future. Nevertheless, ambitious attempts to replace the professional search intermediary with a machine should be encouraged. At this point it is obvious that larger machines than micros are required for such attempts. Micro front-ends can't realistically attempt to do what the good searcher does, but they can make that searher's life a lot easier and, perhaps more importantly, they can help the new searcher learn to become a good searcher. It remains to be seen which side will emerge triumphant. We'll place our money on the micro.

Micro Front-Ends and Experienced Searchers

Even among the group of products courting experienced searchers (who may or may not be information professionals), there is widespread variation. We're talking about the programs that provide their users with full access to that Gee Wiz search software in places like Palo Alto. Other programs simplify the search process to the extent that it becomes a different sort of experience. Programs for the professional searcher provide a direct link to the native search languages of host systems. But they are usually more than communications programs, although they do provide full communications capabilities including downloading (capturing search results on a disk), uploading (sending prerecorded search strategies), and automatic log-on. Most of them have been designed to aid the searcher with capabilities that ordinary communications software doesn't have.

Some help the searcher by mapping commands from one system on to commands from another. Others place subject terms provided by the user into syntactically correct search statements, which are then transmitted. Some have accounting capabilities and others offer specialized editing and file management options. There are programs that claim they can handle all stages of the search process. Some specialize in database selection. Some focus on offline preparation of searches, and others help the search manager keep track of search activity and expense. Let's look at some of them.

Sci-Mate

Sci-Mate is the grandaddy of personal computer front-ends. Eugene Garfield, resident doyen of the online industry and founder of the Institute for Scientific Information, has had a front-end on the market for over five years now. The fourth version of *Sci-Mate* is divided into three modules: the Searcher, the Manager, and the Editor. The folks from ISI insist that it is designed for the end-user, but the scientific clientele for whom it was designed can hardly be described as neophytes in the information arena. The program is easy to use, so it definitely does qualify as a tool for the novice searcher. But *Sci-Mate* is as useful a tool for the experienced searcher as it is for the novice.

So, despite the fact that it is being marketed as a tool for end-users, let us consider *Sci-Mate* as a tool for the veteran searcher. *Sci-Mate* provides sophisticated command translation among five major search services in addition to the usual uploading, downloading, and telecommunications whistles and bells. Menus allow the user of this software to formulate a search in the offline mode that can later be executed on an unfamiliar system. User responses to menu prompts are automatically translated to the appropriate system language. Search profiles can be stored as files on a disk. Experienced searchers may take advantage of the native mode of the system of their choice.

ISI's process tool, *The Searcher*, is totally menu driven. The face it presents to the user is similar in many ways to that presented by *Smartcom*. And like *Smartcom*, *The Searcher* works well and is easy to use. The choices on each menu, the sequence of the menus, and the ability to move back and forth between menus are logically structured. Status lines for *Searcher* commands and information about the connection with a host appear at the top of the screen rather than at their usual spot at the bottom. The main menu provides the option of receiving a tutorial on search basics. The printed manual is excellent and includes tutorials for each of the major "supermarket" online services. Support for those services is one of the major differences between front-ends and the fancier communications programs.

```
              WELCOME TO THE ISI SCI-MATE SYSTEM

          Today's date:         6/27/86
          WORK file status:     WORK file exists
    Do you want to:

          1. Use the Searcher -- for Online Databases
          2. Use the Manager -- for Your Files
          3. Use the Editor -- for Bibliographies

          4. Enter or Change Today's Date
          5. Delete the WORK file

          6. Receive instructions on SCI-MATE
          7. Leave the SCI-MATE System

    Select a number or enter ? for help:

  SCI-MATE (R) V2.0  Copyright 1985  Institute For Scientific Information (R)
```

Sci-Mate's use of menus makes the program easy to use for inexperienced searchers.

```
          SCI-MATE * SEARCHER
    ----------------------------------------------------------------
    Do you want to:

          1. Search an Online Database

          2. Use Search Profile Subsystem before going Online

          3. Use your Microcomputer to access another Host

          4. Receive Instructions in the Basics of Online Searching

          5. Leave the Sci-Mate Searcher

    Select a Number:
```

Sci-Mate's Searcher module provides options for searching, search preparation, telecommunications, and self-instruction.

The Searcher comes with communications parameters, type of prompt, and so forth already specified for five major online services: DIALOG, BRS, SDC ORBIT, NLM, and QUESTEL. Preparing to use those services is as easy as entering phone numbers, baud rates, and passwords when *The Searcher* is installed. Within the module for each online service, there are templates for heavily used files available on that service. Information on each database is provided and at the point when a strategy is being constructed, a menu allows the searcher to fill in the blanks of searchable fields that vary from one file to another.

```
SCI-MATE * CREATE A SEARCH PROFILE
-----------------------------------------------------------------

Access has been defined for the following hosts:

    1.  BRS         (includes ISI databases SOCIAL SCISEARCH and
                                            ARTS & HUMANITIES SEARCH)
    2.  DIALOG      (includes ISI databases SCISEARCH and
                                            SOCIAL SCISEARCH)
    3.  NLM

    4.  ORBIT

    5.  QUESTEL     (includes ISI database INDEX CHEMICUS ONLINE)

    6.  Return to the SEARCHER menu

Select a Number:
```

Sci-Mate comes preconfigured for five major online services.

```
SCI-MATE * CREATE/USE A SEARCH PROFILE       ESC = Return to SEARCHER Menu
HOST: DIALOG
-----------------------------------------------------------------
    Sci-Mate menus list searchable fields for the following:

        ISI DATABASES                       OTHER DATABASES
        ---------------------               ---------------------
    1.  SCISEARCH 1984-                 8.  ABI/INFORM 1971-
    2.  SCISEARCH 1981-1983             9.  BIOSIS PREVIEWS 1981-
    3.  SCISEARCH 1978-1980            10.  CA SEARCH 1982-
    4.  SCISEARCH 1974-1977            11.  COMPENDEX 1970-
    5.  SOCIAL SCISEARCH               12.  ERIC 1966-
    6.  ONTAP SCISEARCH                13.  MAGAZINE INDEX 59-70, 73-
    7.  ONTAP SOCIAL SCISEARCH         14.  MANAGEMENT CONTENTS 1974-
                                       15.  MEDLINE 1980-
                                       16.  NTIS 1964-
                                       17.  PSYCINFO 1967-
                                       18.  WORLD PATENTS INDEX 1981-
            ( MORE - Enter 'N' for Next Screen )

Enter a number from above, or <CR> to select another DIALOG database:
```

Sci-Mate comes set up to deal with the quirks of several core files.

The search profile subsystem represents a viable approach to solving the problems of building a query string for uploading. The menu that asks the user to specify logical connections will accommodate complex, mixed, AND, OR, NOT logic within a search request. It is possible to combine two OR clauses with a NOT clause, for example, simply by responding to prompts on a menu. If you plan to use a really hairy parenthetical statement, you'd probably be better off in the native mode where you wouldn't have to worry about the order in which terms were input. However, the Search Profile Subsystem does allow the searcher at any time to enter a logical statement of his or her own, making the process more open ended. Proximity of terms may also be specified by using the Create Query menu.

```
CREATE QUERY                                    ESC = Done Query
HOST:DIALOG     DATABASE:SOCIAL SCISEARCH       Search Profile: NEW
-----------------------------------------------------------------
What do you want to SEARCH By:

    1. Set Number ( Current = 0 )      6. Corporate Source
    2. Subject Term or Phrase          7. Journal Name
    3. Title                           8. Language
    4. Author                          9. Document Type
    5. Cited References
              10. Your Own Logic Expression
                  (using AND, OR, NOT, and host system's field labels)
              11. Return to DEVELOP SEARCH PROFILE Menu
Select a Number:
```

The searcher is prompted by Sci-Mate for the information needed to build a query. Prompts vary with the database selected.

The Searcher substitutes its own truncation symbol for those used by the various host services, making it necessary to deal with only one truncation symbol when you're using the program. There is certainly a precedent for standards in the electronic information industry. When are the host services going to agree on something like this? Surely a standard truncation operator, once agreed upon, wouldn't be that hard to implement and it would be one small step toward the universal search language that could cause our civilization to blossom. A searcher's Esperanto would allow the developers of front-ends to focus on more important problems.

Profiles can include more than one line and can be stored on a disk and edited later if necessary. This program does provide a facility for editing stored search profiles. A profile can include several search statements that can be easily edited and rearranged without having to employ a word processor or a line editor. An individual could maintain and update searches on different topics, while an institution could use this capability to provide an SDI service for its clients.

```
    CONTINUE/END QUERY                          ESC = Done Query
    HOST:DIALOG     DATABASE:SOCIAL SCISEARCH   Search Profile: NEW
    -------------------------------------------------------------
    QUERY:   CR=bush v, 1945? OR memex

    Do You Want to:

    1. End Query Construction
    2. Continue with OR Logic
    3. Specify Proximity Term

    Select a Number:
```

Sci-Mate allows the searcher to use the full range of logical and proximity operators to connect terms and ideas.

```
SCI-MATE * EDIT SEARCH PROFILE
HOST:DIALOG      DATABASE:SOCIAL SCISEARCH          Search Profile: bush
-------------------------------------------------------------------------
Developed for Host: DIALOG      Database: SOCIAL SCISEARCH
 1  CR=bush v, 1945?




                     ----------- END OF PROFILE -----------------------
     Edit Options:
         I=Insert Query Lines        R=Reorganize Sequence   K=Keep Changes
         D=Delete a Query            N=Next Page             Q=Quit
         A=Append Existing Profile   B=Back to 1st Page

     Enter Option:
```

Sci-Mate allows the searcher to maintain a library of search profiles.

Once online it is possible to selectively download, going with a default print format or using a menu to redefine the default format. It is also possible to use the Browse command to expand an index and view a list of neighboring terms, many which will have the same root. This capability is useful for identifying descriptor phrases and other terms that are alphabetically adjacent in the index to the specified term.

Menus can be awkward while online. Sometimes it feels like you're taking a multiple choice test and doing a search at the same time. Having to move back and forth between menus to gain access to some commands certainly doesn't save the searcher any money in online connect charges. A command mode available from within the search assistance mode while online would be nice. Achieving simplicity at the expense of speed is one of the trade-offs all menu-driven systems must make. At least *The Searcher* hasn't sacrificed many of the more powerful capabilities of host systems on the altar of simplicity, as have so many other front-ends.

Sci-Mate also features a file manager for downloaded information and locally developed databases. A text editor designed for the communication and publication of scientific and scholarly research rounds out the package. ISI was the first software developer to market a family of search-related software products. Each module in the package is sold separately and can function independently of the others; yet they are designed to work together. ISI's experience in the front-end game and emphasis on the needs of the scientific community make *Sci-Mate* a formidable contender.

The Menlo Corporation

The Menlo Corporation was once considered to be one of the major players in the online game. Menlo's first product, *In-Search* was directed toward the novice searcher. The process of connecting to a database was simplified. A simple fill-in-the-blanks on the workform approach was taken to building a search strategy while in the offline mode. *In-Search* used a screen-oriented approach to the user. Flashy graphics (especially in the color version) and pull-down menus made for an impressive way to select a database and design a search. *In-Search* had received rave reviews and sold over a thousand copies when, in April of 1985, Menlo introduced *Pro-Search*, a front-end directed to the professional searcher. Less than a year later, in March of 1986, Menlo announced that it was cashing in its chips. What went wrong?

Pro-Search, a direct descendent of the much heralded *In-Search* represented a fundamentally different approach from that taken by both *Sci-Mate* and its predecessor. The search manager who spends hours at the terminal extracting information from a variety of files for a diverse clientele was the target of Menlo's marketing strategy. *Pro-Search* was definitely designed for the person who does a lot of searching. It handles the mechanical details of searching exceptionally well, moving information between a buffer, disk files, and a printer with ease. Other features, like the ability to type ahead of the host computer and enter new commands before receiving the next prompt, have obvious value for the searcher.

Though it was designed for the experienced searcher *Pro-Search* does have a menu-driven mode called the High-Level Interface for easy offline preparation of BRS or DIALOG searches. Query translation of BRS and DIALOG commands is also possible. Command emulation permits the experienced DIALOG searcher to search BRS using DIALOG commands and vice-versa.

A database describing databases supplied with the package and regularly updated by Menlo was intended to help the user with the database selection process. Accounting software was supplemented by a mailing label program and the ability to produce invoices.

Pro-Search seemed destined to find a niche among the group of heavy hitters who do the majority of searching nowadays. The busy search manager who has to keep track of search activity at her facility seemed like a natural customer for the product. Its future seemed assured. The reviews were good; there was even an announcement in the *DIALOG Chronolog*. The program was basically solid and its emphasis on graphics placed it among the newest wave of software products. Menlo's advertising was slick; the program was even sold at Computerland stores. *Pro-Search* attracted flocks of searchers at the major online trade shows. What caused its demise? We can only speculate. Perhaps it was the price. *In-Search* sold for $399 and *Pro-Search* went for a hefty $495. At almost five hundred dollars, the program might have lost out to quite capable general purpose programs that sell for much less. And it costs a lot of money to develop and market a software product nowadays.

Having to update database descriptions to keep up with developments in the online industry must also have placed a drain on Menlo's resources. *Pro-Search* included an accounting module, but otherwise its postprocessing capabilities were pretty slim. Maybe the professional searchers who would have been its natural customers weren't ready to pay a lot of money for a program that helped them do something they were already able to do (select a database) while not addressing the problems of creating a more acceptable search product. Most of the *Pro-Search* modules came out of the drawer labeled *Process Tools*.

Menlo has not totally disappeared from the scene. Its influence is still being felt in a stripped-down version of *Pro-Search* that is being sold by that online behemoth, DIALOG. Also, Professional Bibliographic Software of Ann Arbor, Michigan, a company best known for its product-oriented tools, has recently purchased *Pro-Search* from Menlo. PBS already produces a variety of text-editing and bibliography production programs. *Pro-Search* will become the online module that had previously been missing from its family of software products.

DIALOGLINK

ISI is not the only database vendor to have entered the personal computer front-end game. DIALOG has announced *DIALOGLINK*, a combination communications and accounting package that with its system-specific features could easily find a ready market among DIALOG's many users. At $125 for the full package, *DIALOGLINK* is quite competively priced. It's too soon to tell whether giant DIALOG's entrance into the front-end game will have the same kind of impact that IBM's entrance into the personal computer marketplace had.

DIALOGLINK, which was developed by Menlo, is a stripped-down version of *Pro-Search*. The program isn't concerned with database selection nor does it provide for command emulation like *Pro-Search*

Specialized Tools for the Searcher 175

did. The emphasis seems to be on an easy-to-use package that concentrates on the communications aspect of the search process and comes preconfigured to work well with DIALOG.

Like *Pro-Search*, *DIALOGLINK* handles communications tasks exceptionally well. A buffer is also used for both uploading and downloading. The windows and pop-up menus have been retained. In use, the program is similar to Microsoft's *Access* in the way commands are invoked by highlighting and hitting the Return key. Two status lines appear at the bottom of the search session screen. One provides information about the program itself--buffer and disk status, printer status, things like that. The other status line indicates whether the program is online and which online service and database are being used.

Function keys are reserved to talk to the program. Pressing function keys causes windows and menus to appear. Context-sensitive help is always available by pressing F1. Pressing F2 displays a window indicating the functions assigned to other function keys, a useful reference within the program. When the connect option is selected, each step in the log-on process is displayed on the screen.

```
F1=Help  F2=Keys  F3=Break  F4=Mark  F5=Connect  F7=Disk  F8=Printer  F9=Menu
   Buffer=   0% Full                                                   Offline
```

DIALOGLINK uses function keys to simplify the search process.

```
HELP INDEX

Select a Help topic by typing its letter (upper or lower case) or number.

A. INDEX TO HELP SCREENS              P. Macro Characters (Table)
B. Accounting--Overview               Q. Mark Key (F4)
C. Accounting--Begin/End Session      R. Online Services Directory
D. Accounting--Session Invoice/       S. Other Online Services (Add,
        Cover Sheet                           Modify, Delete)
E. Account Manager Reports            T. Printer Menu (F8)
F. Break Key (F3)                     U. Retrieve Buffer--Overview
G. Buffers--Overview                  V. Retrieve Buffer--Save/Clear
H. Change Drive or Directory          W. Retrieve Buffer--Print
I. Connect Key (F5)                   X. Service Overview--DIALOG
J. Disk File--View or Print           Y. Service Overview--KI
K. Disk File--Erase                   Z. Service Overview--DIALMAIL
L. Disk Menu--(F7)                    1. Session Menu (F9)
M. Editing Keys                       2. Status Messages
N. Function Keys--Overview (F2)       3. Type-Ahead Buffer--Overview
O. Macros (Auto logon for other       4. Type-Ahead Buffer--Save/Clear
        services)                     5. Type-Ahead Buffer--Load

     Press 'A' to view an index of help screens.  Press Esc to exit help.
  Buffer=   0% Full                                                  Offline
```

DIALOGLINK makes extensive use of online help messages.

176 Microcomputers for the Online Searcher

```
                    Online Services Directory
   Service Name                                  Type-Ahead

   DIALOG (Version 2)                            Yes
   DIALMAIL                                      Yes
   KNOWLEDGE INDEX                               Yes




   Highlight the desired service by using the cursor keys, then press ↵ .
   Buffer=  0% Full                                            Offline
```

DIALOGLINK comes preconfigured for DIALOG's online services.

```
                    Online Services Directory
   Service Name                                  Type-Ahead

   DIALMAIL                                      Yes
   .NOWLEDGE INDEX                               Yes



               Online Services Directory Menu

               1.  Add a New Online Service
               2.  Modify an Existing Service
               3.  Delete an Existing Service

               8.  ·Exit From Menu
               9.  Exit to DOS


   Use the cursor movement keys to select a command, then press ↵
   Buffer=  0% Full                                            Offline
```

DIALOGLINK provides menus for a variety of search functions, including setting up the program for additional services.

Phone numbers, passwords, and log-on protocols are entered as part of the installation procedure. Of course, everything is pre-configured for DIALOG services. Passwords are protected, something that is routinely done by search assistance software. Each packet-switching network can be provided with a primary and a secondary phone number. The searcher can also specify which network should be dialed first, which should be dialed second, right on down the line.

Specialized Tools for the Searcher 177

```
                    Online Services Directory
    Service Name                                      Type-Ahead
                          Disk Menu
    DIALOG (Ver                                          Yes
    DIALMAIL       1.  Start Saving to Disk             Yes
    KNOWLEDGE I    2.  Save Retrieve Buffer to Disk     Yes
                   3.  Save Type-Ahead Buffer to Disk
                   4.  Load Type-Ahead Buffer
                   5.  Change Drive or Directory
                   6.  View a Saved File
                   7.  Erase a Saved File

                   8.  Exit From Menu
                   9.  Exit to DOS


     Use the cursor movement keys to select a command, then press ⏎ .
Buffer=  0% Full                                                  Offline
```

DIALOGLINK permits downloading to buffers or files.

```
                    Online Services Directory
    Service Name                                      Type-Ahead

    IALOG (Version       File Type                       Yes
    DIALMAIL                                             Yes
    KNOWLEDGE INDEX  1.  Saved Output                    Yes
                     2.  Saved Search Strategy

                     8.  Exit From Menu
                     9.  Exit to DOS



     Use the cursor movement keys to select a command, then press ⏎ .
Buffer=  0% Full                                                  Offline
```

DIALOGLINK is set up to create and work with stored search strategies and stored search results.

Macros are limited in length to forty characters, and in number to ten (created by assigning values to Alt Function Key combinations), plus an automatic log-on macro. A facility for creating and editing search profiles for uploading is provided. The same cursor movement and editing keys used by *WordStar* are employed.

Among the program's features is a type-ahead feature like the one available with *Pro-Search*. The type-ahead feature comes configured for use with DIALOG but can be added for any service that supplies a consistent prompt character. Files and previously typed statements are uploaded from the type-ahead buffer. Entire search strategies can be uploaded from the type-ahead buffer (capacity: 20,000 characters).

The program can be loaded, instructed to log-on to a remote service, and told to upload a stored profile from the DOS command line. An entire search from start to finish can thus be represented by a single line in a batch file. This capability increases the possibility of integrating *DIALOGLINK* with other applications.

DIALOGLINK itself, minus its companion program the *Account Manager*, includes some accounting features. The program captures the cost estimate sent by DIALOG when a log-on message is sent by pressing the Connect/Disconnect function key or sending a log-off message from the keyboard. The elapsed time of the search, the date, time, file(s) searched, and estimated cost are extracted. *DIALOGLINK* may be used to produce two types of reports, an invoice for a search session, or a cover sheet describing the search to a client. The invoice it produces includes a breakdown of all charges incurred on all databases used during the session. The total session cost and the total connect-time are provided. The cover sheet can include a description of the search, the date, and the names of the searcher and the client.

An accounting session can be started at any point during a search, allowing the searcher to batch searches and still produce invoices for separate clients. After an accounting session has been started, the searcher can fill in the subject, a charge code, the client's name, and the searcher's name.

Reports summarizing the use of DIALOG services for one session, multiple sessions, or an entire month's searching can be generated with a separately purchased accounting module called the *Account Manager*. The information from each month's accounting sessions is placed in a separate file. Summary reports can be produced by client, by charge code (each department in a university might have a separate charge code, for example), by database, by searcher, or by DIALOG service.

Such summary reports could be very useful for analyzing the activity of a search center. The *Accounting Manager* is a nice extra, but remember that it won't keep track of accounts receivable or send out dunning notices to delinquent clients.

Overall, the advantages of *DIALOGLINK* include a relatively low cost, an easy-to-learn, functional program that presents a friendly face to the searcher, and basic record-keeping capabilities. *DIALOGLINK* is copy-protected but it can be installed on a hard disk, eliminating the major aggravation associated with many copy-protected programs. It can even be de-installed from a hard disk once if its purchaser wants to move it to a different computer than the one for which it was originally purchased.

SearchMaster

SearchMaster, SDC's entry in the front-end game, represents yet another philosophy--a philosophy that has intriguing implications for search managers and their clientele. *SearchMaster* offers the usual uploading, downloading, and autolog-on features plus the ability to respond automatically to prompts from SDC's ORBIT system. At $299, *SearchMaster* falls into the same price range occupied by many of the other front-end products.

SearchMaster does, however, hold one trump card that none of the other players possess. *SearchMaster* allows its users to create "scripts." *SearchMaster* scripts are prerecorded searches that enable searchers "playing" them to pause and fill in the blanks at appropriate points during the search. The scripting capability was designed to allow the experienced searcher to store his knowledge about searching for the use of the neophyte searcher. So far, this is the only search assistance package that provides a script language specifically designed for searchers. While *Crosstalk* and *Access* both come with prerecorded scripts, neither program includes scripts geared toward the "supermarket" retrieval services. Of course, *SearchMaster* has many features intended to directly support ORBIT, just as *DIALOGLINK* favors the DIALOG services.

A *SearchMaster* script can contain prompts and comments provided in advance by an experienced searcher. Such flexibility gives the user of *SearchMaster* a great deal of control over the search process without sacrificing any of the capabilities of the host system. Scripts can be created interactively while online just as they can in Microsoft's *Access*.

Search managers can use such programs to design strategies that meet the unique needs of their clients. *SearchMaster* can be used to provide decreasing levels of assistance to end-users who, as they become more competent at searching, can be gradually weaned from the online prompts, comments, and prerecorded strategies that had been developed by the search manager. One of the exciting things about micros is that they bring the power of the computer to a personal level. Programs such as *SearchMaster* encourage locally developed front-ends that have been designed to meet local needs.

It would be nice if a common script language could be developed with the needs of searchers in mind. Imagine being able to buy a script or *Access* custom menu designed to solve a specific search problem. Who knows, maybe eventually we'll see scripts freely traded and given away in the public domain. *SearchMaster* is so far the only online searching assistance software that provides this capability. If *Access* becomes popular, look for other online vendors to add scripting capabilities. Menlo was working on a program for developing custom-designed front-ends when it went broke. There were rumors that it was being considered by one of the big online vendors.

PC/Net-Link

The relationship between price and value in the software industry has always been something of an enigma. Incredible bargains can be had. Versatile and powerful programs can be had for a song from renegade geniuses like Andrew Flugelman or from forward-thinking software houses like Borland International. Unfortunately, however, there are also products whose cost and capabilities are way out of line--products that for a steep price do far less than their cheaper brethren. At $550 (plus $100 for communications software and $30 for a manual) *PC/Net-Link* from Informatics General Corporation fits comfortably into that category.

PC/Net-Link purports to help the searcher at the database selection stage of the search process by providing "a single integrated directory of databases from all services." A run-time version of *dBase II* is used to accomplish this miraculous feat. A run-time version of a program like *dBase II* is a version whose full capabilities are unavailable to the user--a program that must be used from within another program. Run-time versions are almost always abridgements of the original package. Could the presence of this product from another company have something to do with *PC/Net-Link*'s hefty price? It's doubly unfortunate that *dBase*'s power wasn't used more effectively.

The database descriptions displayed within the program fare poorly when compared to the printed documentation provided by most online services. The module that used an online menu to help searchers select an appropriate database seemed much more simplistic than it could have been. Furthermore as new databases are introduced and new features added to existing files, it is incumbent upon the user to update *PC/Net-Link*'s database of databases. Despite the fact that it is done on a computer, keypunching is far from a joyful task. Filing the occasional "bluesheet" is a piece of cake by comparison.

Pro-Search, which also includes a file of database descriptions, saved the user from the tedious job of updating the file by offering updates on a subscription basis. *PC/Net-Link*'s literature boasts of its uploading, downloading, and stored search capabilities. Remember that popular user-oriented programs like *PC-Talk* ($35 from Headlands Press, manual included) perform the same functions for a fraction of the cost. Remember also that all of the other micro-based front-ends perform the same functions at least as well as *PC/Net-Link*, usually better. It is indeed ironic that *PC/Net-Link* bills itself as a tool for the experienced searcher. The experienced searcher would have a lot more money for searching experience if she bought a program like *PC-Talk* and used the savings for connect charges.

SearchWorks

SearchWorks is the newest program in the lot, and at only $150, it is a good value. *SearchWorks* brings a strong hand to the front-end game and should end up among the winners. There's something for everyone. A nice price, a solid communications program, and postprocessing abilities usually available only in separately purchased modules complement an approach to the analysis of search results that reflects some of the most interesting research now being done.

SearchWorks was designed for the experienced searcher and that fact is reflected in the initial screen it presents. The first thing seen is an empty screen with a call prompt at the bottom. Once the program is configured and installed, getting online is as simple as entering the first letter of the desired service in response to that initial prompt. If the searcher wanted to quickly begin searching on BRS, for example, she would simply enter a "B" and a connection would be made.

The program is great for the run-and-gun searches often done by experienced searchers as preliminary forays into a topic. And its postsearch text analysis and manipulation abilities will help the searcher analyze and refine strategies in addition to producing a high-quality printed product. An accounting module further increases the appeal for the search manager.

SearchWorks comes preconfigured to work with BRS, DIALOG, NLM, and SDC ORBIT. Once phone numbers and other parameters have been entered as part of a simple installation and configuration procedure, logging on to a service becomes a two-keystroke operation. The program will automatically switch from one packet-switching network to another until a connection is made.

When the program is installed, subdirectories are created for its different functional modules. Like most front-end programs, *SearchWorks* performs best on a system equipped with a fixed disk. The *SciMate Searcher*, for example, fills up most of a double-sided, double-density floppy disk. It just isn't very practical to use most of the front-ends on a system with limited disk storage or RAM. The ability to store profiles and to manipulate results just isn't there on floppy disk systems.

A system of menus and prompts is used to communicate with the searcher. The main menu is always available by pressing the Esc key. When the program is first loaded, if the searcher doesn't want to go online immediately, all she has to do is press the Esc key. The main menu provides the options of creating an offline strategy for uploading, processing search results, or initiating a call. Commands and responses to prompts are entered beneath a double line at the bottom of the screen.

```
              SearchWorks by Online Research Systems, Inc.



                   a  -  Edit search strategy
                   b  -  Call
                   c  -  Process search results
                   d  -  File management
                   e  -  Print a file
                   f  -  Accounting & reports
                   g  -  Record editor
                   h  -  Modify profile
                   i  -  Help
                   j  -  Exit
```

SearchWorks provides assistance with all of the tasks professional searchers perform.

```
      NLM TIME 15:35:58 DATE 86:179 LINE 67A

      WELCOME TO THE NATIONAL LIBRARY OF MEDICINE'S ELHILL RETRIEVAL SYSTEM.
      YOU ARE NOW CONNECTED TO THE MEDLINE (1984 FORWARD) FILE.

      SS 1 /C?
      USER:

      Enter file name, F1 to list, or RETURN to upload "upfile" _:
```

SearchWorks asks the user to specify a file for uploading to NLM.

It is possible to create, maintain, and edit search profiles. A line editor approach is taken to creating a profile in the offline mode. Each stored profile may include up to ninety-nine lines, each having a maximum length of eighty characters. Profiles are uploaded one line at a time, waiting for a response from the host before sending each line. Lines waiting to be sent may be edited while the searcher is online.

It is possible to scroll through information that has already been received while still online. Downloading is a little more awkward than with some of the other programs. A default downloading file called "downfile" becomes raw material for offline processing. As the searcher is downloading, he has to be concerned with the requirements of the program's postprocessing modules. *SearchWorks* also includes a record editor that can be used to prepare downloaded searches for further manipulation.

The Online Guide--Search Assistance for the Searcher

SearchWorks really adds to the search process with a unique help feature called the Online Search Guide. The Online Search Guide is a summary of the commands, formats, and syntax of the search languages used by the four services supported. Information on all aspects of those search languages is available interactively from within *SearchWorks*. The searcher specifies a reference system when *SearchWorks* is installed. The selected system is the default system used to provide examples and formats relating to different search functions. The examples relating to the reference system can be compared to the syntax and commands which perform the same functions on an unfamiliar system.

```
FILE SELECTION AND CHANGING FILES
────────────────────────────────────────────────────
     NLM
              Default file is Medline.

              To change files:
                   file filename

     DLG
              Default file is file 1 (ERIC).
              To change files:
                   b fileno

              To change files and later return to original
              file (set numbers are saved):
                   .file fileno

              To list all available files:
                   ?files
```

SearchWorks allows the user to review commands for the currently logged system alongside a reference system while online.

PRINT FORMAT CODES

    NLM

        The following print format options are available:
```
          prt    author, title, source)
          prt ar (author, title, source, abstract)
          prt fu (author, title, source, mesh headings, lang)
          prt dl (full record)
          prt indented (with field labels spelled out)
          prt compressed (entries printed across page)
```
        Tailor print commands by specifying fields to be printed.

    DLG

        Print formats vary by database. A typical bibliographic database format follows:
```
          1 - Dialog accession number
          2 - full record except abstract
          3 - bibliographic citation
          4 - tagged output
          5 - full record
```

Information provided by SearchWorks' online guide reduces the need to consult manuals while online.

    There are few truly multilingual searchers. Each searcher is most familiar with the system he learned on, or the system that he uses frequently. When searching on a "foreign" system, he keeps handy a crib sheet or brief guide, which serves as his Berlitz. The Online Search Guide, which is part of *SearchWorks*, is the equivalent of four immediately available crib sheets. The guide is available in both the offline and the online modes. It can be used to help prepare an offline profile in an unfamiliar search language or as a quick reference while online.

    Pressing the F1 key causes a prompt requesting a term to be displayed. The searcher then enters a term for the search function in which he or she is interested. If a term such as "printing" is entered, for example, the searcher will see a list of all guide entries relating to printing commands and formats. After a specific entry has been selected, the searcher will see an explanation of the command as well as examples of how it is used in two of the four systems supported.

    If the searcher is online when the guide is called, examples relate to the reference system as well as the service currently being used. It is also possible to mark an example in the search guide and move it onto the online session screen while online. The searcher can then use the example displayed as a model for constructing syntactically correct statements in the unfamiliar language. For example, the searcher who was unfamiliar with NLM print commands could cause an example showing the proper format to be displayed on the screen while she was online with NLM. The searcher can specify which services to use as examples when the guide is being used in the offline mode. The BRS searcher could view DIALOG commands and their BRS equivalents to help in preparing a DIALOG search.

Each service has its own group of examples, but the examples provided for all services often relate to the Medline database because it is so prominent and so widely used. Medline is also supported in the search mode by a feature that allows the software to respond automatically to the "Continue Printing?" prompt. Database-specific information is provided for some other files as well. When file-specific information is available about a search function, the user of the program is prompted to enter the name of the file being used. Thereafter, examples displayed will relate to the options available on that specific file within the primary and secondary online services chosen. The *SearchWorks* manual states that updates to the guide, including file-specific information for heavily used databases, are being considered.

The Permuted Index

In addition to selecting specific terms, it is possible to use the Online Search Guide in much the same way one expands on an inverted index in most of the online sytems. The skilled searcher who is already familiar with that technique will have no problem using the permuted index within the *SearchWorks* program. The Online Search Guide takes a little getting used to, but the searcher who becomes familiar with it will discover that it's quick and easy. It really beats having to thumb through a manual while online looking for the correct format to use in a foreign search language.

```
                                                                     Number
         REVIEWING A SAVED    SEARCH                                     55
         EXECUTING A SAVED    SEARCH                                     56
        CANCELLING A SAVED    SEARCH                                     57
                  ENTERING    SEARCH COMMANDS                            09
   STEPS COMMAND see ENTERING SEARCH COMMANDS    ^SELECT                 09
                              SEARCH HISTORY                             52
                  LIMITING    SEARCH RESULTS                             37
                              SEARCH RESULTS (POSTINGS) DISPLAY          10
       STACKING COMMANDS OR   SEARCH STATEMENTS                          15
                   PURGING    SEARCH STATEMENTS                          53
                   NESTING    SEARCH TERMS OR STATEMENTS                 14
     PARENTHESES see NESTING  SEARCH TERMS OR STATEMENTS                 14
                    STORED    SEARCH see SAVING A SEARCH                 54
  FREE-TEXT AND SPECIFIC FIELD SEARCHING                                 16
                   SUBHEAD    SEARCHING                                  20
          PUBLICATION DATE    SEARCHING                                  35
           REGISTRY NUMBER    SEARCHING                                  36
  UPDATE & ACCESSION NUMBER   SEARCHING                                  41
                      TREE    SEARCHING (MEDLINE)                        22
                    AUTHOR    SEARCHING (MEDLINE)                        28
Enter number, scroll key or index letter.  ESCape returns online _:
```

A permuted index allows the user of SearchWorks to select examples of search techniques.

ENTERING SEARCH COMMANDS

    NLM

Default is search mode.

Use "find" to return to search mode (e.g., after "nbr" command).

Unqualified terms will default to being searched on all directly searchable fields except (in Medline): TI (title), AB (abstract), TA (title of journal abbreviation), JC (journal code), PX (pre-explosions), NM (name of substance), NF (name fragment), (or equivalent fields in other files).

To change fields searched:
    elements apply field, field

To exclude fields from being searched:
    elements exclude field, field

Much of SearchWorks' tutorial material emphasizes the Medline system.

Besides simplifying and adding to the search process, *SearchWorks* can add to the search product. The program includes modules designed with a more attractive and more useful search product in mind. It is possible to sort, rank, and index records from an online search. In fact, this is the area where the searcher will really get her $150 worth. However, the product-oriented modules work best when the raw material consists of structured records with labelled fields and little or no line noise present.

    a - Rank search results: y
    b - Sort search results: n
    c - Index search results: y

        d - Minimum occurrence of index term: 4

        e - Maximum occurrence of index term: 15

        f - Approximate total number of records: 100

Enter letter of item to modify, RETURN to continue, ESCape to cancel

SearchWorks allows its users to index and rank or sort search results while offline.

Before an index can be created or records can be sorted or ranked, it is necessary to create a template for the file from which the records were extracted. In the template, the searcher specifies the field labels used in the file and the words with which to replace them in the printed product. For processing to occur, each record must be delimited from others. This is done by specifying the label of the first field in a record and looking for lines separating records from one another. A cost statement entered by the searcher indicates the end of a file and enables *SearchWorks* to capture information for its accounting module. Unfortunately, if fields aren't labeled, or if a field is obscured by line noise, or if a blank line gets into a record, or if a cost statement isn't sent to indicate the end of a file, erratic results can occur. But when things are going smoothly, which is usually the case with tagged records, *SearchWorks* is capable of printing a very high-quality and useful product.

```
      File: lefty            Template: NLM           Vendor:

                   RS Search/Replace: AU =Author(s)
                   EOF Marker       : show cost
      LA =Language
      MH =Index Terms
      SO =Journal
      TI =Title




      Enter ESCape to select a different template, or RETURN to continue
```

Before processing search results, the searcher must create a template specifying record delimiters and field labels and replacements.

Search statements, host prompts, and other messages are automatically filtered from downloaded files, leaving only records as raw material for further processing. Up to thirteen files created by searching as many as thirteen different databases may be merged into a single output file. Each search processed must be ended with a cost request and downloaded into a separate file, things the searcher must remember to do while online.

Records can be sorted by marking the field to sort on. *SearchWorks* will replace field labels such as AU with words such as Author, if told to. Each field will be separated from the others and indented under the new label in the final printout. The program helps its user search several overlapping databases for information on a single topic and then merge all of the records retrieved into a single sorted and formatted printout accompanied by an automatically produced index.

SearchWorks uses a simple algorithm to rank search results according to relevance. Weights are assigned to search terms by the searcher. Every time a weighted term is encountered, the weight assigned to it is added to the relevance value of the record where it was found. Records are then printed out in rank order from highest to lowest weight. It is recommended that narrower terms than the ones used for the search be used to rank results. It is possible to identify new search terms by looking at descriptors associated with high-ranking records, as well as to sort search results according to some secondary topic covered in the search.

The ability to generate a printed index to search results is one of *SearchWorks*' nicest features. Indexing may be done independently or in conjunction with either sorting or ranking. The indexing algorithm selects keywords by looking for terms which fit into a range between a minimum and a maximum number of occurrences specified by the searcher. The size of the index created is related to the size of the file being processed, available disk space, and the amount of RAM available. Multiple-term index phrases are not accommodated. Since the indexing algorithm is applied to the full text of records, authors' names that show up more than the specified minimum will be incorporated in the index created. This is a quick and easy way to identify authorities in a subject area.

SearchWorks also provides a fund accounting capability similar to that offered by *DIALOGLINK*. The client gets a clean, nicely formatted printout with results which have been merged from several searches and sorted or ranked. A keyword index whose limits are defined by the searcher is possible. A combination cover sheet/invoice accompanies the printout. An extra copy is provided for the search manager. The search manager also gets accounting records stored in their own subdirectory on a hard disk and the ability to generate a variety of accounting reports.

Imagine a topic that is locally important and which comes up again and again, the topic of children and television in a College of Education, for example. Using *SearchWorks*, a search manager could create profiles for the topic and do several searches on different but related databases such as ERIC, PsycInfo, Medline, PAIS, and Sociological Abstracts. Results could be cleaned up and merged into a single file. Records could be arranged by author or journal title or some other bibliographic element, or ranked by a subtopic, such as aggression. An index could be included to make the big printout more useful by allowing clients to identify records dealing with

-01-
Author(s)
    Salcedo JR ; Spiegler BJ ; Gibson E ; Magilavy DB
Title
    The autoimmune disease systemic lupus erythematosus is not
    associated with left-handedness.
Language
    Eng
Index Terms
    Adolescence ; Child ; Female ; Human ; *Laterality ; Learning
    Disorders/DIAGNOSIS ; Lupus Erythematosus, Systemic/*DIAGNOSIS ;
    Male
Journal
    Cortex 1985 Dec;21(4):645-7

-02-
Author(s)
    Shea V ; Mesibov GB
Title
    The relationship of learning disabilities and higher-level
    autism.
Language
    Eng
Index Terms
    Autism, Infantile/*DIAGNOSIS/PSYCHOLOGY ; Cognition ; Female ;
    Human ; Intelligence ; Interpersonal Relations ; Language ;
    Laterality ; Learning Disorders/*DIAGNOSIS/PSYCHOLOGY ; Male ;
    Play and Playthings ; Support, U.S. Gov't, P.H.S.
Journal
    J Autism Dev Disord 1985 Dec;15(4):425-35

-03-
Author(s)
    Livingston R
Title
    Depressive illness and learning difficulties: research needs and
    practical implications.
Language
    Eng
Index Terms
    Cerebral Cortex/PHYSIOPATHOLOGY ; Child ; Depressive Disorder/
    *COMPLICATIONS ; Human ; Laterality/PHYSIOLOGY ; Learning
    Disorders/*COMPLICATIONS ; Risk
Journal
    J Learn Disabil 1985 Nov;18(9):518-20

-04-
Author(s)
    Geschwind N ; Galaburda AM
Title
    Cerebral lateralization. Biological mechanisms, associations, and
    pathology: III. A hypothesis and a program for research.
Language
    Eng
Index Terms
    Animal ; Antinuclear Factors/ANALYSIS ; Autoimmune Diseases/
    COMPLICATIONS/PHYSIOPATHOLOGY ; Brain/ABNORMALITIES/*IMMUNOLOGY/
    METABOLISM/PHYSIOLOGY ; Brain Chemistry ; Brain Diseases/
    CONGENITAL/IMMUNOLOGY/PHYSIOPATHOLOGY ; Circadian Rhythm ;
    Delivery ; Dementia/PHYSIOPATHOLOGY ; Dementia, Presenile/
    PHYSIOPATHOLOGY ; DNA/PHYSIOLOGY ; Epilepsy/PHYSIOPATHOLOGY ;
    Hoof and Claw/PATHOLOGY ; Human ; Immunologic Diseases/
    PHYSIOPATHOLOGY ; Infection/IMMUNOLOGY ; *Laterality ; Learning
    Disorders/PHYSIOPATHOLOGY ; Lobsters ; Mental Disorders/FAMILIAL
    & GENETIC ; Spinal Cord Diseases/CONGENITAL/PHYSIOPATHOLOGY ;
    Support, Non-U.S. Gov't ; Support, U.S. Gov't, Non-P.H.S. ;
    Support, U.S. Gov't, P.H.S. ; Sympathetic Nervous System/
    IMMUNOLOGY
    RN - 9007-49-2 (DNA)
Journal
    Arch Neurol 1985 Jul;42(7):634-54

SearchWorks allows the search manager to rank search results and replace field labels.

                    Loyola University Library

        Date................05-21-86
        Patron..............Jane Doe
        Dept................Psychology

        Search Topic........Laterality and Learning Disorders
        Databases searched...Medline 1980-

        Results:
              Ranked   _x_
              Sorted   ___
              Indexed   _x_

        Invoice:
              Amount due 3.00
              Due date   06-20-86

        Search Analyst.......Reference Dept.
        Phone................865-3390

SearchWorks automatically generates two copies of a cover sheet/invoice using a predefined format.

            ABNORMALITIES: 04,05,13,14,16,17
            ADOLESCENCE: 01,10,12,14,17
            ATTENTION: 06,08,11,14,15
            BIOLOGICAL: 04,05,13,17
            BRAIN: 04,05,07,13,14,17
            CEREBRAL: 03,04,05,06,07,10,13,18
            CHILD: 01,03,08,09,10,12,14,15,16,
                  17,19
            CHILDREN: 09,10,14,15,19
            COGNITION: 02,07,16,18
            COMPLICATION: 03,04,05,12,13,15
            CORTEX: 01,03,06,13
            DEFICIT: 06,11,14,15
            DIAGNOSIS: 01,02,06,14
            DISABIL: 03,08,09,12,14
            DISABILITIES: 02,09,12,17
            DISABLED: 08,10,14,19
            DISEASES: 04,07,11,13
            DISORDER: 01,02,03,04,05,06,07,08,
                  09,10,11,12,13,14,15,16,17,
                  18,19
            DOMINANCE: 07,10,13,18
            DYSLEXIA: 06,07,13,17
            FACTOR: 04,05,06,07,17,18,19
            FAMILIAL: 04,11,13,16,17
            FEMALE: 01,02,05,06,07,10,11,13,14,
                  16,17,18,19
            GENETIC: 04,11,13,16,17

SearchWorks automatically generates an index to search results.

aspects of the larger topic. Regular updates could be merged into the file and a new printout created on a periodic basis. How long would it take to make *SearchWorks* pay for itself in value added to the search product?

SearchWorks has great potential, but it would be even better if it were easier to learn to use. The manual is well written, but it could have been a little better organized and more detailed about how the program actually works. More information on the subdirectories used would have been nice as would have progress reports during the installation procedure. A tutorial providing concrete examples of the program in use would also have been welcome. None of the menus and screens used by the program are to be found in the manual. Despite those minor drawbacks, the program provides a good combination of process and product tools at a very reasonable price.

IT Data-Ease, Userlink, and OASIS

Another package that uses textual analysis to assist in the search process was introduced to the market in 1984 by Samuel Wolper, the Cleveland entrepreneur who developed and headed the Predicasts family of databases. Wolpert's product, called *IT* for Information Transfer incoporates a database selection module called Data-Ease which was developed by former Predicasts staffers as well as modules based on pioneering work done by P.W. Williams in Great Britain.

Williams developed and marketed a program called *Userlink* which was intended to assist experienced searchers. *Userlink* has been implemented as part of *IT*. Williams also developed a program for nonsearchers called *OASIS* (Online Access System for Inexperienced Searchers) which has also been implemented within *IT*. *IT* can be used on a high-end micro, but minicomputer users seem to be its primary clientele.

Userlink differs from other front-ends by analyzing retrieved sets and suggesting additional terms to improve the recall of the search. The analysis is based upon terms associated with records deemed relevant by the searcher. *OASIS* engages the searcher in a dialog which results in a query string that includes terms selected by the user from lists provided by the program. These and other largely experimental programs that address the higher level conceptual part of the search process will be discussed in Part Three.

Processing Results--The Sci-Mate Manager

That just about covers the front-ends. Occasionally, a front-end will include postprocessing capability. *SearchWorks* is an example. For the most part, though, postprocessing software must be purchased separately. Some programs, while purchased separately, are nevertheless designed to work closely with other programs as members of the same software family. Other product-oriented software has never been associated with a communications/searching program.

Sci-Mate's program, *The Manager*, was designed to accompany *The Searcher* and another program called *The Editor*. *The Editor* is basically a word processing program designed to produce and work with different bibliographic formats. *The Manager*, which has been on the market now for as long as any other postsearch program, is a full-featured program designed to allow its users to create, maintain, and manipulate primarily bibliographic databases. The end product of this program is a searchable database rather than a printed document, though the program can be used to generate printed reports as well.

Like *The Searcher*, *The Manager* is menu driven and is accompanied by an excellent manual with a tutorial. *The Manager* makes it possible to create a local database that can be searched the same way an online database is searched. Templates are used to define the record structure of the new database. Fields can be specified to correspond to fields found in online files. Templates for all of the ISI databases are included with the program, making the program especially useful for creating databases using records downloaded from one of ISI's online citation indexes.

Once templates have been defined, online records may be created by filling in fields just as they would be created within any other database manager. Other than ISI files, there is no built-in facility for moving downloaded records into a database. Local files may be indexed and searched in a variety of ways, often resulting in a product that shares many similarities with its commercial online counterparts. Separate indexes for different fields are possible.

Menus make the search process relatively easy. Both truncation and full Boolean searching with nested parentheses are provided for. The searcher can also create report formats that can be stored in a report library and used to generate reports from local files.

Perhaps *The Manager*'s strongest feature is its ability to move output from ISI databases directly into a local database by using a predefined template. ISI's online files offer a unique form of

Specialized Tools for the Searcher 193

access. Citation searching methods lend themselves well to analysis of the literature. Combine records from citation indexes with a local database manager and it is possible to recognize patterns and identify connections. Used with ISI files, *The Manager* becomes a powerful analytical tool for scholarly research.

A search was done using *The Searcher* on DIALOG with the Social Scisearch database. It was a cited reference search looking for papers that had cited Bushe's classic article on the memex. *The Manager* was used to move the hundred or so records that were downloaded from a work file into a user file named memex. A pre-existing template for ISI-DIALOG was used to provide the structure of the database.

It was then possible, in the offline mode, to do Boolean searches of the records in the local file. Searching for the term "librar#" yielded records that cited the memex and also dealt with libraries. Searching on the root "comput#" yielded references that mentioned computers in addition to citing the memex paper. Searching for "librar#" and "comput#" yielded papers that dealt with both concepts and cited Bush. Searching the full text of the database for the root "medi#" produced a surprising number of references to the memex in the medical literature.

The memex database was sorted in descending order by publication date and a report was generated listing the date and the title in separate columns. It was easy to see how the publications were distributed over time. Apparently, interest in the memex has been steadily increasing along with the power of personal computers. The memex article was cited only four times in 1974. It was cited fifteen times ten years later in 1984, even though it was first published in 1946 and should theoretically be cited less frequently as it ages.

The Manager's report-generating ability was used to produce a variety of reports related to the literature on the memex. One report was set to display the author and title of each reference sorted by author's name to provide an idea of which authors were frequently citing the memex paper (there were a few who cited it more than once, including ISI's Garfield). One report displayed the papers' titles and the title of the journal each appeared in sorted by journal title, providing at a glance an indication of which journals were consistently including references to the memex. It was interesting to see how many different disciplines have been influenced by the idea. Of course, the library literature was well represented as well as the literature of computer science. Other disciplines ranged from radiology to sociology.

Year	Author	Title
1985	DEGENNARO R	INTEGRATED ONLINE LIBRARY SYSTEMS - PERSPECTIVES, PERCEPTIONS, + PRACTICALITIES
1985	MCCLURE LW	THE PROMISE OF FRUIT ... AND LIGHT
1984	ANONYMOUS	MIDWINTER MUSING ON MICROCOMPUTERS AND MEMEX
1984	IVIE EL	DESIGNING MICROCOMPUTER NETWORKS
1984	GALVIN TJ	THE SIGNIFICANCE OF INFORMATION-SCIENCE FOR THE THEORY AND PRACTICE OF LIBRARIANSHIP
1984	SCHRADER AM	IN SEARCH OF A NAME - INFORMATION-SCIENCE AND ITS CONCEPTUAL ANTECEDENTS
1984	ZAAIMAN RB	DIFFERENCES IN EDUCATIONAL-PROGRAMS FOR LIBRARIANS AND INFORMATION OFFICERS
1983	DAVIES R	DOCUMENTS, INFORMATION OR KNOWLEDGE - CHOICES FOR LIBRARIANS
1983	CRAWFORD S	HEALTH-SCIENCE LIBRARIES IN THE UNITED-STATES .1. OVERVIEW OF THE POST WORLD-WAR-II YEARS
1983	STEVENS N	LIBRARY TECHNOLOGY - THE BLACK-BOX SYNDROME
1982	WILLIAMSON NJ	IS THERE A CATALOG IN YOUR FUTURE - ACCESS TO INFORMATION IN THE YEAR 2006
1982	MATHESON NW; COOPER JAD	ACADEMIC INFORMATION IN THE ACADEMIC-HEALTH-SCIENCES-CENTER - ROLES FOR THE LIBRARY IN INFORMATION MANAGEMENT
1982	KOENIG MED	THE INFORMATION CONTROLLABILITY EXPLOSION
1981	BOTTLE RT	LEGISLATION, TECHNOLOGY AND CURRICULUM REQUIREMENTS FOR OPEN AND CLOSED INFORMATION-SYSTEMS
1981	BALL AJS	VIDEOTEX - CHIMERA OR DREAM MACHINE
1981	SMITH LC	CITATION ANALYSIS
1981	DILLON M	SERVING THE INFORMATION NEEDS OF SCIENTIFIC-RESEARCH
1979	GARFIELD E	HOW WILL NEW TECHNOLOGY CHANGE CHARACTERISTICS OF LIBRARIES AND THEIR USERS
1979	AGUOLU CC	ASPECTS OF THE PROBLEMS OF BIBLIOGRAPHIC ACCESS TO UNIVERSITY-LIBRARY COLLECTIONS
1979	DEGENNARO R	RESEARCH-LIBRARIES ENTER THE INFORMATION AGE

Sci-Mate's manager was used to search a database of downloaded social SciSearch record to produce this list of articles which cited the memex paper and included the root "librar#". (Courtesy ISI)

Memex References - 1974

6/27/86

Year	Author	Title
1974	ROSENBER.V	SCIENTIFIC PREMISES OF INFORMATION SCIENCE
1974	DARLING L	CHANGES IN INFORMATION DELIVERY SINCE 1960 IN HEALTH SCIENCE LIBRARIES
1974	OVERHAGE CF; REINTJES JF	PROJECT INTREX - GENERAL REVIEW
1974	MILLETT JD	PUBLIC INTEREST IN GRADUATE EDUCATION

Memex References - 1984

6/27/86

Year	Author	Title
1984	SCHRADER AM	IN SEARCH OF A NAME - INFORMATION-SCIENCE AND ITS CONCEPTUAL ANTECEDENTS
1984	BULKLEY BH	PROTECT THE SHIFTING PARADIGM - BIOMEDICAL-RESEARCH AND EVOLUTION
1984	WYNGAARDEN JB	SCIENCE AND GOVERNMENT - A FEDERAL-AGENCY PERSPECTIVE
1984	LESK M	COMPUTER SOFTWARE FOR INFORMATION MANAGEMENT
1984	ZAAIMAN RB	DIFFERENCES IN EDUCATIONAL-PROGRAMS FOR LIBRARIANS AND INFORMATION OFFICERS
1984	GALVIN TJ	THE SIGNIFICANCE OF INFORMATION-SCIENCE FOR THE THEORY AND PRACTICE OF LIBRARIANSHIP
1984	HOUNSHELL DA	SCIENCE AND INVENTION
1984	LEWIS IJ	A VIEW OF ACADEMIC MEDICAL CENTERS
1984	ANONYMOUS	MIDWINTER MUSING ON MICROCOMPUTERS AND MEMEX
1984	BECKER J	AN INFORMATION SCIENTISTS VIEW ON EVOLVING INFORMATION TECHNOLOGY
1984	HERNER S	BRIEF-HISTORY OF INFORMATION-SCIENCE

Memex references compared for 1974 and 1984. (Courtesy ISI)

Journals Citing the Memex
6/27/86

Journal	Year
ADMINISTRATION & SOCIETY , V10, N4, P437-464	1979
ADMINISTRATION & SOCIETY, V7, N3, P328-365	1975
AMERICAN JOURNAL OF ROENTGENOLOGY , V145, N6, P1109-1112	1985
AMERICAN PSYCHOLOGIST , V39, N9, P1053-1055	1984
AMERICAN SOCIOLOGIST, V11, N3, P160-164	1976
ANNALS OF THE NEW YORK ACADEMY OF SCIENCES , V424, MAY, P183-192	1984
ANNALS OF THE NEW YORK ACADEMY OF SCIENCES, V260, OCT3, P32-40	1975
ANNUAL REVIEW OF INFORMATION SCIENCE AND TECHNOLOGY , V18, P277-304	1983
ANNUAL REVIEW OF INFORMATION SCIENCE AND TECHNOLOGY , V15, P67-105	1980
ANNUAL REVIEW OF INFORMATION SCIENCE AND TECHNOLOGY, V12, , P249-275, 19- 77	
ARCHIVES OF INTERNAL MEDICINE , V145, N7, P1241-1244	1985
ASLIB PROCEEDINGS , N6, P264-269	1980
AUSTRALIAN AND NEW ZEALAND JOURNAL OF SOCIOLOGY, V12, N3, P219-227	1976
BATTELLE MEM INST, COLUMBUS LABS,INFORMATION SYST SECT/COLUMBUS//OH/43201 ; OHIO STATE UNIV,COLL RES/COLUMBUS//OH/43210 , V11, N4, P75-82	1975
BIOSCIENCE , V36, N3, P158-159	1986
BULLETIN OF THE MEDICAL LIBRARY ASSOCIATION , V71, N1, P16-20	1983
BULLETIN OF THE MEDICAL LIBRARY ASSOCIATION , V72, N2, P214-216	1984
BULLETIN OF THE MEDICAL LIBRARY ASSOCIATION , V73, N4, P319-329	1985
BULLETIN OF THE NEW YORK ACADEMY OF MEDICINE , V59, N1, P9-20	1983
BULLETIN OF THE NEW YORK ACADEMY OF MEDICINE , V60, N5, P494-503	1984
CANADIAN JOURNAL OF INFORMATION SCIENCE, V2, N1, P93-105	1977
CANADIAN LIBRARY JOURNAL , V38, N1, P11-15	1981
CLINICAL RESEARCH , V32, N3, P354-359	1984
COLLEGE AND RESEARCH LIBRARIES, V34, N2, P103-125	1973
CURRENT CONTENTS , N16, P5-12	1980
CURRENT CONTENTS , V1979, N3, P8-12	1979
DAEDALUS , N1, P65-81	1980
DAEDALUS , V107, N2, P75-92	1978

Journals citing the memex. (Courtesy ISI)

Author	Year
AGUOLU CC	1979
ANDERSON B	1980
ANONYMOUS	1984
ARTHURS E; STUCK BW	1982
ATKINSON RC; BLANPIED WA	1985
BAKER CG	1977
BALL AJS	1981
BECKER J	1984
BENDAVID J	1977
BERNIER CL	1978
BERNINGER DE	1982
BERNINGER DE	1982
BORMAN L; HAY R	1977
BOTTLE RT	1981
BROOKS H	1982
BROOKS H	1980
BUD RF	1978
BULKLEY BH	1984
BURNS C	1981
CASE D	1983
CAWKELL AE	1980
CAWKELL AE	
CHUBIN DE	1986
CRAWFORD S	1983
CULNAN MJ	1981
DAMMERS HF	1975
DARLING L	1974
DAVIES R	1983
DEDIJER S	1972
DEGENNARO R	1985
DEGENNARO R	1979
DILLON M	1981
ENGLAND JM	1976

Authors citing the memex. (Courtesy ISI)

The dedicated individual researcher could build a larger, more sophisticated database, including templates created to help with specific research problems. A report library could be developed to reflect any individual's interest in the literature. Records could be grouped together in databases according to criteria established by the researcher. What was that about "associative trails"?

Professional Bibliographic Software

Professional Bibliographic Software began as a system for producing printed bibliographies. Since it has purchased *Pro-Search* from Menlo, Professional Bibliographic Software is now a software family like Sci-Mate, including a full complement of tools for the search process and the search product.

The Professional Bibliographic System allows variable-length records and fields for efficient storage and searching. Boolean searching is possible. However PBS's forte is the printed word, and it may have been the first bibliographic software on the micro market. PBS is capable of generating bibliographic citations for twenty different document types including journals, books, dissertations, and musical scores. Data from a local bibliographic database can be reformatted to conform to any one of several bibliographic standards, including ANSI, APA, MLA or the format used by *Science* magazine. PBS can accommodate up to 30,000 records on a hard disk system.

Biblio-Link, a separately purchased companion program, reformats downloaded records so they can be put into a PBS database and used to generate bibliographies. Despite its name, *Biblio-Link* is not a communications program but a reformatter. It works well with bibliographic utilities like OCLC or RLIN. Like most post-processors, it can't deal easily with untagged records such as those in most DIALOG files.

PBS didn't originally come with a communications package. For awhile, *PC-Dial*, a low-end, shareware communications program, was offered for $25. Then a specialized communications module called *Data Transfer* was offered for $200. *Data Transfer* was designed to download and reformat MARC records from OCLC and RLIN. Direct support isn't provided for downloading from "supermarket" online vendors with their numerous differently structured files. Soon we should expect to see some kind of variant of the original *Pro-Search* offered by PBS.

Another program called *Index Plus* may also be obtained as part of the PBS family of software. *Index Plus* can be used to create different types of indexes to PBS bibliographic files.

Finder

Another of the product-oriented search tools is *Finder* from Aaron/Smith Associates of Atlanta. In this case, the product is a database instead of a printed bibliography. *Finder* allows tagging of fields within unstructured files, such as those downloaded during an online search. The contents of tagged fields may then be moved into a database designed to accommodate them.

The module used to mark and move fields from online records into local files used to be called *The Search Companion* and is now known as *FINDERlink*. *FINDERlink* must be purchased separately. It is not a communications program; no communications programs are offered with *Finder*. A third, separately available program, *PR*, is geared toward generating sorted, reformatted, printed reports from *Finder* databases.

Finder offers the capabilities provided by online services for databases at the micro level. Full Boolean searching is possible. Truncation, range searching, and limiting the search to a specific field are also possible. Sorting and multiple display formats are supported.

Finder includes a database manager, a reformatting utility, a text editor, and indexing utilities. All it needs to move it into competition with other search assistance packages is a search-oriented communications program.

References/Recommended Reading

Blanchard, Mark. "Pro-Search." *OCLC Micro* 1, no.3 (July 1985): 20.

Garfield, Eugene. "Introducing Sci-Mate--a Menu-Driven Microcomputer Software Package for Online and Offline Information Retrieval. Part 1: The Sci-Mate Personal Data Manager." *Current Contents*, 21 March 1983, 5-12.

_____. "Introducing Sci-Mate--a Menu-Driven Microcomputer Software Package for Online and Offline Information Retrieval. Part 2: The Sci-Mate Universal Online Searcher." *Current Contents*, 4 April 1983, 5-15.

Hawkins, Donald T., and Louise R. Levy. "Front End Software for Online Database Searching, Part 1: Definitions, System Features, and Evaluation." *Online* (November 1985): 30-37.

Karten, Howard A. "In Search of a Significant Dialog [In-Search]." *PC Magazine*, 21 August 1984, 265-270.

Levy, Louise. "Gateway Software: Is It for You?" *Online* (November 1984): 67-79.

"Menlo Seeks Pro-Search Buyer, Future Uncertain." *Information Today* 3, no.3 (March 1986): 1.

Pisciotta, Henry. "Sci-Mate: A Review." *Reference Services Review* (Summer 1985): 11-16.

Stout, Catheryne, and Thomas Marcinko. "Sci-Mate: A Menu-Driven Universal Online Searcher and Personal Data Manager." *Online* (September 1983): 112-116.

Wilbur, Helen. "The ORBIT SearchMaster System: A Search Management Tool." In *Downloading/Uploading Online Databases and Catalogs*, edited by James A. Benson and Bella H. Weinberg, 22-24. Ann Arbor, MI: Pierian Press, 1985.

PART THREE
PEOPLE AND MACHINES

CHAPTER ELEVEN
END-USERS AND GATEWAYS

The Era of the End-User

"End-user" is the somewhat logically ambiguous term applied to the consumer of electronic information. Information rarely has a final destination, nor does its supply decrease as it is consumed. Almost always, it is transformed and passed on. Despite the enthusiasm in the literature, especially the marketing literature of the online vendors, end-user online searching will probably not catch on in the home computer market anytime soon.

When micros were first introduced, they were touted as the solution to a variety of household problems from tax preparation to recipe management. How many people do you know who keep recipe files on a micro? The traditional professional, academic, and corporate clients of online services are the end-users everyone is talking about. Eventually, we might have searching in the home, but for now the term "end-user" is mostly associated with those who stand under the umbrella of some larger body like a university, a hospital, or a corporation.

End-users are an institutional phenomenon. And most of the institutions with which end-users are associated have in their employ some sort of search manager, usually a librarian. In the short term, then, the end-user phemenon will result in an increased rather than a decreased demand for the services of professional searchers. The term "end-user" is, besides being logically inconsistent, somewhat grating on the ear. It seems more relevant to international arms deals than to information transfer. Richard Janke, one of the first proponents of self-service online searching, prefers the term "client searcher."

Call them what you will, client searchers are beginning to have an impact on search managers. References to online searching now can be commonly found in newspapers and popular magazines. The folks who run the training seminars for the big online vendors report that the proportion of attendees who are not trained information specialists is steadily increasing. Why the sudden interest in online searching after so many years? Could the fact that people are beginning to use personal computers as a communications medium have something to do with this phenomenon?

A debate rages on the effectiveness of end-users as searchers. No one seems to be sure whether subject knowledge or system knowledge is more important to successful searching. Certainly both are important. Most of the early experiments with client searching focused on specialized professionals who were familiar with the technical literature and its vocabulary. While many were able to learn the craft of searching, many still preferred that searches be performed by a trained intermediary.

Now we are beginning to see end-user training efforts directed toward less specialized groups, such as college undergraduates. Much of the impetus for this has come from the products and services directed toward the personal computer market. This newest group of online searchers presents both problems and opportunities for the search manager. Personal computers provide a solution to many of the problems and a medium for realizing opportunities.

Management Problems

Let's examine some of the problems first. Security may be the number one problem facing the manager of a micro-based client searching program. Security problems exist at different levels. The most obvious problem is password protection. Most search assistance packages provide a means for securing passwords. General purpose communications programs aren't as consistent.

Protecting hardware from theft is another security concern, especially in public settings or in libraries that maintain late hours. It may be necessary to physically secure the equipment itself. There are a number of companies providing cables and lock boxes designed to protect computer hardware. Doss Industries, 1224 Mariposa St., San Francisco, CA (phone: 415 861-2223) sells a specially designed security enclosure for IBM equipment. Anchor Pad International, 4483 McGrath St., Ventura, CA 93003 (phone: 805 658-2661) offers adhesive pads designed to protect all types of computer equipment.

Protecting software and data from piracy and tampering is an even tougher problem than protecting hardware. The problem becomes especially severe where several people share, or have access to, a hard disk-equipped machine. A number of different solutions are available. The simplest involves buying a relatively inexpensive utility program like *MagLock*, $89 from Finder Software Laboratories in Tonawanda, New York. Such programs permit their users to restrict access to files, to encrypt files, and to specify passwords at the local level.

Security programs can be used to limit access to specified subdirectories and to make it difficult for the pirate to copy software kept on a hard disk. Public microcomputers will require libraries to take more active measures against copyright violation than they take with photocopying. It's so much easier to copy an enormous volume of valuable information with a micro than it is to pirate printed information with a photocopier.

Another software solution builds protection into the storage medium itself. The Vault Corporation of Westlake Village, California sells disks marked with an electronic "fingerprint" that prevents the unauthorized copying of files stored on them. A pack of ten FILELOK disks sells for $84.95. Vault's hard disk protection software called *PROLOK* uses the same principle with hard disks, and its *TELELOK* program encrypts software for transmission over phone lines.

The software-only approach to security is supplemented by products combining hardware and software components. Some require the addition of an expansion card which works in tandem with a program supplied on a disk. Others come with a peripheral input device. United Security of Vienna, Virginia, makes available with its security program, *Privacy Plus*, a hand-held wand called LASER-LOCK, which is required to supply an electronic password in combination with a password sent from the keyboard.

For the ultra secretive, there is the Gordian Systems Access Key from Gordian Systems of Palo Alto, California. Central control of security is provided by a Key Cutter, which encodes hand-held peripheral devices with electronic access codes. Each key can be supplied with a different level of access. The user must touch the key to the surface of the screen and the code on the key must be verified along with a keyed password before access is provided.

It is possible to buy a disk protection utility program for less than a hundred dollars or to spend thousands on a more sophisticated scheme. Even if security is never breached, accounting can be a real headache. Some of the search assistance packages do provide fund accounting and invoicing capabilities. Third computer gateway systems can be used to consolidate accounting records and maintain individual records for a group of clients. A few of the end-user gateway services charge a flat rate per search, simplifying accounting.

Passing costs to users can be a problem. It's hard to collect for something, the cost of which is not known until after it's been purchased and the value of which may be doubtful to its purchaser. Making change and collecting for searches performed by others will take time away from the professional searcher, time that might be spent more productively in other ways.

The magnetic strip card now being used with many library photocopiers provides a possible solution. Searches could be paid for in advance by clients who would buy credit on the card which would be encoded at a central accounting location. A black box between the card reader and the micro would poll the micro to determine how much time had elapsed since the card was inserted. A formula built into the software would be used to debit the card based on some predetermined rate. When the amount of credit on the card was close to exhausted, a warning could be displayed on the screen and the client given the option to save his strategy before buying more time on the card. This approach would work best with services that charged a single, flat connect rate.

Hardware and software maintenance can also present problems for search managers. The more people using a machine, the more likely it is to break. The search manager running a large-scale client searching center will want to assign hardware and software maintenance tasks to a trained staff member. The era of the end-user is likely to result in other organizational changes with more emphasis on training, consultation, and computer services.

The problems associated with client searching are counterbalanced by exciting new opportunities. Personal computers provide a convenient medium for training clients to become searchers. Micros also make possible a variety of gateway products and services for inexperienced clients. A microcomputer can be used to provide an inexpensive way to train novice searchers. The search process can be simulated in the offline mode; computer-assisted instruction (CAI) can be provided. Experimental search assistance and training programs originally developed on large computers are bound to show up eventually in microcomputer versions. A few of the packages designed for searchers, most notably *Sci-Mate* and *SearchWorks*, provide tutorials or ready reference relating to search techniques. Almost all of the end-user gateways to be discussed later incorporate some tutorial material.

The imaginative search manager who knows her way around DOS could use batch files and locally developed menus to provide custom-designed tutorials. Actual examples of different techniques and the use of specific files could be cut from downloaded searches and pasted into tutorial modules with a word processor.

Librarians are already beginning to develop and use their own tutorial material. Clyde Grotophorst, systems librarian at George Mason University in Fairfax, Virginia, has written a BASIC program designed to introduce online searching. The program, called *GMUTANT*, is available as shareware through the OCLC Microcomputer Program Exchange (OMPX). The program is described along with many others in the OMPX Catalog, which is available from OCLC Microsystems, 6565 Frantz Rd., Dublin, OH 43017-0702.

Client training, whether with the machine or by more traditional means, provides an opportunity for search managers to bolster their role as information consultants. Among the things search managers have to consider are which parts of the search process lend themselves to being taught by the machine and which aspects should be delegated to the person. Why bother to train clients to log on when the process can be so easily automated?

One of the questions which remains to be answered is how effective micro-based CAI will be for training end-users. Should tutorial developers focus on strategy development, languages and commands, database selection, or the idiosyncracies of specific databases? Search training has traditionally been provided by system vendors who have a vested interest in their own product. If nothing else, micros will allow search managers to develop tutorial material that isn't designed to emphasize one system or database while excluding all others.

Beyond the opportunity to train clients are opportunities to develop new services geared toward client searchers. The search manager may eventually move into the role of memex consultant, advising clients on hardware, software, and online services. One day the professional searcher's major responsibility may shift from performing searches to designing a search environment. Among the tasks performed by the search manager will be developing macros, templates, tutorials, scripts, and stored profiles for a more sophisticated clientele. The search manager will continue to be responsible for delivering electronic information, but she will also be charged with using the micro to transform the process and the product.

End-users have been the target of a major marketing push by traditional online vendors in addition to an assortment of third party entrepreneurs. The result has been an abundance of new products and services, all of which fall under the rubric "gateway."

Enter the Gateway

A term often heard in circles where front-ends and end-users are being discussed is the word "gateway." Apparently, there is some sort of a distinction between the two but it involves a subtle nuance that is difficult to describe. Ask any three players in the game to define those terms and you'll almost certainly get three different answers. A group of the major contenders for the niches in the front-end marketplace participated in a panel discussion at Online Inc.'s Online '85 conference. Lloyd Kreuzer, then president of Menlo Corporation, offered the following definition of gateway, which was concurred with by the other participants on the panel:

> A gateway takes more than one online service and blends them together so that they appear uniform to the user. A front-end may not be a gateway but a gateway is always a front-end.

A gateway is, therefore, a variant of the front-end. In addition to gateways that provide access to more than a single system, there are those front-ends that have been designed by database producers to work with specific databases or groups of databases.

Who's It For?

Such front-ends are almost always designed to be used by the inexperienced searcher. They represent the marketing strategy of the database producer who wants to increase the number of people who use his database by providing software that simplifies the use of that database. Some notable examples are Wilsearch, which acts as a front-end to the databases produced by H.W. Wilson, MicroDisclosure, which is designed to be used with the Disclosure database on DIALOG, and Search Helper, which provides simplified access to the databases available from the Information Access Corporation. There is a fundamental difference between personal computer software that is designed to be used by people who are accustomed to dealing with a retrieval language, and that which is designed to be used by the uninitiated. Unfortunately, much of the software designed for new searchers doesn't begin to take full advantage of the system with which it was designed to work.

Those who work without benefit of programmed mediation are often those who are best served. As the number of neophyte searchers (i.e., end-users) increases along with the computing power of micros, there is likely to be an increase in the number of elegant and versatile programs designed for those who aren't familiar with the formalities of asking system vendors for information.

Mainframe Gateways

Before examining end-user software designed for micros, let's take a quick look at some of the end-user software developed by system vendors and others for use on mainframe computers. Gateways residing in remote mainframes don't require a micro at the other end of the line; any terminal will do. Nevertheless, mainframe gateways owe their existence to personal computers, which popularized searching among those who had previously relied upon intermediaries.

End-user gateway software superimposes upon an existing search language a different, somehow "friendlier" way of querying a database or, in many cases, simply connecting to a database. This is often accomplished by displaying menus and prompts to which the inquirer is asked to respond. Sometimes the full capabilities of the host are available. Other times features are sacrificed for simplicity. Simplicity is one of the operative principles of end-user software. Another principle is transparency--the user of the gateway logs on with the gateway service instead of the system actually being used. Some gateways go to great lengths to conceal the identity of the system vendor actually being used. Reduced cost is another benefit attributed to many gateways, but that, as well as other claims, has to be examined critically.

System Vendors and End-Users

BRS introduced the first front-end software directed toward nonprofessional searchers. BRS After Dark first made its appearance early in 1983. After Dark, as implied by its name, is only available during nonprime evening hours. After Dark offers only a subset of the full complement of BRS databases. Most customers pay by credit card, and rates are substantially lower than those charged for the full service. After Dark, though it was intended for individual consumers, is also used in institutional settings. Its low rates and relatively broad selection of files made it especially popular in academia.

After Dark provides menu-driven access to almost fifty of the BRS databases, including a handful of full-text files. Databases are grouped together into broad categories such as Education and Social Sciences. The menu-driven approach can become tedious, just as it can when it is employed by general purpose communications software such as *Smartcom*, or micro front-ends like *Sci-Mate*.

Despite the use of menus, little of the interactive nature of the search process is sacrificed by BRS After Dark. Truncation and full-text word proximity searching are supported. Field qualification for more precise searching is also possible. The user of the software is able to modify strategy based upon output from the host. The searcher is given the option of seeing detailed instructions throughout a search. If the detailed instructions option is chosen, explanations of commands and database descriptions are made available. After having chosen a subject category and a database, the searcher is prompted to enter search terms or a command. Commands are summarized on the screen.

BRS has continued its commitment to end-user searching. Since the introduction of After Dark, BRS has been involved in a collaborative venture with W.B. Saunders, the medical publisher. The Colleague system is a joint venture directed toward health care professionals. More recently, BRS introduced BRKTHRU, a full day and night service that adds to the capabilities of After Dark while retaining a menu-driven approach. BRKTHRU is somewhat more expensive than After Dark and provides access to over sixty-five databases. It is also now possible for a searcher to use the BRS native system in a menu-driven mode for a slightly higher connect rate.

BRS continues to be the leader among host system developers of software for novice searchers, most of whom are PC owners. BRS has spiffed up its documentation and training materials and continues to add the full-text files that enable end-users to do all of their information shopping in a single place. Labelled fields for postprocessing, an emphasis on client searchers, and attractive rates add to BRS's appeal as a search service that meets the needs of PC owners. BRS has not yet introduced a micro software product for searchers but is reported to be working on one.

Knowledge Index

Not to be outdone, DIALOG introduced its end-user, after-hours service, Knowledge Index, shortly after BRS After Dark was made available. Knowledge Index, which includes about thirty of DIALOG's most popular files, is somewhat less comprehensive than After Dark. Knowledge Index is menu-driven and uses a simplified version of DIALOG's command language. Field qualification and proximity searching are not permitted. One of the really nice things about Knowledge Index is that all of the files offered are available for the single, flat rate of $24 per hour with no monthly minimum. The flat rate makes it easy to predict in advance the amount of money a client search will cost.

Rather than introducing new end-user services, DIALOG seems to be concentrating on adding end-user-oriented capabilities to files that are available through its full service. The report generation software that accompanies many numeric and directory files is one example. DIALOG also serves as a gateway for other services that are menu driven and targeted toward information consumers. Menus developed for use with specific databases are made available to those accessing those databases through DIALOG. Two of the databases to which DIALOG provides a menu-driven gateway are OAG (the Official Airline Guide), and Quotes and Trading, which allows investors to retrieve financial information and place orders with a broker.

Combining the information raw material with the software tools to manipulate it is reminiscent of the "object" concept pioneered at Xerox PARC for the Smalltalk operating system and later embodied in Apple's Macintosh. Rather than dealing with files and programs, the computer deals with entities known as objects. Objects are defined as the combination of data with the instructions needed to manipulate the data. An object-oriented online system would merge each database with the instructions required to manipulate the data it included. DIALOG files such as Media General or Donelly Demographics, which are accompanied by special report generation software, can be thought of as "objects" with which the searcher can work.

Third Party Gateways

DIALOG and BRS are not the only online vendors offering gateway and end-user services. An article in the May 1985 issue of *Online* lists several pages of "databanks which market to microcomputer owners and other information end-users." There are also third party online vendors that mediate for end-users by providing a gateway to the online services from which source data is available.

EasyNet is a Narberth, Pennsylvania-based, public dial-up service that provides access to databases available from nine different online services. A phone call to EasyNet results in a series of prompts designed to elicit information that will help its gateway software select an online service and a database. The user also has the option of bypassing menus and choosing his own database by selecting EasyNet II.

EasyNet simplifies accounting by providing a single, monthly invoice for all the services to which it acts as a gateway. Searching is made more predictable by charging a flat rate of $8 per search plus a $1 access fee. If a search yields no hits, there is no charge other than the access fee. Hits are displayed without abstracts. The searcher is charged the rather steep price of $2 for each abstract requested.

EasyNet does not require a microcomputer since the gateway software resides in its mainframe computer in Pennsylvania. EasyNet constructs a query string by inserting terms selected by the user into syntactically correct search statements before connecting to a host and uploading them. A feature called SOS enables the puzzled searcher to receive assistance through his terminal from a trained searcher at EasyNet's console in Pennsylvania.

The major problem with EasyNet is the lack of control provided to its users. Much of the interactive nature of the search process is lost. It is not easily possible to modify strategy based on the response from the remote system. It is true that there is no charge for searches that don't produce hits, but it is also true that there is a charge for searches yielding false or irrelevant hits. EasyNet, while it is definitely an online, interactive service, tends to function much of the time in a batch mode reminiscent of searching's early years.

Both the BRS and DIALOG gateways are designed to work with a single parent search language. EasyNet, on the other hand, must be capable of speaking the search languages of nine different online services. It's no wonder that the EasyNet software is mounted on a mainframe rather than a micro. Trying to deal with several different systems must add considerable overhead to the software.

Gateways for Personal Computers

The California-based Business Computer Network was among the first gateways to be directed specifically to micro users. BCN lived a short, eventful life. Its demise, while possibly related to poor management, under-capitalization, and the other financial and marketing problems that plague software developers, may also be seen as an object lesson for developers of gateways.

BCN was announced in a flurry of publicity. Its aggressive marketing campaign included some of the slickest, most graphically appealing promotional material on the micro scene. BCN gave away communications software to potential customers and offered modems at discounted rates. Reviews that were more favorable than usual appeared in the micro literature. But despite all the hoopla, by the end of 1985, just two years after it was introduced, BCN was bankrupt. What went wrong?

BCN produced its own microcomputer telecommunications software, *SuperScout*, which dialed up its gateway computer in California. The BCN gateway provided access to virtually all of the major online services. BCN's approach was based on the notion that end-users would be interested in having access to an incredibly large array of online services while only receiving a single monthly invoice, from BCN of course.

BCN was a wholesaler of online information. BCN bought blocks of online time at discounted rates and planned to take its profit from the difference between its discounted price and the retail cost passed along to its customers. BCN's customers would pay the same rates they would have paid if they had established accounts with the vendors they used without having to worry about monthly minimums (except BCN's $5 minimum). Nor would BCN customers have to bother with keeping track of invoices from several different vendors. BCN did provide a gateway to more services than anybody else; BCN made it easy to log on to and pay for searches done on numerous services.

However, once the user was connected to a service by BCN, he was on his own. BCN did not provide any search assistance other than making the connection. Simply providing access to a variety of online services was not enough, especially with those customers who searched so infrequently that they were reluctant to take on the accounting responsibilities of dealing with more than one service. True, the single invoice did make paying the bills easier, but the ability to log on easily to a variety of services could have been handled as easily by a micro communications program. And once the user was online, he could quickly get beyond his depth, and beyond the depth of his pocketbook.

If an end-user product is to succeed, it must do something more than simply connect its users to source databases. Ironically, one possible cause for BCN's demise may have been the variety of files it offered. Even experienced searchers have difficulty keeping track of the intricacies of more than a single service. End-users may benefit more from products that provide assistance with a single online service, or, even more specifically, with a single database or database family.

SearchWare

Before moving on to stand-alone microcomputer software, let's look at another micro/third party gateway hybrid. SearchWare is a California-based company that picks up where BCN left off by assisting its users in building search profiles for later uploading. Though it does add to the capabilities offered by BCN, SearchWare still does not provide a sufficiently viable justification for the micro/gateway mainframe approach to end-user software.

SearchWare--unlike BCN, which was comprehensive to the nth degree--is designed to serve as a gateway only to those databases that are available through the DIALOG system. However, its designers have attempted to conceal from its users the fact that DIALOG is the source of the information they are retrieving. Users are given the impression that the databases they are searching are SearchWare rather than DIALOG databases.

Users of the software established a DIALOG account through SearchWare and pay SearchWare instead of DIALOG. The approach makes some sense when several vendors are involved, as is the case with EasyNet and as was the case with BCN, but one wonders why it is necessary to deal with a single vendor such as DIALOG through an intermediary like SearchWare.

There are about fifty different SearchWare disks. The only substantive difference among them is that each is designed to work with a select group of DIALOG databases within a specialized subject area. At $290 for the first disk, $290 for the second, and $100 for each subsequent disk, it would cost the search manager a substantial amount of money to cover even a few of the fifty or so available subject areas.

The idea of grouping databases together into subject categories to make the search process less confusing and to meet the needs of those in specialized fields is a sound idea. After all, how many client searchers are likely to be interested in more than a few databases or subject fields. Front-ends residing in host systems also often take the strategy of grouping files into subject categories. Context sensitivity can be achieved by designing separate software modules to take advantage of database-specific searchable fields, limiting capabilities, and other idiosyncracies.

Despite the underlying validity of the approach, SearchWare's method of marketing the disks leaves something to be desired. Why not make the database-specific parts of SearchWare available on a separate disk for a lower cost, or allow the user to select the databases to be supported and merge the modules for them into the main program? Further problems are caused by the failure of the subject disks to take in-depth advantage of the files they were designed to support.

The only specific DIALOG/Medline search field accounted for on the Biomed disk is the human/nonhuman check tag. No prompts were provided to allow the user to specify sex, age group, chemical Registry Number, or any of the other fields searchable on DIALOG/Medline. Nor was any mention made of the subheadings that are so important to Medline searching. The BIOSIS module prompted for Concept Codes, but not for Biosystematic Codes.

SearchWare works on three levels. Level One involves the familiar tactic of building offline queries by responding to menus and prompts. After a Level One search has been prepared, it is uploaded to DIALOG. Level Two searching is basically offline batch searching with DIALOG commands. All DIALOG conventions from Prefix= to /Suffix are retained. To perform a Level Two search, the searcher must be familiar with the DIALOG language. Level Three searching is simply DIALOG searching with SearchWare's cryptic prompts substituted for DIALOG's.

Level One and Level Two, the "friendliest" search modes, are basically batch modes. Level One, besides prompting the user to enter a strategy, also asks her to specify the number of hits to print or download, the format to use, and whether or not to log off automatically after the search is completed. Level Two uses the line-editor-on-the-screen approach to creating an offline profile.

The SearchWare documentation provides an introduction to DIALOG searching that isn't nearly as effective as DIALOG's own material. The DIALOG Pocket Guide is much more thorough and professionally done. A glossary includes basic terms like disk, menu, and command, which should already be familiar to any micro user, while neglecting to include terms like record, field, descriptor, and many of the other terms that are important to information storage and retrieval. Nor did the manual make any mention of thesauri or search guides that are available for the databases supported by the subject disk and which would be of real use to the searcher who concentrates on a few databases from a subject field.

The software itself also seemed determined to mystify the search process. While logging on, messages appear briefly on the screen and then are replaced, all to the accompaniment of much beeping. The strategy that's uploaded isn't displayed as it's sent, and SearchWare prompts on top of DIALOG's added to the confusion.

For $290 per disk the client searcher might be better off taking the DIALOG training seminar, investing in thesauri and search guides for heavily used files, and buying a good general purpose communications package. Gateways available from the vendors themselves provide advantages in terms of cost and usability that just aren't available from third parties like SearchWare.

References/Recommended Reading

Dagani, Ron. "On-Line Literature Searching Catches on Among Researchers." *Chemical and Engineering News*, 7 May 1984, 29-30.

"Databank Directory." *Online* (May 1985): 99-108.

Eisenberg, Michael. *The Direct Use of Online Bibliographic Information by Untrained End-Users: A Review of Research*. Syracuse, NY: ERIC Clearinghouse on Information Resources, 1983. ERIC Document, ED 238 440.

Gaffner, Haines B. "Personal Computers: Key to Mass Market Online Database Market." In *National Online Meeting: Proceedings--1983*, compiled by Martha E. Williams, and Thomas H. Hogan, 147-158. Medford, NJ: Learned Information, 1983.

_____. "PC Software and Online Databases." *Publishers Weekly*, 23 November 1984, 44-50.

Glossbrenner, Alfred. "A Low-Cost Database Pool [BCN]." *PC Magazine*, 2 April 1985, 315.

Guy, Robin Frederick. Training Aids for Online Instruction: An Analysis. Paper presented at the International Online Information Meeting (7th, London England, Dec, 1983). ERIC Document ED 248 900.

Haines, Judith S. "Experiences in Training End-User Searchers." *Online* (November 1982): 14-23.

Hamilton, Dennis. "Library Users and Online Systems: Suggested Objectives for Library Instruction." *RQ* 25, no.2 (Winter 1985): 195-198.

Janke, Richard V. "Online After Six: End User Searching Comes of Age." *Online* (November 1984): 15-29.

Moskowitz, Robert A. "Gateways to Online Information." *Computer Decisions*, 10 September 1985, 36-40.

Ojala, Marydee. "End User Searching and its Implications for Librarians." *Special Libraries* (Spring 1985): 93-99.

Smith, Bev. "BCN Out of Business; Bankruptcy on Horizon?" *Information Today* 2, no.9, (October 1985): 1.

Stone, David. "Getting On-line at the Database Supermarket [BCN]." *PC Magazine*, 5 March 1985, 50.

Taylor, Jared. "On-Line House Calls [Knowledge Index and BRS After Dark]." *PC Magazine*, 16 October 1984, 135-138.

Tenopir, Carol. "Systems for End Users: Are There End Users for Systems?" *Library Journal*, 15 June 1985, 40-41.

CHAPTER TWELVE
SOFTWARE FOR BEGINNERS

Micro Software for End-Users

So far, software that is designed to work with a specific database has been the most successful. It's pretty hard to fit instructions that cover even the most common databases on a floppy disk--and the floppy disk, even when four or five of them must be copied onto a hard disk to properly use a program, is still the way most software is marketed. Database specific end-user software has many advantages. Less overhead is required to cover all of the possibilities. Greater depth can be achieved. More file-specific features can be supported and more tutorial material can be included. Modules for communications and automatic log-on are included. Sometimes downloading is facilitated; other times it is not possible. But logging on and downloading are not what end-user software is truly about. Searching is. The big disadvantage of much end-user software is not in its communications capabilities but in its search capabilities.

The ability to interact with a database in real time, to modify strategies and base decisions upon the symbols pouring in over the wire, lies at the very core of online searching. Many end-user programs, in an effort to simplify the process, save money, and provide users with advance knowledge of how much each search will cost, resort to a batch approach, abandoning the online capabilities that make searching what it is.

There is strong evidence that even experienced searchers rarely take full advantage of the interactive capabilities of online searching. Many searchers fix on a strategy and either refuse to deviate from it or overspecify when it yields more hits than anticipated. Several investigators have studied various aspects of the searcher's mentality. Professional searchers often fail to take advantage of interactive capabilities, preferring not to deviate from preconceived notions of how to proceed and what to expect. How can we expect client searchers to approach the process any differently, especially if we provide them with software that encourages a batch mentality?

But is it possible to develop software that encourages clients to take advantage of online interactivity without discouraging them by presenting them with disastrously expensive searches? How can options such as expanding the basic index, browsing through online thesauri where they exist, and choosing searchers' display formats be incorporated in search assistance programs for naive searchers?

Knowing in advance the fixed cost of each search is one of the desirable facets of several of the end-user programs. But the fixed cost idea militates against emphasis on interactivity and results in a batch mentality. A batch mentality may reduce costs, but it is also likely to result in less than satisfactory results. The batch approach is still the most common tactic taken by personal computer software for end-users. Until connect charges are significantly reduced or programmers become more sophisticated, this trend is likely to continue.

SearchHelper

SearchHelper was among the first micro-based, end-user products designed to provide simplified access to a single family of databases. *SearchHelper* was designed by the Information Access Corporation to provide access to its files on the *DIALOG* system. In addition to logging on, the program provides client searchers with assistance in constructing search strategies.

Users of *SearchHelper* prepurchase searches on a subscription basis. The price paid for each search is determined by the number of searches subscribed to. Each search costs a predetermined amount, usually $2.50 or $3.50. Each search unit will yield up to twenty hits. Each subsequent group of up to twenty hits is paid for as a separate search. However, the search unit fee is levied regardless of whether or not a search yields any hits.

The two big advantages of *SearchHelper* are its fixed cost and its simplicity. *SearchHelper* provides access to seven of IAC's databases, including Magazine Index and National Newspaper Index. It was intended for client searchers in libraries, and since each search carries a fixed fee, it can be coin operated. All the search manager has to do is initialize the program by providing passwords, phone numbers, and so forth. IAC will even supply all necessary equipment for a fee.

The program provides a brief description of the databases it supports and gives the client the option of selecting which file to use. Strategies are constructed in an offline batch mode. Clients specify search terms by responding to menus and prompts. Clients are first asked if they are interested in researching a person or a subject. Depending upon the choice made, additional explanatory material and prompts are provided. The program automatically inserts proximity operators between the terms in multiple word search phrases. Truncation is also supported. Field qualification is also possible, but the Advanced Search Tips section of the manual has to be consulted for specifics.

Unfortunately, only the Boolean AND operator is supported. Client searchers are thus unable to broaden the search by entering synonymous terms for individual facets. Consequently, searches are often too narrow, producing few or no hits. Clients tend to eliminate possibly useful material by overspecifying with more AND clauses than are needed.

Once a profile has been created, it is displayed for the client's approval before it is uploaded. *SearchHelper* will try each packet network in the order specified by the search manager until a connection is achieved. Any hits yielded by a search are downloaded into a RAM buffer and may be printed immediately or after the search has been completed and the client has disconnected. Downloading to disk is not provided. Once a search has been completed, any results evaporate into the same ozone that is the final destination of all volatile information.

The manual accompanying *SearchHelper* is clearly written and logically organized. Advanced searching tips discuss the many file-specific features associated with IAC's databases. The program itself is easy to use and works well considering its limitations. IAC has long been a pioneer in the development of electronic information products, and as we shall see, is moving into new modes of delivery.

However, *SearchHelper* does fall victim to the very simplicity that is one of its major selling points. Deprived of the ability to use the OR operator, the searcher is placed in the position of hoping that her search terms match those of the controlled vocabulary being used or coincide with terms found in the titles of articles. A good controlled vocabulary and a certain amount of advance preparation are crucial to the success of "batch mode" searching.

MicroDisclosure

Another early file-specific software package for micro users was *MicroDisclosure*, which was designed to work with the Disclosure II database of business and financial information. *MicroDisclosure* was one of the first programs to integrate information retrieval with other functions. Users of the program are provided with the ability to retrieve records from the Disclosure II database as well as the ability to manipulate data contained in downloaded records.

Users of *MicroDisclosure* are given the option of looking for information on a specific company or of compiling a list of companies that meet specified criteria. Once again, a query string is built by responding to a series of menus and prompts. Disclosure II is a numeric/text database rather than a bibliographic database. It has many more searchable fields than the average bibliographic file, and the information contained in many of them lends itself more readily to manipulation and analysis by computer.

MicroDisclosure comes on three disks. One disk enables the user to search the Disclosure II database. Since the program is specialized for that file, it is possible to specify which of almost one hundred searchable fields is to be examined. Once a search has been performed with the search module of the program, downloaded data are stored on a specially formatted database disk. A third disk contains the Reports and Analysis module, which may be used to manipulate the financial information on the database disk.

MicroDisclosure comes with preformatted reports designed to permit the quick comparison of companies using such common variables as balance sheet data or financial ratios. It is also possible to specify custom-designed reports for a single company or reports that compare the performance of a few companies. Financial attributes of companies may be sorted and ranked by a variety of criteria. Data downloaded from Disclosure II can even be converted to an appropriate format and exported to a spreadsheet program, where it can be used for financial modeling.

At $45, *MicroDisclosure* is quite inexpensive for a front-end. The real commodity being sold here is the information from Disclosure II, not the tool for manipulating it. Eventually electronic information, the structure for its organization and exchange, and the tools for transforming it may all be parts of the same entity.

Numeric files lend themselves especially well to post-search manipulation. It takes a much smarter computer to manipulate words than it takes to juggle numbers. Since it is so easy to accomplish, we can expect to see more specialized software designed to work with numeric and directory files. Downloading also becomes less problematic when the front-end vendor and the data vendor are one and the same. Front-ends like *MicroDisclosure* and ISI's *Sci-Mate* are examples of programs that incorporate data structures for processing downloaded records from the parent company that produced them.

In the future, we can expect to see an increasing number of low-cost front-ends designed for a single file or file family and intended to be sold as an adjunct to the online data that is their producer's main line of business. *MicroCambridge*, at $45 from Cambridge Scientific Abstracts, is another example of the low-cost front-end provided as an incentive to get potential searchers to use the parent vendor's files. In the case of *MicroCambridge*, the files offered by the parent company are bibliographic rather than numeric. Other vendors of numeric and financial data offer combination manipulation/retrieval capabilities of the same sort offered by Disclosure. The *DunsPlus* package of software from Dun and Bradstreet offers even more analytical capabilities at a substantially higher price.

Wilsearch

H.W. Wilson, that stalwart of the indexing business, was a late entry into the online field. Its *ELHILL*-based service, Wilsonline, entered the field in 1985. Wilson's late entry into the field did give it the opportunity to capitalize on the most current developments in user-friendly search assistance software. *Wilsearch*, the microcomputer end-user software introduced by Wilson in 1985, will help to justify the company's choice of the *ELHILL* system. The program is quite capable of taking advantage of *ELHILL*'s strengths and compensating for many of its weaknesses. Wilsearch and the National Library of Medicine's somewhat whimsically named program, Grateful Med, are obviously cut of the same *ELHILL* cloth.

Neither program's manual is longer than fifty pages. Each software package provides the requisite simplicity while sacrificing little of the mother language's power. Both programs are quickly learned and easy to use. This is the state of the art when it comes to search software for the infrequent searcher.

Wilsearch uses a series of menus to assist the novice searcher in selecting and querying files from the Wilson family of databases (most of which correspond to Wilson's familiar printed indexes). It is possible to use the menus and a search formulation screen to build an offline batch strategy in the familiar manner. It is also possible to use the software to connect directly to Wilsonline for a search in the native mode. Extensive tutorial and descriptive information is provided by the software itself. Even the most hesitant or computer-shy bibliophile will have no problem becoming adept with *Wilsearch*.

After selecting the *Wilsearch* option from the main menu, the searcher is presented with a selection menu that asks him to choose a Wilsonline database or database category. Some of the categories allow the searcher to query more than one file simultaneously. The Business and Legal Literature category, for example, will cause the program to search the online versions of both the Index to Legal

Periodicals and the Business Periodicals Index. Once any file or category has been chosen, pressing the HOME key will cause a detailed description of its contents to be displayed on the screen.

```
            <  M A I N   M E N U  >

               1. WILSEARCH
               2. Overview of System
               3. Review Results of Last Search
               4. Direct Access to WILSONLINE
               5. Setup
               6. Quit
               7. Exit to DOS


      To make your selection, type a number, or use ↓↑ keys
      to highlight the desired option and hit the ↵ key.

      WILSEARCH will help you to search for authors/names,
      title and subject words, journal names, organizations,
      Dewey numbers, and dates in the WILSONLINE databases.
```

Wilsearch is a menu-driven search program intended for inexperienced searchers.

```
            < S E L E C T I O N   M E N U >

               1. Books
               2. Book Reviews
               3. Readers' Guide and Popular Literature
               4. Business and Legal Literature
               5. Science and Technology Literature
               6. Biology and Agriculture Literature
               7. Education Literature
               8. Art and Humanities Literature
               9. Social Sciences Literature
               a. Select Your Own WILSONLINE Databases
               b. Go to the RESTART MENU
               c. Quit

      To make your selection, type in a number or letter, or use
      ↓↑ keys to highlight the desired option and hit the ↵ key.

      With this you will search Business Periodicals Index
      and the Index to Legal Periodicals. Hit the HOME
      key for more detailed information.
```

Wilsearch provides detailed information about the database it supports from within the program.

Once a file has been selected, a screen designed to help the user create a strategy is displayed. The searcher can fill in authors' names, title words, subject words, journal titles, and other search keys on appropriate lines of the search screen. Each line on the query construction screen corresponds to a different searchable field of the selected database. As the searcher moves from one line to another, a display window explaining the proper form of entry can be seen at the bottom of the screen. At any point, pressing the HOME key will produce a more detailed explanation with examples. This and other tutorial features offered by *Wilsearch* make the program especially easy to use for the unitiated searcher. At any point during the program, it is possible to request a specific explanation of the search task being addressed.

```
       Enter your search request for    4. Business and Legal Literature

       Author/name

       Title words

       Subject words    /TELECOMMUTING
         2ND subject    ANY UNIONS LABOR EMPLOYEES BENEFITS
         3RD subject

       Journal Name
       Organization
       Dewey number
       Earliest date
       Latest date
              Type only on lines applicable to your search.  Hit⏎
              to go to the next line.  Hit HOME for entry instructions
              and examples.  Hit ESC to return to the SELECTION MENU.

              Type words on one or separate lines. Type ANY then
              like terms all on one line. Precede Wilson subject
              headings with a slash(/) each on a separate line.

              [End] End input & start search
```

Wilsearch provides a help window at each step of the query-building process.

The *Wilsearch* query construction module supports the OR as well as the AND logical operator. Synonymous terms for a single concept may be used to create a broad search facet by preceding them on the same line of the search screen with the word "ANY." Truncation and wild card characters are also supported. It is possible to limit the search to subject headings used in the Wilson indexes by preceding subject heading terms with a slash (/). In fact, using Wilson subject headings is the only way to search for multiple-term descriptor phrases or heading/subheading combinations.

Both Wilsonline and NLM use the same *ELHILL* software and neither supports the full-text proximity and adjacency features supported by most other search languages. The databases offered by both services rely very heavily on precoordinated heading/subheading combinations for index terms. Understanding the relationship between the printed products and the online files is vital to using both systems.

The Wilsonline indexes don't include abstracts, further reducing the likelihood of getting good results with a natural language strategy. Therefore, using the subject headings found in the printed Wilson indexes will greatly increase the likelihood of performing a successful search. Using the slash to indicate a subject term search is the only effective way to search for multiple-word index terms.

After a search has been formulated by filling in the blanks on the search screen, *Wilsearch* dials the Wilsonline computer and uploads and executes the stored profile. The batch approach is vulnerable to line noise. While testing both *Wilsearch* and *Grateful Med*, at least one search for each program blew up because of line noise. In situations where clients are able to perform their own searches and asked to pay for them, this could be a problem.

```
I am now using the telephone numbers and WILSEARCH ID
and password entered via "Setup" to access WILSONLINE.

If any number is busy or fails to bring a response, I
will automatically go to an alternate number if one
was given to me.
```

```
I am now dialing the WILSONLINE computer via: 8,5244094

If there is no response within 2 minutes, hit the ESC
key to go to the RESTART MENU.
```

Wilsearch logs on automatically.

As the search proceeds, the searcher is able to see displayed on the screen the number of items matching each line in the query. If there is a problem, the searcher has the option of directly viewing the strategy as it was reformatted by the program and sent to the host. This is a nice feature for the experienced searcher who wants to peek behind the scenes and examine the inner workings of the program.

```
Database(s): Business Periodicals Index(*)
             Index to Legal Periodicals(*)
(*) Copyright 1983 The H. W. Wilson Company.  All Rights Reserved.

   Step              Search Formulation                          #FOUND
     1     TELECOMMUTING:                                            79
     2     (bi) UNION# or LABOR or EMPLOYEE# or BENEFIT#          18553
     3     1 and 2                                                    9
```

```
Type in a number that does not exceed the total
number of references found, then hit the⏎ key.

9 reference(s) found.  How many do you want to see?
```

Wilsearch asks the user how many references to display.

Once a target set has been created, the user is asked to specify how many references he is interested in seeing. Each set of ten references is delivered for a fixed fee, which varies depending upon whether a prepayment agreement has been made. Without a prepayment agreement, the cost for each ten references is $5. With a prepayment option, depending upon the size of the advance deposit, the charge ranges from $1 to $3 per search. A search yielding no hits won't be charged to the searcher. The search manager also has the option, when configuring the program, of limiting the maximum number of references that can be downloaded during any single session.

After references have been downloaded, *Wilsearch* reformats them for printing and offers the searcher the option of printing them selectively. As each reference is displayed, the searcher, in addition to being given the option to print it, is asked if it is related to the topic in which she is interested. After the entire search has been reviewed, *Wilsearch* presents the searcher with a list of subject headings that were associated with the references in which she indicated an interest.

```
Based on the citations you responded yes to, the following subjects
may be of further interest to you:

    LABOR LAWS AND LEGISLATION
    TECHNOLOGY AND LABOR
    TELECOMMUTING
```

```
                        TYPE ANY KEY TO GO ON.


    End of Execution
```

Wilsearch analyzes records deemed relevant and extracts potential search terms.

This is a very useful feature, especially in situations where the printed Wilson indexes are not available as sources for potential search terms. After doing a preliminary search, the searcher can use the terms suggested by the program to achieve greater precision or higher recall than was initially achieved.

Wilsearch devotes attention to the higher-level aspects of the search process instead of focusing on the mechanics of communications and offline query construction. Tutorial material available from within the program adds to its value. It's also nice to finally see a micro program that addresses the problem of term selection. All of its features, when combined with a flat-rate pricing strategy, make *Wilsearch* especially appealing to search managers interested in establishing a program for client searchers.

Grateful Med

Grateful Med is NLM's friendly front-end for the Medline database. *Grateful Med* is esentially the same program as *Wilsearch*. Differences between the two programs reflect differences between the Medline database and the Wilsonline databases. *Grateful Med* adds some whistles and bells intended to take advantage of the structure of the Medline database. Until recently, anyone wanting to establish an account with Medline was required to complete an extensive training course. It was assumed that the NLM system was simply too complex to be used by someone who hadn't been properly trained. The training requirement was recently dropped. Now anyone can get a Medline account. The most likely reason for the change in policy is the availability of programs like *Grateful Med*.

Though programs like *Wilsearch* and *Grateful Med* are intended for client searchers, they may also find an audience among those experienced searchers who use NLM or Wilsonline less frequently than they use other systems. The searcher who never received NLM's Medline training course is now able to search the database with the assistance of *Grateful Med*. And the program only costs $30 and can be learned in less than an hour.

The *Grateful Med* manual is one of the simplest software manuals ever written. Ten or so large-type pages walk the user through the program; the rest of the manual is comprised of search tips and installation instructions. The program itself is so straightforward and easy to use that no further documentation is required.

Grateful Med does include a larger amount of tutorial material than *Wilsearch* includes. The greater complexity of the Medline database warrants the additional material. *Grateful Med* also permits and encourages downloading for postprocessing. Search results are automatically stored in a buffer and dumped in a disk file called OUTPUT. The output file can be renamed with DOS and then manipulated with a word processor or text editor. *Grateful Med* also permits the searcher to store search profiles that are initially placed in a file called SRCH. The SRCH file can also be renamed and edited in the same way the OUTPUT file can.

Anyone who has used NLM/ELHILL knows how unwieldy its printing commands can be. One of *Grateful Med*'s strongest features is its ability to generate a clean, clearly labeled printed product. The search product obtained from *Grateful Med* is a considerable improvement over the usual Medline printout. Nor does *Grateful Med* neglect the search process. It allows the experienced Medline searcher to take advantage of tree structures, subheadings, even pre-exploded terms. The searcher always has the option of limiting output to English. It is also possible to specify review articles only. Both techniques are suggested as ways to narrow a search that yields more than the expected number of hits.

Both *Grateful Med* and *Wilsearch* represent a substantial improvement over previous generations of microcomputer software for inexperienced searchers. Both programs have much to offer the experienced searcher as well. The main thing to remember when using these programs is the importance of taking advantage of MESH terms and Wilson subject headings when devising search strategies. Both programs move beyond the mechanistic approach taken by earlier software and allow the novice searcher to take advantage of more sophisticated system features as she gains experience.

The next generation of software for client searchers will move beyond describing databases and suggesting terms to selecting databases, querying them, and modifying the initial query based upon the client's perception of the results obtained. Truly powerful, experimental front-ends have not yet entered the micro arena. Personal computers haven't yet attained the storage and processing power to accommodate the more sophisticated front-ends. Let's look at some of them anyway. It is only a matter of time before micros will be able to handle the highest level of user friendly software.

GRATEFUL MED

A SEARCH ASSISTANT FOR MEDLINE & CATLINE

The GRATEFUL MED program allows you to select a database and then helps formulate a search on the MEDLARS system of the

United States National Library of Medicine

After the search has been formulated, the program calls the MEDLARS system and runs the search. After it has been run, the retrieved references to articles or books will be displayed for your review.

Version 1.0
Version Date: February 20, 1986

Copyright 1985 by Online Information International, Inc.

TYPE ANY KEY TO GO ON.

Grateful Med was developed to provide easy access to Medline.

INSTRUCTIONS FOR SEARCHING

1. The next two screens will let you select a file and enter a search.

2. To get help on these screens, hit the HOME key.

3. To start over, hit the escape(ESC) key.

4. After selecting, fill in ONLY the applicable lines on the form screen.

5. To go to the next line on the form, hit ENTER ,

6. To correct your errors, hit the D or DEL key.

7. The SEARCH SYSTEM reformats your input, if necessary.

THE SYSTEM DOES ONLY ONE SEARCH AT A TIME.

This system will formulate your search and run it on the MEDLARS system.

If you want to print these instructions, hit Shift-PrtSc .

TYPE ANY KEY TO GO TO THE NEXT STEP

Help screens are available at all levels of Grateful Med.

SELECT THE ACTION YOU WANT TO TAKE

1. Search recent journals (MEDLINE) using the form screen.

2. Search books (CATLINE) using the form screen.

3. Go directly to search bypassing the form.

4. Review results of last search again.

5. See the system overview description.

6. Run SETUP to enter new telephone numbers/login codes.

7. Quit

ENTER TOP ROW NUMBER OR FUNCTION KEY FOR YOUR CHOICE

Menus provide users with options including the ability to log on to Medline in native mode.

INPUT YOUR SEARCH
FILL IN THE APPLICABLE LINES, E.G., TYPE AUTHOR'S NAME IN THE AUTHOR LINE.
HIT ENTER TO GO TO NEXT LINE. FOR HELP HIT HOME . TO START OVER HIT ESC

AUTHOR/NAME

TITLE WORDS

SUBJECT WORDS

  2ND SUBJECT

  3RD SUBJECT

  4TH SUBJECT

ENGLISH ONLY

REVIEW ONLY

JOURNAL ABBREV

Grateful Med uses a workform approach to building a query.

```
                       INPUT YOUR SEARCH
        FILL IN THE APPLICABLE LINES, E.G., TYPE AUTHOR'S NAME IN THE AUTHOR LINE.
        HIT   ENTER   TO GO TO NEXT LINE. FOR HELP HIT   HOME . TO START OVER HIT   ESC

        AUTHOR/NAME
                               ENTER TITLE WORDS
        TITLE WORDS
                          ENTER ALTERNATIVE SUBJECT WORDS FOR THE FIRST CONCEPT.
        SUBJECT WORDS     laterality or handedness
                and       ENTER ALTERNATIVE WORDS FOR NEXT CONCEPT, IF ANY.
          2ND SUBJECT     autoimmune or immunology or embryology
                and       ENTER ALTERNATIVE WORDS FOR NEXT CONCEPT, IF ANY.
          3RD SUBJECT

          4TH SUBJECT
                          ENTER ANY CHARACTER TO SEARCH ONLY ENGLISH LANGUAGE.
        ENGLISH ONLY      y
                and       ANY CHARACTER FOR ONLY REVIEWS. USE HOME FOR DEFINITION.
        REVIEW ONLY
                          ENTER JOURNAL ABBREVIATION. USE HOME KEY FOR LIST.
        JOURNAL ABBREV

                    DO YOU WANT TO RETRIEVE THE ABSTRACTS (Y/N)?
```

Grateful Med places ORs between terms on each line and places ANDs between lines.

```
        SS 1 /C?
        USER:
        LATERALITY (mh) or LATERALITY (tw) or HANDEDNESS (mh) or HANDEDNESS (tw)

        PROG:
        SS (1) PSTG (1472)

        SS 2 /C?
        USER:
        AUTOIMMUNE (mh) or AUTOIMMUNE (tw) or IMMUNOLOGY (mh) or IMMUNOLOGY (tw) or

        PROG:
        CNT 2

        USER:
        EMBRYOLOGY (mh) or EMBRYOLOGY (tw)

        PROG:
        NP (AUTOIMMUNE (MH))
        SS (2) PSTG (1920)

        SS 3 /C?
        USER:
        1 and 2 and not for (1a)
```

Grateful Med allows its users to view the actual search transmitted to the host based on the search workform responses.

```
1                             MEDLINE
Salcedo JR; Spiegler BJ; Gibson E; Magilavy DB
The autoimmune disease systemic lupus erythematosus is not associated
with left-handedness.
Cortex 1985 Dec;21(4):645-7
Unique Identifier: 86134688


   Medical Subject Headings:
Adolescence
Child
Female
Human
Laterality
Learning Disorders--DIAGNOSIS
Lupus Erythematosus, Systemic--DIAGNOSIS
Male




     IS THIS ONE RELATED TO WHAT YOU WANT (Y/N/*)?
        HIT  *  TO PRINT WITHOUT STOPPING OR  ESC  TO END.
```

Grateful Med allows selective printing while analyzing records for possible search terms.

```
1                    BACK83
James WH
Twinning handedness and embryology.
Percept Mot Skills 1983 Jun;56(3):721-2
Unique Identifier:  83272820

Medical Subject Headings:

Embryo--PHYSIOLOGY
Female
Human
Laterality--PHYSIOLOGY
Pregnancy
Twins, Monozygotic


1                    BACK80
Marx JL
Autoimmunity in left-handers. Left-handedness may be associated with an
increased risk of autoimmune disease. Is testosterone the link between
the two? [news]
Science 1982 Jul 9;217(4555):141-2,4
Unique Identifier:  82223773

Medical Subject Headings:

Animal
Autoimmune Diseases--PHYSIOPATHOLOGY
Brain--EMBRYOLOGY--PATHOLOGY--PHYSIOLOGY
Dyslexia--PATHOLOGY
Female
Human
Laterality
Learning Disorders--COMPLICATIONS
Major Histocompatibility Complex
Male
Rats
```

Grateful Med allows storing a search profile and running it against backfiles.

References/Recommended Reading

Fenichel, Carol Hansen. "The Process of Searching Online Bibliographic Databases: A Review of Research." *Library Research* 2, no.2 (Summer 1980): 107-127.

King, Joseph, and Peter Brueggeman. "Matrix of Frontend Software, Gateways, and User-Friendly Systems." *Database End-User* 2, no.6, 20-21.

O'Leary, Mike. "Gateway Software to the Information Stars." *PC Magazine*, 20 August 1980, 181-188.

Tenopir, Carol. "Software for Online Searching." *Library Journal*, 15 October 1985, 52-53.

CHAPTER THIRTEEN
EXPERT SYSTEMS AND THE SEARCHER

Some of the most interesting research going on right now involves the development of expert systems for information retrieval. While the majority of experimental systems described in the literature have been mounted on mainframes, they are still of interest to the PC owner. Small computer hardware is evolving at such a rapid pace that programs based upon research now being done should soon be available as personal computer tools. Already programs like *Sci-Mate*, *SearchWorks*, and *Wilsearch* incorporate features first seen on experimental front-ends.

Expert systems are mostly directed toward the novice searcher. If everyone were an expert, there would be no need for these systems. Mediation takes place at a higher level. The search process is treated at a conceptual level, not an electrical level. Certainly there are levels of these programs which handle electrical information, but way above them are layers which are concerned with the meaning of the interaction. Expert systems, because they work in a more ambiguous area--some would call it a fuzzy area--require substantially more computing power. The developers of expert systems are as concerned with searcher behavior and the psychology of searching as they are with the syntax of search languages.

Expert system programs are nonlinear. The program is able to respond in a purposeful way to messages coming in from the host and messages from the searcher. Each expert system is different because each is closely bound to the task it's assigned to perform. An ideal expert system for online searching would provide the same kind of mediation provided by an expert human. The program would be able to deal equally well with the syntax and structure of the retrieval system and the subject being investigated.

Expert system programs depend upon heuristics rather than algorithms. Emphasis is on the general rules of thumb followed by an expert searcher as he interacts with an online system. An attempt is made to mimic the thought process of the skilled searcher. The "rules" for good searching are stored in a knowledge base that is comprised of a series of IF ... THEN propositions intended to cover all of the possible situations a searcher may encounter. For example, the following rules might be associated with an unexpectedly high number of hits:

If the initial search results in too many hits:

- eliminate terms from OR clauses
- try limiting to the descriptor and title fields

- look for more precise descriptor terms

If more precise descriptors are needed:

- expand the basic index
- expand the online thesaurus
- create a narrow set with a full-text strategy and examine some records in a searcher's format

Along with the knowledge base are problem-solving strategies--gambits that have proven successful in the past. Principles of artificial intelligence are applied to enable the program to add to its knowledge base and list of rules. The ideal expert system for searching would be capable of "learning" which strategies yielded the best results in different search millieus and would be able to take advantage of knowledge gained through experience.

Microcomputer front-ends do most of their work in the offline mode. The program interacts with the searcher. The online system is usually approached in a batch mode. The current crop of front-ends are able to respond to messages from the searcher but unable to take initiative and respond to any but the simplest messages from the host computer. Programs such as *Grateful Med* that analyze records identified as relevant and extract possible search terms from them are moving in the right direction. An expert system would not only identify search terms, but act upon them, modifying the initial strategy and sending appropriate messages to both the host system and the human inquirer.

An Expert Query Translator

Front-ends for PCs address the problems of query building and file handling. Expert systems address higher-level problems. Programs such as *Sci-Mate* begin to address the problem of what Gerard Salton calls "language normalization." The electronic world brain we're working with today is a conglomeration of data structures and retrieval languages. We have seen the problems associated with confusion over standards at the lower levels of computing. There have been eloquent pleas for a universal search language. So far there is no Esperanto for searchers. Automatic translation is one of the tasks addressed by expert systems.

The CONIT system developed by Marcus at MIT was one of the first attempts to provide searchers with a common retrieval language. Users of CONIT were able to talk to NLM, SDC, and DIALOG with a single virtual system. CONIT also provided search aids for specific databases. Instruction relating to searching was also provided. Instruction was provided in stages. The most basic search commands were introduced first. Additional capabilities were explained as they were needed by the searcher.

CONIT's performance compared favorably to the performance of skilled searchers in a series of controlled experiments. CONIT generally achieved higher recall of relevant items while suffering from longer connect times. Marcus and his colleagues are now working on an expert system based upon CONIT. The name of CONIT's descendent is EXPERT.

An Expert Tutor

Almost all of the personal computer front-ends include a certain amount of tutorial material. Some even provide context-sensitive help. IIDA (Individualized Instruction for Data Access), an experimental program developed at Drexel University by C.T. Meadow and others, goes considerably beyond the instructional capabilities provided by PC front-ends. IIDA used the CONIT hardware and software to connect graduate students and industrial engineers to the DIALOG system. CONIT's cross system translation capabilities weren't required, since DIALOG was the only service supported by IIDA.

IIDA added tutorial material and search assistance features to CONIT's capabilities. In its offline instructional mode, IIDA provided computer-assisted instruction in the basics of online searching. In its online assistance mode, IIDA helped the inquirer with a DIALOG search. IIDA was designed to analyze search technique, recognize faults, and suggest more appropriate or productive strategies. The program is able to diagnose simple problems like syntax errors. However, its most impressive feature is its ability to diagnose and suggest remedies for larger strategic problems like creating too many sets or failing to display potential target sets. In the assistance mode, the search is analyzed as it progresses; problems are recognized and possible solutions are presented. Help is offered only when the program perceives it is needed by comparing rules for searching to the content of a specific search.

IIDA maintains a history of each search--storing both messages sent by the inquirer and received from the host. A record of all sets created is kept. The search history is analyzed to diagnose problems with search technique. A record is also kept of actions taken by the searcher that resulted in fault diagnostics being triggered. Though its primary purpose was to serve as a teaching/learning tool, IIDA also proved useful as an intermediary for untrained searchers.

SAM and FRED

It seems that many front-ends have names that are acronyms and acronyms that are names. Ol' SAM (Online Database Search Assistance Machine) was among the first of the front-ends to take advantage of microcomputer technology. Ol' SAM was developed by David Toliver and marketed by the Franklin Institute in Philadelphia. Toliver, who had worked with Meadow on IIDA, later went on to become manager for development at ISI. There is no denying that Philadelphia has been a hot bed for research and development of front-end systems. Ol' SAM ran on a NorthStar microcomputer and included diagnostic features, conference searching with two terminals, and a virtual language for connecting to NLM, SDC, and DIALOG. In 1982, the programs sold for $995.

Among the other pioneers in PC front-ends was CAST (Chemical Abstracts Searching Terminal), a specialized hardware/software package for searching the Chemical Abstracts database. Another early micro-based front-end was UserKit, a hardware/software package developed in Great Britain by P.W. Williams.

FRED (Front End for Databases) was a prototype front-end described by computer scientists at GTE in 1982. One of the capabilities proposed for FRED was the ability to "select target databases automatically based on information in the user query," a pretty neat trick. FRED was comprised of a user interface subsystem, a database interface subsystem, and a knowledge base.

Content Analysis

CONIT was designed to connect to several different databases and systems. Consequently it employed a natural langauge approach to searching. Other programs attempt to take advantage of controlled vocabularies used by many databases. Such programs assist in the search process by analyzing the content of the search and helping the searcher select and combine search terms.

A considerable amount of research and development has focused on the problems of term selection. P.W. Williams developed a system that emphasizes the processing of search output. Williams's system was designed to improve recall by extracting potential search words and phrases from the database being used. The system, which combines search assistance and search analysis features, was most recently known as UserLink. Williams was among the first to see the potential of the personal computer for dealing with the higher-level problems faced by searchers. An earlier version of UserLink called UserKit was marketed as a hardware/software package just as CAST was. The more recent trend (since IBM became a dominant force) is to design software for IBM-compatible machines and sell it separately at a much lower cost.

Term selection is one of the toughest problems faced by those seeking to automate the search process. One approach has been to store the indexes and thesauri for a number of files in a single program that is able to map natural language terms onto terms from an appropriate controlled vocabulary. Another approach requires judgment calls that are now beyond the ken of the machine. Such an approach requires a human to be included in the loop. Almost always the searcher is asked to select relevant items from the output of an initial search. The contents of those items are then subjected to analysis by the program. Two analytical approaches have been taken: a statistical approach and a linguistic approach.

The statistical approach is more typical. A frequency table of terms associated with records deemed relevant is generated. Unfortunately, the frequency with which a term appears in relevant documents is no certain indication of the value of using that term to increase the yield of relevant documents while eliminating irrelevant items. As programs like *Grateful Med* are showing, the technique does help to improve recall. When used with a database employing a consistently applied controlled vocabulary, the approach can be very useful for identifying terms which will yield relevant material.

Full text or more loosely indexed files may be more appropriate for linguistic analysis. The computer is programmed to parse sentences and analyze text. An attempt is made to understand the meaning of different classes of terms and the relationships between them. However, the computer processing required to "understand" natural language is far more complex than that required to statistically analyze term frequencies. Salton differentiates between database management, bibliographic retrieval, and question-answering systems. As bibliographic files are supplemented by full-text files, there is bound to be a greater interest in programs which help inquirers extract "answers" to questions by analyzing textual material. A project developed at the National Library of Medicine centered around the development of a Hepatitis Knowledge Base, which was intended to provided answers to questions concerning hepatitis.

Practical solutions to problems of relevance and recall are made more difficult by the nature of commercially available databases and search systems. The data structures and search languages of today were developed for the technology of twenty years ago. Each database uses a different way of organizing and describing its contents.

The type of Boolean searching used by most online systems can be unforgiving in its rigidity. Salton and others have experimented with automatic query formulation. One of the major problem areas has been the inability of Boolean logic to accommodate the ambiguity of the process by which humans determine relevance. Salton points out that an OR clause including several terms will give the same consideration to an item including only a single term as it does to an item including all of them. An AND clause will eliminate the item missing just one of the AND'ed terms along with items containing none of them. Boolean searching, unlike the type of searching done by humans examining printed indexes, is often an all or nothing proposition.

Various attempts have been made to weight search terms and rank search output. For a long time now, searchers have been using tricks such as limiting to a specific field or using proximity operators to build a highly precise, natural-language search phrase. Experimental programs have assigned weights to terms based upon their frequency of occurrence. Infrequently occurring terms are assumed to be more meaningful and are assigned higher weights. Complex algorithms are used to calculate relevancy values for retrieved documents. Among the microcomputer front-ends *SearchWorks* allows offline ranking of search results based upon term weights assigned by the searcher.

Another interesting approach to ranking search output and compensating for deficiencies of Boolean logic incorporates what is known as fuzzy set theory. Mathematical models are used to assign ranks to items that overlap only partially with the precise specifications of a Boolean query. Items are assigned numeric values based on the degree of relevance calculated by the system. Both Salton and Bartschii provide excellent overviews of fuzzy set retrieval and other efforts to automate the search process.

Another area of concern for the developers of expert systems is the creation of user interfaces that are suitable for both the novice and the skilled searcher. Of all the problems associated with expert systems for searching, this is the one that lends itself most readily to being solved with microcomputer technology. Burns and Robinson have proposed a multilevel adaptable user interface that is able to guage the needs of the user and present an appropriate mode of interaction based upon its appraisal. The inexperienced searcher would be provided with extensive menus and help screens while the experienced searcher would be required to use a minimum number of keystrokes.

Scott Preece and Martha E. Williams developed at the University of Illinois a prototype microcomputer system for online searching. Called The Searcher's Workbench (TSW), it incorporates many of the features found in other expert systems. Among the software tools proposed for the Searcher's Workbench are a "single interface to various search systems and user aids . . . tutorial capabilities and search behavior monitoring," the ability to reformat and merge output from several databases, and direct access to "a family of vocabulary access tools" and a "database Selector."

TSW is a screen-oriented system that allows input from a touch pad on the screen as well as from the keyboard. A special window on the screen is reserved for "query results, user options, and result citations." A single uniform interface is proposed for the searcher who really needn't be concerned with the particular system or file being used. Williams and Preece designed a *Smalltalk*-like language to handle search tasks.

> A complete TSW would be implemented as a set of objects and rules for their intercommunication. One such object would be the user interface, and it would request services from objects corresponding to hardware and software components. Further standardization would be incorporated so that adding new features would amount to defining them in high level terms.

Peter Noerr and Kathleen Bivins Noerr are also working on a microcomputer device that would provide a user interface for the searcher. Called the Electronic Scroll, it would also apply the principles of object-oriented programming to the interaction of a searcher at a micro with a database in a remote computer.

Full-text, numeric, and directory databases, many of which are intended to provide the information end-user with one-stop online shopping, are also likely to have an impact on the user interface. Summit and Meadow point out that an increase in the number of sources as opposed to bibliographic files, will result in better search systems, improved methods of presentation and display, and greater postprocessing capabilities. Developments in the database industry are likely to have implications in other areas. The way in which electronic information is produced, distributed, and consumed has changed radically since personal computers made their appearance.

Technology is affecting the economics of the industry. It is beyond the scope of this book to analyze legal and economic issues with the depth they deserve. However those developments prompted by the PC cannot be ignored.

References/Recommended Reading

Bartschi, Martin. "An Overview of Information Retrieval Subjects." *Computer* 18, no.5 (May 1985): 67-84.

Bates, Marcia J. "The Fallacy of the Perfect Thirty-Item Online Search." *RQ* 24, no.1 (Fall 1984): 43-50.

Bernstein, LM; Siegel, ER; Goldstein, CM. "The Hepatitis Knowledge Base: A Prototype Information Transfer System." *Annals of Internal Medicine* 43, no.1 (1980): 165-222.

Burns, A. and J. Robinson. "Tools and Techniques for Adaptable User Interface Development." In *Online Information Meeting* (8th International, London England, December 1984), 255-262. Medford, NJ: Learned Information, 1984.

Crystal, Maurice I. ""FRED, a Front End for Databases." *Online* (September 1982): 27-30.

Fidel, Raya. "Online Searching Styles: A Case-Study Based Model of Searching Behavior." *Journal of the American Society for Information Science* 35, no.4 (July 1984): 211-221.

Harter, Stephen P. "Online Searching Styles: An Exploratory Study." *College and Research Libraries* (July 1984): 249-258.

Marcus, Richard S. "An Experimental Comparison of the Effectiveness of Computers and Humans as Search Intermediaries." *Journal of the American Society for Information Science* 34, no.6 (November 1983): 381-404.

Meadow, Charles T., et al. "A Computer Intermediary for Interactive Database Searching. I. Design." *Journal of the American Society for Information Science* 33 (September 1982): 325-332.

_____. "A Computer Intermediary for Interactive Database Searching. II. Evaluation." *Journal of the American Society for Information Science* 33 (November 1982): 357-364.

Noerr, Peter, and Kathleen Bivins Noerr. "The Electronic Scroll." In *The Application of Mini- and Micro-Computers in Information, Documentation, and Libraries*, edited by C. Keren, and L. Perlmutter, 41-53. Elsevier, North-Holland, 1983.

Preece, Scott E., and Martha E. Williams. "Software for the Searcher's Workbench." In *American Society for Information Science, Proceedings of the 43rd Annual Meeting*, 403-405. ASIS, 1980.

Salton, G. "Some Characteristics of Future Information Systems." In *The Application of Mini- and Micro-Computers in Information, Documentation, and Libraries*, edited by C. Keren, and L. Perlmutter, 11-22. Elsevier, North-Holland, 1983.

Summit, Roger K., and Charles T. Meadow. "Emerging Trends in the Online Industry." *Special Libraries* (Spring 1985): 90-92

Toliver, David E. "OL'SAM: An Intelligent Front-End for Bibliographic Information Retrieval." *Information Technology and Libraries* (December 1982): 317-326.

Vigil, Peter J. "The Psychology of Online Searching." *Journal of the American Society for Information Science* 34, no.4 (July 1983): 281-287.

Williams, PW. "A Model for an Expert System for Automated Information Retrieval." In *Online Information Meeting* (8th International, London England, December 1984), 139-149. Medford, NJ: Learned Information, 1984.

_____. "Recent Developments in the Use of Microcomputers to Access Online Systems." *The Application of Mini- and Micro-Computers in Information, Documentation, and Libraries*, edited by C. Keren, and L. Perlmutter, 645-653. Elsevier, North-Holland, 1983.

Yaghmai, N. Shahla, and Jacqueline A. Maxin. "Expert Systems: A Tutorial." *Journal of the American Society for Information Science* 35, no.5 (September 1984): 297-305.

CHAPTER FOURTEEN
DATABASE PRODUCTS FOR MICRO USERS

Online/Offline

We've seen how the expanded use of personal computers has increased the number of potential customers for online services. We've also seen a host of new software products for microcomputers --tools that enhance or compete with capabilities previously provided only by online search services. Functions once offered only as services by centralized mainframe computers are now being taken over by software products at the local level. Now we are seeing another consequence of the end-user phenomenon. There is a fundamental change in the way electronic information is being distributed. Databases themselves are being offered as microcomputer products. Personal computers are encroaching upon what had previously been the exclusive domain of the centralized mainframe. Information raw material that used to come in over the wires can now be purchased directly and stored locally.

The first databases for micros didn't appear to present any threat to the online giants. The first mammals probably weren't perceived as a threat by the huge reptiles with which they co-existed. The first personal computer databases were small subsets of much larger online files--subsets that were delivered on floppy disks.

The idea of the database subset on a disk has obvious appeal both for individuals and for libraries. The database subset places the data and the software for searching it on the same medium. The cost is usually fixed and known in advance. The database--once it's been physically delivered--is under the complete control of its purchaser. There are no surprises when the invoice arrives. Client searchers can be provided with unlimited access to the database. Mistakes or hesitancy at the terminal need no longer be intimidating or expensive.

Database subsets are generally prepackaged to reflect a subtopic of the larger subject dealt with by the mother file. Occasionally it is possible to store a profile with a database producer and subscribe to a database subset that is custom-designed to match the profile. The customized file approach has particular appeal to the individual researcher or the special library. BIOSIS is among the database producers that offer customized subsets on floppy disks.

ERIC MICROsearch

ERIC *MICROsearch* was the first of the database subsets to be developed for personal computer users. ERIC began development of its micro product in 1980. At that time, the number of PCs in the educational institutions that were ERIC's major clients was increasing exponentially. Along with the increasing number of micros came an increasing interest among information consumers in direct access to the ERIC database. MICROsearch represented a way of alleviating the high costs and the learning difficulties associated with client searching of traditional online services. MICROsearch was originally developed for the Apple II, which had come to dominate the educational market. In 1985, a faster, more powerful version was introduced for the IBM.

The IBM version of *MICROsearch* requires a software disk, which sells for $34, and a database disk. Database disks are provided for two broad subject areas, appropriately, Educational Technology and Library/Information Science. Database disks are issued quarterly and sold on a subscription basis. Depending upon the number of items added to the ERIC database, each subject area will be covered by one or more disks each quarter. Each disk holds approximately 575 citations (not including abstracts) and sells for $10. It is also possible to purchase a demonstration set including the program disk, the manual, and one database disk for $49.

Database disks include citations along with three inverted indexes: a basic index, an index of descriptors, and an author index. The inverted files are similar to those employed by centralized online services. Abstracts were not included due to floppy disk storage limitations.

MICROsearch is another example of a menu-driven program that prompts its users to enter search specifications. Windows and highlighting, popular features of many programs nowadays, are also employed. Pressing the F1 function key will generate a help message related to the current task being addressed by the program. Pressing the key labeled F2 yields an explanation of the keys used by the program for different tasks.

A command line on the screen gives the user the opportunity to highlight the desired search option. Depending upon which option is selected, the program will display additional prompts. If the Find option is selected for example, a list of indexes will be displayed and the searcher will be given a chance to select the Basic, Descriptor, or Author index, or to Expand the Basic Index that is the default. As a query is constructed, the terms selected are displayed at the bottom of the screen along with their logical connectors. The program does not permit manipulation of stored sets. As each operation is performed, the contents of the target set are changed. The Combine command permits full Boolean AND, OR, NOT logic. In addition, search features like truncation and expanding an index are permitted.

```
ERIC MICROsearch    Version 2.0
Find  Combine  Show  New  Quit  Options
Change search strategy (author/descriptor/title)
```

```
Current index              Occurrences
Search strategy
D[Current Drive: A]
```

ERIC MICROsearch, since it uses highlighting and windows, is difficult to represent on the printed page.

```
ERIC MICROsearch    Version 2.0
Find  Combine  Show  New  Quit  Options
Combine words with operators NOT/AND/OR
        OR
        AND
        NOT
```

```
Current index BASIC         Occurrences 6
Search strategy  B:TELECOMMUNICATIONS OR B:COMMUNICATIONS OR B:ONLINE AND B:SOFTWARE
D[Current Drive: A
```

ERIC MICROSearch supports full Boolean searching.

248 Microcomputers for the Online Searcher

ERIC MICROsearch   Version 2.0

Find Combine Show New Quit Options

Show current records

        Short Form

        Long Form

        Print All

        Store

Current index BASIC   Occurrences 6
Search strategy   B:TELECOMMUNICATIONS OR B:COMMUNICATIONS OR B:ONLINE AND B:SOFTWARE
D[Current Drive: A]

MICROSearch permits search results to be displayed in one of three formats or stored in a file.

    Eric Number: EJ322503
    Title: Software Tools: A One-Semester Secondary School Computer Course.
    Author: Bromley, John;Lakatos, John
    Journal: Computing Teacher;v13 n1 p21-23 Aug-Sep 1985
    Descriptor: Computer Graphics;*Computer Literacy;Computer Software;*Course Content;Course Descriptions;Merchandise Information;*Microcomputers;Secondary Education;Student Evaluation;Telecommunications;Word Processing
    Identifier: Apple IIe;Integrated Software;Operating Systems;Spreadsheets

    Eric Number: EJ322621
    Title: Software Reviews.
    Author: Smith, Richard L., Ed.
    Journal: Journal of Computers in Mathematics and Science Teaching;v4 n3 p60-67 Spr 1985
    Descriptor: Anatomy;*Biology;*Computer Software;*Elementary School Mathematics;Elementary Secondary Education;*Fractions;Laboratory Animals;Mathematics Education;Science Education;*Secondary School Science;*Telecommunications
    Identifier: *Frogs;Software Reviews

    Eric Number: ED257442
    Title: An Economic Assessment of Electronic Text. Report Number Six of the Electronic Text Report Series.
    Author: Carey, John
    Descriptor: Computer Software;Cost Effectiveness;*Cost Estimates;Databases;Higher Education;*Information Networks;*Information Services;Information Systems;Surveys;*Telecommunications;Teleconferencing;Use Studies;*Videotex
    Identifier: *Electronic Mail;*Electronic Publishing

    Eric Number: ED258543
    Title: Information Society and General Education.
    Author: Lariccia, Giovanni;Megarry, Jacquetta
    Descriptor: *Computer Literacy;Computer Software;Developed Nations;Educational Development;Equal Education;*Information Science;Microcomputers;Museums;Program Descriptions;Programing Languages;School Business Relationship;*Sociocultural Patterns;Teacher Education;Telecommunications;Videotex
    Identifier: *Information Society;LOGO Programing Language

Records on communications software from the ERIC MICROSearch educational technology database

At any point the searcher can request a display of items in the target set by choosing the Show option. The searcher can then select the Short Form, which displays only author and title, or the Long Form, which displays the full bibliographic record. The New command erases the current search and allows the client to begin a new one.

Although it doesn't have the fanciest typography, the manual is clearly written, but this kind of program is so simple to use that a manual is hardly required. Like many screen-oriented programs that feature highlighting and windows, ERIC *MICROsearch* is easier to use than it is to describe. There is something about the dynamic nature of the screen display that makes it difficult to write about without becoming excessively verbose. Nor is it easy to illustrate the program by dumping the screen display to the printer. The interaction encouraged by the program is not evident in a picture of one of its screens on a printed page.

The database subset may not be large enough for any but the most specialized application and serious searching would probably require continually moving disks in and out of the machine. Nonetheless, low-cost alternatives to online searching should be welcomed. *MICROsearch* holds special promise as an inexpensive way to teach clients through experience, the principles of Boolean searching. For those in the educational and library/information science fields, it offers the added bonus of being an inexpensive, micro-based current awareness service.

MICROsearch databases are sold on a subscription basis, eliminating the cost uncertainties that have been the major obstacle to widespread acceptance of online searching. At only $10 for almost 600 citations, it represents one of the all-time bargains among electronic information products.

BIOSIS B-I-T-S

Not too long after *MICROsearch* was introduced, BIOSIS, another major database producer launched a floppy disk product called *B-I-T-S* (for BIOSIS-Information-Transfer-System). *B-I-T-S*, which made its debut in 1983, offers a fuller product line and a somewhat more flexible approach. *B-I-T-S* offers some seventeen or so subject subsets called pre-profiles. *B-I-T-S* pre-profiles cover topics ranging from weed control to human immunopharmacology. Other topics covered are as diverse as poultry science, aging, and sexually transmitted diseases.

Floppy disks covering the selected topics are issued on a monthly instead of quarterly basis. In addition to prepackaged subject profiles, *B-I-T-S* provides its customers with the opportunity to develop a customized profile. The results from executing the profile are delivered on a floppy disk. Once again, we see the familiar macro--script--template--custom-design idea being associated with personal computers. This time the customized entity is a floppy disk full of information instead of a bunch of instructions or a structure in which to place data.

B-I-T-S is not the low-cost product ERIC *MICROsearch* is. Nor is there any way to know in advance how much each monthly update will cost. Costs are levied on a unit-of-information basis rather than as a flat rate subscription. Charges include a fee of $2.70 for each disk and $.44 for each record accompanied by an abstract or $.22 for each record without an abstract. Buy more than ten thousand citations and the price drops to $.33 for each citation with an abstract or $.17 for each basic bibliographic record.

The software to search and manipulate the data on the disks is called *BioSuperfile* and costs $100. It's impossible to tell in advance how much a custom profile or for that matter a pre-profile will cost. BIOSIS will prepare a free estimate for those interested in developing a custom profile. If research suddenly heats up in a profile's subject area or interest subsides, the cost of *B-I-T-S* will fluctuate accordingly. It is not unusual for *B-I-T-S* customers to receive twelve disks a month. At $2.70 per disk, the $32.40 the disks cost is nowhere near the $600 or so the information on them is likely to cost.

Both ERIC *MICROsearch* and *B-I-T-S* are delivered on floppy disks via the mail. Disks are probably produced at the "database factory" by uploading the records matching the profile at high rates of speed (probably 9600 baud or higher). Predefined profiles can be mass produced once the original set of disks has been mastered. An alternative mode of delivery would involve a high-speed, off-hours upload from the vendor's computer to the subscriber's micro. Speed limits imposed by packet-switching networks have thus far made this approach impractical.

A Software/Database Alliance

A minor variation on the database subset theme is the alliance between the producers of the Cumulative Index to Nursing and Allied Health Literature and Knowledge Access Inc., a California-based software house. Knowledge Access, developer of the *KAware* retrieval system supplies the retrieval software, and CINAHL supplies the database subset on floppy disk. The resulting product, called NURSEARCH will become available on an annual subscription basis beginning in the summer of 1986. Knowledge Access also cooperated with Database Services, the current producer of Microcomputer Index, to produce a one-shot index to software reviews derived from the 1984 Microcomputer Index database. Knowledge Access is an example of a software producer that develops retrieval software designed to work with floppy disk subsets from a variety of database producers.

The floppy disk subset has the potential to become an important component of a personal information system. The predefined subset can be viewed as a prefabricated house in our city of information. The institutional information consumer or the individual with the right kind of hardware storage capacity could upload information from floppies onto a locally controlled mass storage medium. Eventually a rather large, specialized database could be created (though no where near as large as the mother file). The customized database derived from a single commercial database could be supplemented by an occasional citation search or interdisciplinary foray into another commercial file. It is also now possible to subscribe to a much larger database or database subset. The optical storage media which make this possible could end up becoming major structures in our city of information.

Optical Publishing

Optical storage technology has been the subject of much speculation in the online literature. There are many who contend that optical publishing portends the end of the online database as we know it. There is no denying that optical storage media provide database producers with the opportunity to deliver database products directly to information consumers, who can search them at leisure on local microcomputers. Whether or not optical products will allow database producers to distribute their wares directly to end-users remains to be seen. It seems as if both online vendors and libraries will continue to play a role as mediators between information users and stores of electronic information. The major customers for optical products are the same institutions that have traditionally been the customers of online services.

Optical storage technology has been around for awhile. And it has been associated with microcomputers for just about the whole time. Optical storage and retrieval is the perfect example of a hybrid technology. One of the first commercial systems, Video

PATSEARCH, which was developed for Pergamon International of McLean, Virginia, is illustrative of the degree of hybridization in the field. Video PATSEARCH linked a traditional online database to a microcomputer and a videodisc player.

Video PATSEARCH was designed to provide electronic access to 750,000 patent documents. A system was required that would provide multiple access points to the full text of patent records located in the PATSEARCH database. Since patent records are accompanied by drawings or chemical structure diagrams, it was also necessary for the system to provide access to the graphic images associated with each patent. Microfiche was considered as a storage medium for patent graphics, but the idea was abandoned in favor of videodisc, an optical storage technology that allows computerized access.

A specially designed microcomputer was developed to solve the problem of delivering both text and images while permitting multiple access points. Searching and telecommunications were emphasized along with graphics display capabilities. The hardware/software front-end provided 1200-baud communication with the mainframe computer in which were stored the 750,000 textual patent records. Drawings and chemical structure graphics (750,000 of them!) were stored locally on a set of eight videodiscs. Software mounted on the micro provided a front-end to the PATSEARCH database and the capability to match records obtained from the online service to graphic material stored locally on a videodisc. Each videodisc was able to store approximately 100,000 graphic images. Software on the host computer provided the search capabilities and multiple access points required for the text records on the mainframe. Two separately located but related stores of information were thus integrated functionally, if not physically. The system enabled its users to view images and text separately or mixed together. Its users didn't have to be concerned with the physical source from which information was obtained. The micro solved the problem of providing a transparent means of supplying the user with both the image and the text contained in every patent record.

Optical technology is also being used commercially as a medium for stand-alone databases. The Information Access Company, whose *Search Helper* was one of the first front-ends directed toward client searchers, was also among the first to introduce a database product based upon optical technology. Instead of employing the more standard 4.75-inch CD-ROM discs, IAC's InfoTrac product is distributed on a twelve-inch laser disc. The laser disc was chosen because high demand for CD-ROMs by the recording industry had resulted in production backlogs among the companies that mastered the disks. The InfoTrac database is issued monthly and IAC, which wanted to assure the timeliness of its product, was unwilling to accept the delays associated with CD-ROM.

InfoTrac is marketed as a hardware/software/database subscription package. The complete package includes:

- A monthly subscription to the InfoTrac database. The database arrives in the mail on a twelve-inch laser disc that resembles a long-playing record album. The disk has a capacity of approximately 800 megabytes and includes approximately 500,000 citations derived from IAC's family of databases. The index is cumulated monthly and covers close to five year's worth of periodical literature.
- Software on a floppy disk that allows clients to search the InfoTrac database.
- Up to four workstations, each consisting of an IBM PC and a Hewlett-Packard ThinkJet printer.
- A security enclosure for each PC workstation from DOSS industries of California.
- A laser disc player and controller manufactured by LaserData Inc. of Cambridge, Massachusetts.
- A cabinet for the laser disc hardware as well as all necessary cables and connectors.

The InfoTrac configuration consists of IBM PCs, an optical disk player, and a silent printer.

The price of the standard four-workstation configuration is a hefty $16,000 per year for the first five years. After the five years, the workstations become the property of the subscriber and the price drops to $9,500 a year, $8,000 for the database subscription and $1,500 for maintenance and updates on the disk player and search software. Upon initial purchase, IAC will install the system to the purchaser's specifications. It is possible to place workstations in separate locations, though all must be connected to the disc player by cables having a maximum length of one hundred feet. It is also possible to connect more than one disk player to the system, allowing clients to connect to more than one database. IAC promises additional databases, each of which will be sold as a separate subscription. Right now the full text of the *Wall Street Journal* is also available. IAC also promises to replace disk players as improvements to the technology become available. The software was designed to be compatible with CD-ROM. As CD-ROM mastering delays decrease, perhaps we'll see InfoTrac being issued in the more standard format.

The search software is simple to use when compared with the more sophisticated programs mounted by online services. Clients are prompted to enter the information required by the program. A set of simple instructions are printed on a panel that is attached by velcro to the front of each PC workstation. The PC's function keys are used to control the action. Specially labeled plastic caps have been glued to the top of the function keys to indicate the operations those keys have been preconfigured to perform. A search is begun by entering a subject word in a box on the screen and pressing the RETURN key, which has been relabeled as the SEARCH key.

Almost instantly, a list of citations associated with the search term is displayed. The process is a breeze when compared to the time-consuming and failure-prone mechanical process of searching Magazine Index and IAC's other microfilm indexes. Each citation is preceded by an equal sign. Function keys enable the searcher to scroll up or down through the list, either one line at a time or one screen at a time. Other function keys permit the searcher to print a single citation or an entire page.

Boolean searching is not provided for, but an online thesaurus of sorts and extensive use of precoordinated heading/subheading terms eliminate most of the problems caused by the lack of Boolean capabilities. In fact, the lack of Boolean capabilities can be viewed as a blessing in disguise, since a nonBoolean system is so much easier to learn for novice searchers. Pressing the function key labeled Subject Guide causes a list of index terms without their accompanying citations to be displayed. IAC's controlled vocabulary is based on the Library of Congress Subject Headings, making InfoTrac easier to use for those who are already acquainted with the LC system. Cross-references are displayed for terms with which they are associated and moving from an entry term to a SEE or SEE ALSO reference is as simple as positioning the cursor on the term referred to and pressing the SEARCH key. The searcher can jump back and forth through the database with surprising speed. Response time is often faster than it is with an online system that is being shared by many more then four users.

The database itself is derived from IAC's online files and is updated and cumulated monthly. Its orientation is toward business literature, though more general sources, such as those indexed in Magazine Index, are also covered. Emphasis is on the serious researcher. For example, many of the homemakers' magazines covered by Magazine Index have been dropped by InfoTrac. Newspapers are covered, though the level of retrospective coverage provided for other sources isn't available. Citations to newspaper articles are regularly purged from the file to leave room on the disk for other material. The assumption behind the policy is that the topics treated in newspaper articles will eventually be covered by other sources if they are truly important. Newspaper citations can be a problem, however. Most libraries buy microfilm of the New York edition of the *New York Times*. InfoTrac indexes the national edition, resulting in inaccurate citations, frustrated clients, and damaged microfilm.

Another source of frustration is the difficulty of obtaining some of the sources covered by InfoTrac. A large number of records are derived from IAC's Trade and Industry Index and Local Business Databank, both sources of specialized business data. If one subscribes to IAC's expensive microfilm Business Collection, many of them are obtainable. Otherwise, it's nearly impossible to obtain some of the more esoteric titles covered. Those in libraries should expect InfoTrac to place a certain amount of pressure on the Interlibrary Loan Department. Many academic and public libraries would probably rather go online or buy a much inexpensive subset on a floppy disk for coverage of winners like *Rubber World* or the *East Podunk Journal of Business*.

The self-service approach does not always make the search manager's life easier. It's easy to initialize the program, but somebody has to do it every morning. Equipment breakdowns aren't as frequent as they are with the ROM COM readers used for Magazine Index and Business Index, but they do occur occasionally. Fortunately IAC's customer service is excellent (as should be expected for a product costing $16,000 a year). The printers that make InfoTrac attractive to clients can cause problems. Plan to spend some of the time you save performing searches for others, or changing paper and ink cartridges. And don't forget to add money to the $16,000 annual budget for the special paper and ink cartridges required. Despite its high cost (which we hope will drop as more subscribers come aboard), InfoTrac is a great equalizer when it comes to providing access to electronic information. Its price puts it out of the range of most individuals, but the institutions that subscribe to it will have partially solved the problem of distributing the online dollars to clients with varying abilities to pay. Institutional searchers may find themselves talking clients out of online searches and steering them toward InfoTrac as an alternative.

Optical Storage of Source Material

Optical technology, in addition to providing a cost-effective way of storing secondary sources, such as indexes and bibliographic databases, offers potential as a medium for the storage of primary source material. Government agencies especially have been experimenting with this technology as a way of storing large amounts of text and graphics for automated retrieval. Among the government agencies experimenting with optical storage are the Library of Congress, the Smithsonian, and the National Gallery of Art, which have used the technology as a method for preserving the intellectual artifacts entrusted to them. Among the agencies developing more utilitarian systems are NASA, the Department of Agriculture, and the National Library of Medicine. Projects have included an electronic "jukebox" from NASA, and a pork handbook combining text and image from USDA.

Several commercial ventures involve optically published source material. COMPACT DISCLOSURE from Disclosure Inc. is a CD-ROM product that is similar in many respects to MicroDisclosure. In the Easy Menu Mode, menu-driven search software is used to query a database containing profiles of more than 10,000 companies. The major difference between the two products is that with COMPACT DISCLOSURE, the database isn't stored on a remote mainframe computer. It sits on a CD-ROM attached to a standard microcomputer. The disk itself can hold 275,000 pages of full text. An annual subscription to the product is $2,200 without quarterly updates or $3,200 including quarterly updates for nonprofit organizations. Corporate subscribers pay $1,300 more per year.

Other publishers of source material have entered the optical marketplace. Grolier offers a CD-ROM version of the *Academic American Encyclopedia* for a mere $199. One of the interesting aspects of the optical revolution is the potential to combine data and instructions on the same medium. The CD-ROM version of the encyclopedia can be indexed and searched in a much more dynamic way than the printed publication can. And it can be offered at a lower price and updated much more easily. However, the speed with which updating can be accomplished can't begin to compare to the time sensitivity of online telecommunications-based systems. That is one reason why optical technology lends itself especially well to "longer lasting" information. It is unlikely to ever become a news medium.

Alliances and Hybrids

It is interesting to note that among the leaders in optical publishing are companies whose previous product lines emphasized the use of microforms. Many are predicting that CD-ROM means the beginning of the end of the traditional online database. Information producers and consumers now have the opportunity to do an end run around the system vendors who are the largest buyers and sellers of electronic information. However, it seems the technology poses as great a long-term threat to microforms as it does to online services. Undoubtedly, all three technologies can and will coexist for awhile.

In the past, we've seen alliances between traditional publishers and electronic publishers. We've seen print publishers move to microform and then to online databases. In the database-subset-on-a-floppy-disk arena, we've seen alliances between the developers of search software and hardware and data producers. An excellent review of optical publishing provided by Norman Desmarais in the May 1986 issue of *BYTE* provides an idea of how many different companies are involved. Everybody is jumping on the optical bandwagon. Among the big players are Disclosure, a database producer; DEC, a computer manufacturer; Grolier, a reference book publisher; and OCLC, an online bibliographic utility. Might all of these diverse categories one day become the same thing?

We are also seeing database producers ally themselves with companies that have sprung into being to develop and market optical products. Silver Platter Inc. of Wellesly Hills, Massachusetts, offers databases from PsycInfo, ERIC, and PAIS on optical disks. Is there an optical disk equivalent of DIALOG, SDC, or BRS waiting in the wings?

The products we'll eventually see may turn out to be offline/online hybrids similar to video PATSEARCH. Wouldn't it be nice to have retrospective indexing on an optical disk combined with online access to the type of current information that can only be provided by an online service? Wouldn't it also be nice to have this accomplished by a standard brand microcomputer in such a way that the inquirer was unaware of which records were being delivered by the online service and which were coming from the local database? The whole process could be made transparent, hiding from the searcher which functions were being performed by software on the micro and which were being performed by the host. The optical disk could evolve into something which is at once a physical object, and an "object" in the conceptual sense. Throw in source data, some from remote sources and the rest available locally on disks, and you have something very much like a memex.

Storage Medium of the Future

Optical storage and retrieval technology has advantages for both database producers and users of machine-readable information. Information consumers have the ability to store databases locally, and pay one price for unlimited use. Information producers have a method of distributing their product directly to customers in a form that permits electronic access but which cannot be easily copied. Data on the disks can be manipulated only if the search software is designed to provide that capability. CD-ROM could eventually make downloading a moot question. The disks themselves are durable and reliable. They offer compact storage that surpasses that of print on paper. The hardware required to use optical disks is relatively inexpensive and easily added to standard microcomputer systems.

Optical memory can perform many of the long-term archival functions performed by books. One of the great advantages of the printed book is its ability to combine text and image in a single medium. Optical disks also provide that capability and, unlike books, can also store moving images. Scientists from the Massachusetts Institute of Technology have developed a video map of Aspen, Colorado on an optical disk. The Aspen Movie Map allows its users to "drive" through the town of Aspen. "Drivers" of the map can navigate the streets of the city, seeing what they would have seen had they actually been there. Interactive video and audio are combined to provide the ultimate vicarious experience. We have databases that provide abstracts of the medical literature. We also have databases that provide the full text of medical journals. Imagine a database that a medical researcher could use to retrieve a video of a surgical procedure, or an image of a beating heart.

Problems Exist

Despite the enormous long-term potential of optical technology, there are problems. Most CD-ROM systems only permit reading from the disk (ROM = Read Only Memory), diminishing their potential as a medium for personal information systems. A scholar can use the information on the disk, and in some cases manipulate it, but the disk isn't able to include custom-designed files created by the user. If the information on the disk is to be re-used in its electronic form, it must first be downloaded onto some other medium that allows both read and write operations. Optical disks are expensive to master and there are few mastering plants in the U.S. Consequently, updates can't be produced as quickly or as easily as they can by online services. Nor does the software used with CD-ROM provide the level of sophistication (Boolean searching, proximity operators, field delimitation, etc.) provided by the online services.

Decisions, Decisions

As the technology improves, we can expect to see some of these problems solved. But technological problems have a way of being resolved eventually. Economic and legal problems are harder to handle. Producing a database is a time-consuming, labor intensive activity. Placing a monetary value on information is still more of an art than a science. How do database producers decide how much to charge for electronic information? Are information consumers justified in re-using information once they have paid for it, or should the producer be paid for each use? How does a library determine when it is appropriate to pay a fixed (usually high) cost for unlimited use of a database on CD-ROM in lieu of online searching? These questions aren't easily answered. As technology moves forward, new questions will arise. One thing is certain. The way in which information is produced and distributed is changing and our options as information managers are increasing.

References/Recommended Reading

Ammon, George J., et al. "A High-Speed, Large-Capacity, 'Jukebox' Optical Disk System." *Computer* 18, no.7 (July 1985): 36-44.

Andre, Pamela. "Evaluating Laser Videodisc Technology for the Dissemination of Agricultural Information." *Information Technology and Libraries* 4, no.2 (June 1985): 139-147.

Carney, Richard A. "Information Access Company's InfoTrac." *Information Technology and Libraries* 4, no.2 (June 1985): 149-152.

Desmarais, Norman. "Laser Libraries." *BYTE* (May 1986): 235-246.

Fantel, Hans. "A Key to the Library of Tomorrow." *New York Times*, 18 May 1986, H26.

Gale, John C. "The Information Workstation: A Confluence of Technologies Including CD-ROM." *Information Technology and Libraries* 4, no. 2 (June 1985): 137-139.

Herther, Nancy K. "CD-ROM Technology: A New Era for Information and Retrieval?" *Online* (November 1985): 17-28.

Lewis, Bryan G. "Encoding Databases on Optical Disks." *Information Technology and Libraries* 4, no.2 (June 1985): 147-149.

Nace, Ted. "Lighting a Path to the Future." *Macworld* (February 1986): 100-106.

Sandberg-Diment, Erik. "Price and Promise of Compact Disks." *New York Times*, 15 April 1986, 21.

Schulman, Jacque-Lynne. "Video PATSEARCH: A Mixed-Media System." *Information Technology and Libraries* 1, no.2 (June 1982): 150-156.

Schwerin, Julie B. "Optical Publishing: Technological Breakthrough as a Marketing Challenge." *Information Times* (Fall 1985): 30-32.

Tenopir, Carol. "Database Subsets." *Library Journal*, 15 May 1985, 42-43.

CHAPTER FIFTEEN
VALUE-ADDED ONLINE SEARCHING

In our electronic civilization, information is the major commodity. And any civilization whose major commodity is information is faced with a big problem that so far we've only skirted around. We have the tools to build our city of information and a medium with which to work. Our biggest problem is not a technical problem. It is a problem of value. There is no way to take the measure of the city we've built, no concrete way to determine its value. Any attempt to evaluate our city must be made in a constantly shifting environment in which it is difficult to separate the value of the machine, the instructions, and the information that have become intertwined with one another.

Value is ultimately measured in economic terms. Before we look at value then, it is first necessary to examine the economics of the online industry in terms of the changes caused by the widespread use of personal computers. There can be no denying that the presence of this powerful new medium has had an important impact on the entire online industry. When micros first came on the scene, there were many predictions concerning their economic impact. Some thought that system vendors and database producers would suffer as more customers saved money on connect-time by using high-speed communication and prepackaged search strategies.

Despite the initial fears, the greatest impact of personal computing seems to have been a dramatic increase in the potential customer base for online services. More people than ever before are aware of the value of electronically delivered information. The new medium has caused changes, but it appears to have helped rather than hurt the industry. It is true that there is more competition now. A host of new products and services are available. We can also attribute to the personal computer a changing price structure and new methods of distributing information.

The idea of downloading was once anathema to database producers and system vendors. But fears have proven to be largely unjustified. Krasny has pointed out that system vendors, who retain the ability to control the speed at which information can be transferred, have in that capability an effective means of protecting their economic interests. Large-scale downloading and piracy are impractical at current transmission speeds and the speed limit is set at the source, not at the destination. Even if charges were calculated solely on the basis of online connect-time, it would be difficult for the pirate to download large numbers of records without incurring substantial expense. Furthermore it would be nearly impossible for a pirate to offer for resale electronic information downloaded from a commercial system without being detected and challenged.

Krasny also discusses other possible responses vendors might take to thwart data pirates. Vendors can limit the number of records delivered during any given search or automatically flag for investigation transactions involving large transfers. When it comes to downloading, online vendors, since they control the flow of information transfer, still hold most of the trump cards. On the other hand, system vendors have no way of knowing if information requested by clients is being printed at a terminal or dumped onto a disk. Downloading is nearly impossible to detect, and as we have seen, it is easy to accomplish. If system vendors are smart business people, and most of them are, they would probably assume that downloading is occurring and take steps to protect their profits. Most of them have.

Let's look at the response of DIALOG, the largest of the system vendors, and of the database producers whose products are distributed by DIALOG. The *CHRONOLOG*, DIALOG's monthly newsletter to its subscribers, is now regularly accompanied by a list of terms and conditions supplied by the data producers whose wares are available from DIALOG. Many database producers are now explicitly stating their policies regarding downloading and electronic re-use of information. Policies vary from file to file and range from totally prohibitive to fairly liberal. The size of the terms and conditions document has steadily increased over the years, reflecting the concern among data producers with downloading. Just about everyone has a policy now. A few years ago, hardly any database producers had policies on downloading.

Changing Price Structures

Another obvious development has been a changing price structure. In the past, most online search charges were based on a flat, hourly connect rate. Before IBM introduced its PC in August 1979, the DIALOG price list included seven of roughly 100 databases that charged for online types--the online delivery of specified records. In 1979, about 7 percent of the files available from DIALOG charged for individual records sent over the wires. By January of 1982, after IBM had introduced its PC and *Time* had named the personal computer "machine of the year," about forty-three files were charging for online types. The total number of files had increased to around 172. Of those, roughly 25 percent had adopted a unit cost pricing scheme. One year later, in January of 1983, ninety-five files were charging for online types--in one year up from 25 percent of the total to 45 percent (not counting ONTAP or other nonapplicable files). By January 1984, about 57 percent of the total applicable files were employing unit pricing. Between 1979 and 1984, a period of less than five years, the percentage of files charging a per-unit-of-information fee had increased from 7 percent to 57 percent of the total.

Was the 50 percent increase indicative of a trend? And if it was a trend, what was responsible for it? If the percentage of files charging for online types were plotted on a graph along with the market penetration of PCs among searchers, the two lines would undoubtedly follow the same sharp upward path. Nowadays, virtually all applicable files charge online type fees. Even government-produced holdouts like Medline and ERIC now charge a unit of information fee for each record delivered online via DIALOG. By 1983, NLM--another major online vendor--had changed its pricing policy to reflect the use of mainframe computing resources in addition to connect charges. Similar changes in pricing strategy have been adopted by other online services and database producers.

The movement toward basing charges on a flat connect rate to unit-of-information fees has tended to eliminate many vendors' concerns about downloading. The willingness of both database producers and online services to market software that encourages downloading is another indication that downloading has become less threatening to them. The rush by database producers to distribute databases and database subsets on media such as optical disks is another sign that those on the production side of the online community recognize the advantages of machine-readable products for consumers. It is only a matter of time before system vendors introduce data products in optical formats.

If database producers are fairly paid for the value they add to their products, and if system vendors are fairly paid for the value they add, why should anyone be worried about whether the information is re-used as long as it's not resold. The trend of reducing connect charges while levying unit-of-information fees may have an unexpected benefit. Searchers may become more discriminating about the items they request, taking advantage of lower connect rates to make good use of the interactive features provided by the host before ordering records. For many files, it has become cheaper to order offline prints than it is to download, even at high rates of speed. The major disadvantage of ordering offline prints instead of downloading is the inability to manipulate those prints, which of course are not delivered in machine-readable form. Consequently, we are seeing more data manipulation functions being built into host system software. Software that used to emphasize retrieval now provides options for sorting, reformatting, and alternative page layouts.

There are many levels and degrees of downloading. Some pose a threat to the producers and distributors of electronic information but most do not. In fact, the ability to manipulate and re-use downloaded data may be an incentive for more people to use online services. Software piracy appears to be a much more severe problem than data downloading. Before examining the implications of different types of downloading and re-use, let's get back to the question of value.

Who Adds Value?

Who adds value in the information marketplace, and how is it added? An author adds value to his or her ideas by recording them for the use of others. A publisher adds value by mass producing and distributing recorded ideas. Indexing and abstracting services add value by summarizing and describing the contents of publications--by making the information they contain intellectually accessible. Online system vendors and database producers add value by providing remote electronic access to information and by providing mechanisms for selecting desired items from a large universe of possibilities. Packet-switching networks add value by providing an efficient mode of delivery for the distribution of electronic messages.

Libraries add value by collecting and organizing the documents (as used here a CD-ROM could be defined as a "document") in which ideas have been recorded. Libraries also provide services to make documents more usable. Intellectual access to information is becoming as important as physical access once was. An idea from the time it is recorded by an author to the time it is published, indexed, abstracted, cataloged, and distributed (whether electronically or physically) has had several layers of value added to it.

The cumulative nature of the process makes it difficult to determine how much value was added at each layer. The difficulty of separating the idea, the medium, and the services associated with both also makes it difficult to assign value. Electronically published and distributed materials especially are subject to transformation and manipulation, making it even harder to separate the raw material from the finished product.

The personal computer as an extraordinarily flexible medium for transforming information also has potential for adding value, especially when it comes to the type of electronic information delivered by online services. The personal computer makes it possible to add value at the point of information consumption. Electronic information, because it is incorporeal, is much more easily manipulated and transformed. Consequently, value is more easily added at the local level.

How is Value Added?

Value is added by changing the contents of messages. Making a message more concise by abstracting or expanding upon it by annotating are both ways of increasing its potential usefulness. Adding graphic images or performing calculations on raw, numeric data are other ways of adding value by changing information content. Is a spreadsheet derived from downloaded numeric data a value-added product? Of course it is. Is a list of records that has been annotated to reflect a researcher's personal interests a value-added product? Certainly.

Reformatting is another way of increasing value. Typesetting, printing, sorting, reporting, and transforming from print to electronic or vice-versa all have been used to add value to recorded information. Is a report that integrates electronic data delivered from diverse sources a value-added product? Is a clean, easily readable printed document a value-added product?

Another way of adding value involves changing the syndetic structure for connecting messages instead of changing messages themselves. Indexing, cataloging, and organizing a database are all ways of increasing the usefulness of pieces of information by connecting them to other pieces of information. Is placing downloaded records into a local database a way of adding value? Is generating indexes to search results?

Value may also be added by improving the mode of delivery for information. Certain kinds of information have a very short "shelf life." Such so-called volatile information lends itself readily to electronic delivery. Is information relating to what the stock market will do today of any good if it can't be delivered until tomorrow? Is a database that is updated daily worth more than one that is updated annually? It depends on the type of information each contains.

Improving the ease with which specific pieces of information can be obtained also adds value. A library card catalog and a user-friendly retrieval language are both services for adding value. Does a twenty-four-hour, toll-free help line add value to an online service? Does a script that walks the novice searcher through a search add value? Is software that includes tutorial material worth more than software that lacks it?

Value can also be added--and this is especially true in the monetary sense--by providing cost efficiencies. Uploading search profiles at high speed to save money adds to the search process. So does downloading during off hours. A micro equipped with a 1200-baud modem is worth more as a search medium than a micro with a 300-baud modem.

Information can be made more useful if it is tailored to match local needs and delivered in manageable quantities. Customization adds value. The search that matches a list of core sources, or sources that are easily available is more valuable than the indiscriminate search. Records that are arranged in user-defined categories are worth more than records that are arranged according to a schema developed by an online service. Is a custom-designed macro file a value-added service? Without a doubt.

Principles for Search Managers

There are some general principles that can be followed by search managers who are interested in adding value to the search process or the search product. Let's look at some of them before considering some examples of systems for adding value.

Emphasize the Local Solution

Value can be added by meeting needs at the local level insofar as is possible. If answers are provided locally, time is saved. Money is also saved. A personal computer connected to local information resources is one way of emphasizing local solutions to information problems. If it is not possible to meet demands for information locally, the PC can be used to develop precise requests that can be presented electronically to the global information system. The personal computer can be the focal point for information distribution within an institution. The inquirer need never know whether requested information is coming from local sources or from outside the organization.

Exploit the Core

Most institutions and individuals rely on a small fragment of the total corpus of recorded knowledge. If the core literature can be identified and circumscribed, the personal computer can be used to obtain a more useful product while cutting costs. Many databases cover obscure and difficult-to-obtain publications. The microcomputer can be used to provide easy access to only those journals of interest. Individual researchers usually have specific authors, subjects, or institutional sources that are of interest. Once the codes and search keys for authors, journals, and corporate sources that constitute the core have been identified (and it isn't always easy), statements for identifying core material can be stored on a disk and used to make the database conform to the local core.

Remember that each individual's memex will be different. Each researcher will therefore have to identify his or her own personal core. The analytic power of the PC can easily be used to identify each individual's personal core of authors, journal titles, institutions sponsoring interesting research, subjects--whatever. Remeber how easy it was to use the *Sci-Mate Manager* to generate reports on the memex literature?

In an institutional setting, such as a university, the core could be designed to make online systems function as teaching tools. Strategies to identify information originating with selected authors, subjects, journals, etc., could be built into the scheme for exploiting the core with a PC. Money could be saved by using the PC to deal with the essence of a discipline while discarding peripheral sources.

Just as everyone has favorite authors, journals, and subjects, everyone has a group of favored databases. A system that seeks to exploit the core would try to identify the core databases as well. An effort would be made to determine which databases consistently cited relevant authors and journals, and which consistently yielded good results. Once again, the analytical power of the machine could be used to isolate a group of core databases. For example, the postings associated with cross-database searches for core items could be put into a spreadsheet model and analyzed to determine which databases were the best choices as core files. Once core databases had been identified, they could be exploited by developing macros, scripts, templates, hedges, and tutorials to take advantage of their features.

An online database can thus be made to function as a dynamic index to sources defined at the local level. The fewer journals, authors, and so forth comprising "the core," the easier this would be to accomplish. The individual researcher has in her power the ability to custom design an "electronic index" to only those sources in which she is interested.

The personal computer can also be adapted as a medium that is able to deal with different information formats. Some core sources can be made directly available in formats like CD-ROM; others can be delivered electronically and others which are delivered in print formats can be made more accessible by online indexing and abstracting services.

Train and Assist

Another principle of value-added searching involves using the personal computer to provide training and assistance. Training and assistance can involve things as simple as buying software that provides extensive help to something as complex as using macros and batch files in a custom-designed user interface. It is relatively easy to purchase and integrate software that will help to simplify the search process. Developing scripts that anticipate the needs of clients is another way to follow the training and assistance principle. Value can be added by reducing complexity. The use of "standard brand" off-the-shelf hardware and software can greatly reduce complexity.

Provide Cost Efficiencies

One of the first reasons many people had for adopting the micro as a search medium was to save money. Changes in the pricing strategies of many of the vendors have made the micro less effective as a money-saving medium. However, there are still ways the machine can be used to provide cost efficiencies. Most cost-saving techniques involve the offline preparation and high-speed uploading of search queries. Money can also be saved by subscribing to databases on disks as an alternative to heavy use of corresponding online files. Are flat rate, per-item pricing strategies a cost efficiency? It all depends.

Provide Tools and Services

There are now a number of computer-based tools and services that search centers had previously been able to provide only at great expense. It is now possible to offer a number of customized tutorial and search assistance services. Assistance with logging on and developing strategies is easy to provide, as are tools for the development of personalized profiles. Database management and bibliography production tools make possible services such as searching of local databases and creation of attractive, printed products. In the future, one of the most important jobs of the search manager will be to create a search environment by gathering together an assortment of tools and media that can be used to solve information problems at the local level.

Paper Chase

Paper Chase, a Boston-based gateway service to the medical literature, although it doesn't require a personal computer, seems to exemplify the approach PC owners should take. Paper Chase was developed at Beth Israel hospital and is now being marketed as a dial-up, third party gateway service. The information raw material available from Paper Chase's computers in Boston is supplied by NLM.

Paper Chase is a program to search the Medline database. Paper Chase doesn't have a user manual. Most help is provided while online. The program works by guiding the user from natural language input to MESH terms. In a way, its success is predicated upon the existence of a consistently applied indexing scheme such as MESH.

The user of the program is prompted for terms to search. Abstracts are available for display but are not searched. Searching for subject words is done on the basic index. Boolean strategies are developed by specifying that references be common to more than one list (AND), or that a list contain any of a group of specified references (OR), or that a list exclude a specific term (NOT). As lists are combined the user is immediately given the option to display the results of the logical combination.

The program forgives spelling errors by searching for terms that are as close as possible to the entry term in spelling and automatically truncating. Just about any form of journal title entry is acceptable. It is possible to limit by date, author, or language, or any of the other search keys that are part of the Medline record. The program even knows which subheadings are permissible with different classes of medical subject headings. MESH terms are obtained for the user by building a frequency table of the nine MESH terms most frequently associated with each natural-language entry term.

Paper Chase automatically exploits the core. Search results are matched to local holdings, which are displayed first. The program used at Beth Israel Hospital not only listed local holdings first, but listed them in the same order that they were arranged on the shelf. This approach adds to the convenience for the inquirer, making it more easily possible to answer questions at the local level.

For individuals not using the program within an institutional setting, Paper Chase matches results to a core list developed by the American College of Physicians, the *New England Journal of Medicine*, and others. This type of precision searching is intended to serve as a "filter" to prevent Paper Chase users from being swept away beneath a deluge of medical references, many to obscure, difficult-to-obtain sources.

All search results are stored in the Paper Chase computer for two weeks, just in case someone changes their mind or wants to review a search. Strategies are stored for six months. Though the program is directed to the uninitiated, the marketing emphasis is on institutional customers. Libraries, hospitals, and medical schools are providing Paper Chase to potential consumers of electronic medical information. However, each individual can be given his or her own password by the managing institution.

The connect rate is $23 per hour, $4 of which goes to NLM for the raw material. Each record displayed or printed is ten cents. Abstracts are ten cents extra. Prints can be ordered offline and document delivery is available as well, reflecting the emphasis on one-stop information shopping. Documents that aren't included in the core can be ordered at $6 each.

Paper Chase, because it is an online service, cannot be a totally self-contained system, but it does attempt to address the total information problem by matching references to local holdings and providing a document delivery service. On the other hand, since it is an online service, it is available at all hours of the day and night from any remote location with access to a telephone. Furthermore, the database can be updated easily and regularly.

A micro-based, value-added system can also seek self-sufficiency by employing precision search tools. Many of the features of Paper Chase could be easily implemented on a PC system, though on a smaller scale. Our next example of a value-added system is something totally different from Paper Chase, but it also embodies many of our general principles.

An Off-the-Shelf Approach

In its June 25, 1985 issue, *PC Magazine* described a project being developed by the Smithsonian Air and Space Museum. Hernan Otano and Rob Martella are developing a system for storing and retrieving documents, drawings, and photographs from the museum's collections.

The most interesting aspect of Otano and Martella's approach is the emphasis on inexpensive, off-the-shelf hardware and software.

The hardware configuration adds a videodisc player and a digitizing camera to a PC. The cost for the hardware required, including a high-resolution thermal printer, is about $10,000. On page 200 of the article, Walter J. Boyne, director of the museum, explained the project's objectives to *PC*'s reporter:

> We wanted our system to incorporate five principles: easy acquisition, mass storage, automatic indexing, easy retrieval, and cheap distribution. We also wanted it all done with off-the-shelf equipment so we wouldn't get locked into using one supplier.

The system is being designed to make it easy to photograph both documents and graphic images with a digitizing camera. Both formats are then stored on a videodisc for easy retrieval. Pictures of words are converted to ASCII text by an optical character recognition program. Document retrieval is accomplished by ASCII text files, but display is accomplished by referring to the same type of bit-mapped graphic image used for photographs and drawings. When a document is displayed, one page at a time is shown. Search terms that resulted in a document being retrieved are highlighted on the display. Photographs and drawings may also be retrieved by the system and displayed or printed.

The museum plans to market videodiscs containing photographs, drawings, and other archival material from its collections for $35 per disk. Each disk can store approximately 50,000 photographs or 100,000 documents per side. Among the material in the museum's collections are the papers of the Wright brothers and Wehrner Von Braun. Otano envisions the system being used by rural libraries eventually. A system for quickly recording images (which is easy) and text (which is not easy) in machine-readable form promises to revolutionize scholarship.

Right now, most of the existing store of machine-readable text is owned by someone and subject to copyright or contract restrictions, or both. The system being developed by the Air and Space Museum makes it possible to transform the information--both text and image--from those many works in the public domain into a format which is understandable to both human and machine. We may soon see an inexpensive new medium for preserving graphic records passed to us by earlier generations. Optical technology may soon provide for the arts and humanities the same volume of electronic information resources that had previously been reserved for the sciences and business. It's not hard to imagine, for example, the graphic and written works of an artist like William Blake being made available on an optical disk of some sort.

The technology used by Otano and Martella sounds somehow familiar. Let's see, first there is a camera for recording text and images. There is a mass storage medium and an indexing scheme. All of it is part of an expensive, desktop machine. Where have we seen this before? Oh yes, the memex.

We've seen Paper Chase, an online service for delivering medical information over the wires. That medical information is volatile, the record is continually updated. PaperChase helps the user deal with the enormous volume of medical data by encouraging custom-designed output. We've also seen the totally self-contained system under development at the Smithsonian. It is a system for handling long-lasting, nonvolatile, archival information. When the memex finally appears on the scene, which system will it resemble? Will it resemble the user-friendly gateway to a remote store of volatile information? Or will it resemble a device for mass storage and retrieval of archival records? Maybe it will resemble both.

Converging on the Memex

Information technology is converging upon an online/personal computer/optical disk device. Databases are getting bigger and computers are getting smaller. It is now possible to distribute an entire database of text and images on a portable medium. We are experiencing a shift from online secondary services and bibliographic databases to a different type of electronic information product. We are now seeing electronic source material. Indexes and abstracts are being supplemented by full-text files. The most recent batch correspond to periodicals and reference works. More recently, we've seen graphic images being included and data being distributed on optical disks.

Many of the latest electronic information products represent something qualitatively different from the usual indexes and abstracts. Many of the latest crop have no printed counterparts. Even on the traditionally bibliographic DIALOG system, full text, numeric, and directory databases are increasing more rapidly than bibliographic files.

Emphasis is also shifting from data to services. We now have the ability to create custom-designed products by merging individual data elements from diverse records. The ability to manipulate information at the level of the field, especially in numeric databases, provides us for the first time with the possibility of on-demand publishing. Numeric fields can be combined to create unique records, records that are produced as they're consumed, records that may be further manipulated at the local level by a personal computer.

The bibliographic record that was once the basic unit of electronic consumption is being supplemented by much larger units, such as full-text files on CD-ROM, and much smaller units, such as individual data elements from a numeric database. The personal computer, which is capable of storing and manipulating the larger information units at the local level and obtaining the smaller units from remote sources for local manipulation, has been a major impetus for these changes. The idea of custom-design is achieving prominence. We already have the tools, the medium, and the raw material. Let's get to work.

References/Recommended Reading

Benson, James A., and Bella H. Weinberg, eds. *Downloading/Uploading Online Databases and Catalogs.* Ann Arbor, MI: Pierian Press, 1985.

Bishop, David F. "OCLC Copyright: A Threat to Sharing." *Journal of Academic Librarianship* 11, no.4 (September 1985): 202-203.

Boyne, Walter J., and Hernan Otano. "Direct Document Capture and Full-Text Indexing: An Introduction to the National Air and Space Museum System." *Library Hi Tech* 2, no.4, 7-14.

Brooks, Kristina M. "The Online Transfer of Machine-Readable Data: A Pandora's Box." *Database* (February 1982): 18-21.

Brown, Rowland C.W. "OCLC, Copyright, and Access to Information: Some Thoughts." *Journal of Academic Librarianship* 11, no.4 (September 1985): 197-198.

Brownrigg, Edwin B., and Clifford A. Lynch. "Electrons, Electronic Publishing, and Electronic Display." *Information Technology and Libraries* 4, no.3 (September 1985): 201-207.

Case, Donald. "The Personal Computer: Missing Link to the Electronic Journal." *Journal of the American Society for Information Science* 36, no.5 (September 1985): 309-313.

Cochrane, Pauline A. "Friendly" Catalog Forgives User Errors." *American Libraries* (May 1982): 303-306.

Grisham, Frank P. "Copyright is Wrong [OCLC]" *Journal of Academic Librarianship* 11, no.4 (September 1985): 199-200.

Henderson, Earl, and George Thoma. "Optical Technology: Impact on Information Transfer." *Bowker Annual of Library and Book Trade Information*, 30th edition, compiled by Julia Moore, 91-102. NY: R.R. Bowker, 1985.

Horowitz, Gary L., and Howard Bleich. "PaperChase, a Computer Program to Search the Medical Literature." *New England Journal of Medicine* 305, no.16, 15 October 1981, 924-930.

Horowitz, Gary L., et al. "PaperChase, Self-Service Bibliographic Retrieval." *Journal of the American Medical Association* 250 (1983): 2494-2499.

Kenton, David. "The Development of a More Equitable Method of Billing for Online Services [NLM]." *Online* (September 1984): 13-17.

Kochen, Manfred. "Technology and Communication in the Future." *Journal of the American Society for Information Science* (March 1981): 148-157.

_____. "Impacts of Microcomputers on Information Use Patterns." In *The Application of Mini- and Micro-Computers in Information, Documentation, and Libraries*, edited by C. Keren and L. Perlmutter, 469-477. Elsevier, North-Holland, 1983.

Krasny, Mitchell A. "Technology--The Problems and the Solutions." *Information Services and Use* 1 (1982): 341-349.

Lemley, Brad. "Preserving the Past on Disk." *PC Magazine*, 25 June 1985, 199-212.

Taylor, Robert S. "Value-Added Processes in the Information Life Cycle." *Journal of the American Society for Information Science* (September 1982): 341-346.

Tenopir, Carol. "The Database Industry Today: Some Vendors' Perspectives." *Library Journal*, 1 February 1984, 156-157.

Warrick, Thomas S. "Large Databases, Small Computers, and Fast

Modems... An Attorney Looks at the Legal Ramifications of Downloading." *Online* (July 1984): 58-70.

Yankelovich, Nicole, and Norman Meyrowitz. "Reading and Writing the Electronic Book." *Computer* 18, no.10 (October 1985): 15-29.

GLOSSARY

Communications Terms

analog--a method of representing information in which the signal varies in proportion to the data being represented.

ASCII--American Standard Code for Information Interchange; the most commonly used code for representing keyboard characters; also used to represent a special group of control characters; there are 128 characters in the ACSII character set; each ASCII character is represented by a unique sequence of seven bits; an eighth bit called the parity bit is usually added.

asynchronous--a form of transmission in which the computers at either end of the line are not synchronized with one another; each character transmitted is individually synchronized by the addition of framing bits called start and stop bits; this is the form of communication that is almost always employed by microcomputers.

baud--a measure of the speed of transmission; expressed mathematically as the reciprocal of the time duration of a single bit; at 300 baud the duration of one bit is 3.33 milliseconds; at 1200 baud the signal duration is 833 microseconds; baud rate is often confused with (and used interchangeably for) the rate of information transfer, which is more properly expressed as bits per second.

bit--the smallest unit for representing information; shorthand for binary digit; in the binary system each bit is represented as either a 0 or a 1.

bits per second--a measure of information transfer; often confused with baud rate; a 300-baud modem transmits 300 bps; what is called a 1200-baud modem is usually a 600-baud modem transmitting at 1200 bps.

carrier--a continuous frequency wave upon which an information-carrying signal is superimposed; this wave is modulated by the modem.

channel--the path along which information-carrying signals are transmitted.

demodulation--the process of converting a modulated analog signal to a discrete digital signal.

digital--a way of representing information as sequences of discrete bits of information; in the binary system the bits are represented as 0s or 1s, unlike analog, in which the method of representation varies with the information being represented.

duplex--relating to the two-way communication of data; see full duplex, half duplex.

echoing--an error-checking technique in which each character received by the host computer is echoed back to the terminal for comparison with the character that was transmitted.

framing bits--bits used to delineate the beginning and end of the bit stream representing a character; also called sync bits; at 1200 baud, a seven-bit ASCII character is framed by a start bit, a parity bit, and stop bit, bringing its total length to ten bits.

full duplex--a communications channel that permits simultaneous two-way communication.

half duplex--a communications channel that permits two-way communication but that does not permit simultaneous sending and receiving.

handshaking--the exchange of control characters between computers required to establish a communications link; among the characters sent are the ACK character, which signals acknowledgement of the receipt of information and readiness to receive the next block of data; handshaking also determines which computer is sending and which is receiving at any given time.

host computer--in online searching, the mainframe computer containing databases and the software required to interact with them.

mark--in digital communications, the term used to represent the binary digit, 1, which is electrically represented by a negative voltage pulse.

modulation--the process by which a digital signal is converted to an analog signal for transmission over a phone line; an information signal is superimposed upon a carrier signal by modulating the carrier signal in one of three ways: amplitude modulation (AM)--for low-speed transmission; frequency modulation (FM)--for medium-speed transmission (e.g., 300 baud); phase modulation--for high-speed transmission.

network--a series of interconnected communications channels that permit remote computers to interact with one another.

node--a point on a network at which signals can be routed, synchronized, amplified, or transferred; this is usually accomplished by a minicomputer called an engine.

packet switching--a method of dividing communications transactions into blocks called packets and routing them on separate lines to achieve maximum efficiency of transmission within a network.

parallel--communications method in which all of the bits representing a character are sent simultaneously over eight parallel lines; form of transmission used within a microcomputer; only effective over short distances; often used to transmit information between main unit and printer or monitor.

parity--an error-checking technique that involves adding an extra (8th) bit to a character so that the total number of 1s in the character is always even or always odd.

protocol--set of rules required to achieve communication between computers; rules generally relate to character length (in bits); bit duration (baud); presence of framing bits, duplex, various error-checking conventions and system-specific requirements.

serial--form of communication in which all of the bits representing a character are sent in sequence along a single line; asynchronous, serial transmission is the most effective method of transmitting data over long distances and is therefore the transmission method used for telecommunications involving microcomputers; used synonomously with asynchronous.

space--in digital communications, the term used to represent the binary digit 0, which is electrically represented by a positive voltage pulse.

start bit--in asynchronous transmission, the bit used to indicate the beginning of a character.

stop bit--in asynchronous transmission the bit used to indicate the end of a character; for transmission at 300 baud, two stop bits are required.

synchronous--a transmission method in which characters are sent and received in blocks; used for very high speed transmission on dedicated lines; start and stop bits are not required for each character, but the operation of both the sending and receiving computers must be closely synchronized; not used with microcomputers.

terminal--a device capable of sending and receiving information over communication lines.

throughput--a measure of the amount of useful information communicated between computers; for example--a seven-bit ASCII character with three framing bits for a total character length of ten bits and a transmission speed of 1200 bps yields a throughput of 120 characters per second. If the average word is six characters long, then throughput could also be expressed as approximately 1200 words per minute.

Hardware Terms

acoustic coupler--the part of a modem that connects directly to a telephone handset by means of rubber cups; subject to external noise and not compatible with certain types of telephones.

Bell 103--a tone-signalling standard for modems operating at speeds of 300 baud or less.

Bell 202--a tone-signalling standard for 1200-baud modems; only capable of supporting half-duplex operation.

Bell 212--a tone-signalling standard for 1200-baud modems; supports both full and half-duplex operation.

buffer--a temporary storage area for data; often used to handle data flowing between computer components having different data transfer rates and capabilities (e.g., a modem and a printer or disk drive).

bus--the physical pathway along which information travels within the computer.

card--a slang term for a printed circuit board that is added to the computer by inserting it into an expansion slot on the computer's mother board.

clock--the part of the computer's processing unit that generates precisely timed electrical impulses that are used to synchronize the flow of information within the computer; also used to refer to a device that can be used to "turn on" the computer at a predetermined time.

CPU (Central Processing Unit)--the part of the computer that interprets and executes stored instructions, controls the flow of data into and out of the machine, and performs logical and arithmetic operations.

DB-25--the standard electrical connector for RS-232-C standard systems; the plug and jack used to connect the modem to the computer; a trapezoidal-shaped connector with twenty-five pins, thirteen on the top row and twelve on the bottom.

disk drive--a peripheral storage device that is used to read information stored on disks or to write information on disks by spinning them between magnetic read/write heads.

dot-matrix printer--a printer that forms characters on paper by extending and retracting pins to create predetermined patterns of dots on a matrix; generally the fastest, cheapest, and quietest printers; print quality is generally low.

expansion slot--a slot on the main circuit board of the computer into which printed circuit boards can be inserted.

floppy disk--a flexible magnetic disk upon which information can be stored; the standard size for microcomputers is 5 1/4 inches; generally capable of storing between 100 and 500 kilobytes (approximately 50-150 pp.).

formatting--the process of dividing a floppy disk into addressable sectors in which data are organized.

function key--a special key that is used to send a complex message or perform a specified operation; function keys may have predetermined functions or they may be programmable; many software packages take advantage of function keys by providing them with functions related to the tasks for which the software was designed.

hard disk--a mass storage device capable of storing large amounts of data; typically accommodates between 5 and 50 megabytes (million bites); high-speed rotation provides rapid access to stored data.

intelligent terminal--a terminal that has a limited amount of memory, programmability, and processing capability.

letter-quality printer-a type of printer that forms characters by striking a metal or plastic die of a fully formed character on the ribbon; expensive, slow, and noisy, but the print quality can't be beaten; also called a daisy-wheel printer.

microcomputer--a small, stand-alone computer whose CPU is a microprocessor; price from $39 to $10,000; size from hand-held to desktop; computing power ranges from minimal to enormous.

modem--modulator/demodulator--a device for converting the digital signal produced by a computer to the analog signal acceptable by the telephone system (modulation) and for converting the analog signal from the phone line to a digital signal that the computer can understand (demodulation).

monitor--an output device used to display information sent from the keyboard and received from the remote system.

motherboard--the main circuit board of the microcomputer to which all other circuit boards are attached.

operating system--the master control software that controls the flow of information within the computer and between the computer and its peripheral devices in addition to providing a variety of utility programs and commands.

port--the point at which data enters or exits the microcomputer.

RAM (Randon Access Memory)--the internal memory of the computer; its contents can be changed at any time; also called volatile memory; its contents disappear when the power is turned off; this is generally the area where programs are being stored during execution and the location of the buffer.

ROM (Read Only Memory)--this is the micro's permanent internal memory; its contents cannot be changed; parts of the operating system are often stored in ROM.

RS-232-C--the electrical standard for the interconnection of computer equipment.

serial card--slang term for the circuit board required for asynchronous, serial communications; also called an asynchronous communications card.

UART (Universal Asynchronous Receiver/Transmitter)--an electrical device that converts the parallel signals within the computer to serial signals required for communication with the outside world and converts incoming serial transmissions to parallel.

Software Terms

applications software--software that is designed to be used for a specific purpose (e.g., word processing or communications); applications can be fairly specialized (e.g., online searching applications software is a specialized type of communications software).

automatic dialing--a modem capability that enables phone numbers to be dialed automatically with a single keystroke.

back-up--a copy of a file or program that is created to ensure replacement if the original is lost or damaged.

break--a control character that is used to interrupt transmission or receipt of data between computers; software for online searchers must have the capability of sending a break signal.

character stripping--the capability of filtering out unwanted characters being transmitted by the host system; often used to remove control characters that could interfere with post-search processing of information received from the host.

command-driven--software that is used by entering commands directly through the keyboard rather than responding to prompts or menus.

command mode--for communications software the command mode is the offline or local mode; this is the mode that is used to set parameters, store protocols, and prepare search statements before going online; when you are online the software is said to be in the terminal mode.

control character--characters that do not print and are not normally displayed on the monitor; control characters are used to initiate or stop some operation of the computer; the break signal, the backspace signal, and the carriage return are all control characters.

database management system (DBMS)--a software package that enables its users to create and manage databases; some database management systems are designed specifically for bibliographic applications; others are much more general and can be used for a variety of purposes.

default--with software that allows the assignment of variable values (parameters, protocols, etc.), default indicates the values that are automatically assigned when the software is loaded if no other values are specified.

display--a term for the way in which information is visually presented to the user; display characteristics include screen width, arrangement of data elements on the screen, presence of status flags, windows, etc.

documentation--a jargon word for the printed manuals, tutorials, and crib cards that accompany computer software; also used to refer to the online Help and Status displays built into many programs.

download--the process of capturing data transmitted by a host computer; downloaded data may be captured in files (permanent) or in a buffer (temporary); downloaded data is used in a variety of ways and may be easily manipulated after a search has been terminated.

end-users--a popular jargon word for the ultimate consumers of information extracted from computer databases; online searches have traditionally been performed by trained search intermediaries acting on behalf of end-users; for a variety of reasons, many end-users have recently begun conducting their own online searches.

file--a collection of data (e.g., search results) that has been given a name and stored on a medium (e.g., a disk).

front-end--software and/or hardware that mediates between a searcher and the host system; front-end software can assume many functions from handling routine communications protocols to sophisticated query language translation.

gateway--software and/or hardware that enables searchers to connect to several different host systems by handling communications functions and that simplifies accounting by producing a single monthly invoice; this term is often used interchangeably with front-end.

global search--in word processing, the ability to search an entire file for the presence of a specified character or string of characters.

macro--a user-defined key; macros make it possible to store a string of characters or a command and then to transmit them with a single keystroke; macros are very useful for the offline preparation of search statements and commands; the length of macros is often limited by software packages that permit macro creation

massaging--jargon word for post-search manipulation of search results to create a more appealing or useful final product.

menu-driven--software that is used by selecting options from "menus" displayed on the screen; easy to learn, but can be very tedious if there is no possibility for over-riding menus and directly issuing commands.

options file--a file containing macros and parameters that may be used with a specific system or for a specific purpose.

parameter--a variable that may be changed depending upon the requirements of the system being used or of a specific application (e.g., baud rate, duplex, etc.)

prompt--the character sent by the host computer to indicate its readiness to receive the next command or search statement (in DIALOG the ? is the prompt).

script--a stored search or protocol that is able to recognize and respond to prompts and messages transmitted by the host system.

sorting--rearranging data (e.g., search results) to make them more useful; some retrieval systems provide the capability of sorting online; sorting can also be done offline if data have been downloaded and if one has software that can sort; some online searching application packages provide a post-search sorting capability.

status line--many software packages provide a status line that displays current values for all parameters (e.g., printer width, baud rate, duplex, etc.).

terminal mode--the condition of communications software when the micro is online with the host system and functioning as a terminal.

toggle--to move back and forth between two conditions; communications software can be used to toggle between full and half duplex or between the terminal mode and the command mode, for example.

utility--a general purpose software package used for routine tasks rather than specific applications; the operating system has utilities for copying, erasing, and moving files; some utilities may be used in conjunction with other software; some utility programs may be used with communications software for the creation of macros.

window--a method of display in which available commands are displayed in a box on the screen.

VENDOR LIST

Note: Prices were provided to allow comparison of relative costs. Prices are subject to fluctuation and are often heavily discounted, especially by mail order houses. Also be aware that software publishing is less stable than book publishing. Software products that are here today could easily be gone tomorrow.

Communications Software

BackComm
LaSalle Micro
1350 Remington Rd.
Suite W
Schaumberg, IL 60195
312-882-5171 $99

Crosstalk XVI
1000 Holcomb Pkwy.
Roswell, GA 30076
404-998-7798 $195

Crosstalk Mark 4
1000 Holcomb Pkwy.
Roswell, GA 30076
404-998-7798 $245

Microsoft Access
Microsoft Corp.
10700 Northrup Way
Bellevue, WA 98004
206-828-8080 $250

Mirror
SoftKlone Distributing
1210 East Park Ave.
Tallahassee, FL
904-878-8564 $49.95

PC-Dial
Buttonware
P.O. Box 5786
Bellevue, WA 98006
206-746-4296 $29

PC-Talk III
The Headlands Press Inc.
P.O. Box 862

Tiburon, CA 94920
415-435-9775 $35

PFS: ACCESS
Software Publishing Corp.
1901 Landings Drive
Mountain View, CA 94043
415-962-8910 $95

Smartcom II
Hayes Microcomputer Products
5923 Peachtree Industrial Blvd.
Norcross, GA 30092
404-449-8791 $119

Front-End and Search Assistance Software

DIALOGLINK
Publications Distribution Center
DIALOG Information Services Inc.
3460 Hillview Avenue
Palo Alto, CA 94304
800-334-2564
Communications Manager, $95
Account Manager, $45

FINDER
Aaron Smith Associates Associates
Suite 312
1430 West Peachtree St.
Atlanta, GA 30309
FINDER (complete system), $1,495
FINDERlink, $295
Search Companion, $295

IT (Information Transfer)
Data-Ease Inc.
3130 Mayfield Rd.
Cleveland Heights, OH 44118
216-831-3749 $500

PC/Net-Link
Informatics General Corp.
Library Services Division
6011 Executive Blvd.

Rockville, MD 20850
800-638-6595 $550

Professional Bibliographic Software
P.O. Box 4250
Ann Arbor, MI 48106
313-996-1580
Professional Bibliographic System, $395
Biblio-Link, $195 per service
Data Transfer System, $200

Sci-Mate
Institute for Scientific Information
3501 Market St.
Philadelphia, PA. 19104
215-386-0100
The Searcher, $399
The Manager, $399
The Editor, $399

SearchMaster
SDC Information Services
2500 Colorado Ave.
Santa Monica, CA 90406
800-421-7229 $299

SearchWorks
Online Research Systems
627 West 113th St.
Suite 4F
New York, NY 10025
212-408-3311 $149

Gateways and Software for Beginners

BRS After Dark
1200 Route 7
Latham, NY 12110
800-345-4277

Colleague
BRS/Saunders Colleague
1290 Avenue of the Americas
New York, NY 10104
800-833-4707

Easynet
Telebase Systems Inc.
134 N. Narberth Ave.
Narberth, PA 19072
800-327-9638

Grateful Med
NTIS
U.S. Dept. of Commerce
Springfield, VA 22161
703-487-4650
order no: PB86-158482/GBB, $29.95
shipping and handling, $3

Knowledge Index
DIALOG Information Services
3460 Hillview Ave.
Palo Alto, CA 94304
800-334-2564

MicroDisclosure
Disclosure Inc.
5161 River Road
Bethesda, MD 20816
800-638-8076 $45

Paper Chase
Beth Israel Hospital
330 Brookline Ave.
Boston, MA 02215
617-735-2253

SearchHelper
Information Access Company
11 Davis Drive
Belmont, CA 94002
800-227-8431 $200/yr.
700 searches, $1,750
300 searches, $1,050

SearchWare
22548 Ventura Blvd.
Suite E
Woodland Hills, CA 91364
818-992-4325 $290 first disk
$100 each additional disk

WILSEARCH
H.W. Wilson Co.
950 University Avenue
Bronx, NY 10452
800-462-6060
Prepayment Options:
2,000 searches, $2,000
1,000 searches, $1,500
500 searches, $1,000
250 searchcs, $750
Without Prepayment, $5 per search

INDEX

ABI/INFORM 138-139
Academic American Encyclopedia 256
Access (Communications program) 140-145
accounting 174, 178, 188
After dark 209-210
amplitude modulation 53
analog 50-52
Anchorpad 205
architecture 24-36, 39
ARPAnet 5, 56
ASCII 42-44, 271
Aspen Movie Map 258
asynchronous 27
AT commands 60-63
autoexec.bat 95

Backcomm 121
batch files 95, 133-134
baud 54-56
BCN 212-213
Bell 103 (signaling std.) 52
Bell 212 A (signaling std.) 52
Bernoulli Box 81
BIOSIS B-I-T-S 249-250
BPS (bits per second) 54-55
breakout box 48
BRS 138, 143-145, 169, 173, 181, 209-210, 212
buffers 12, 34, 61
Bush, Vannevar 2-3

cables 48-49
CAST 238
CCITT 52
CD-ROM 73, 82-84, 252-259
channel 46-47
character stripping 126, 155
CINAHL 250
clock 25
clock/calendar 25
clones 19-20
coding 42-44
command-driven software 123-124, 127
command mode 119-120
communications interface 10
communications software 117-149
Compaq 19-20
COMPACT DISCLOSURE 256
compatibility 19-20, 90

CONIT 236-237
content analysis 238-239
control characters 117, 126
core literature 266-268
costs 259, 262-263
Crosstalk 49, 134-140
custom design 272-273
custom menus 142-143

data communication 42-59
data processing 6-7
database management 157-160
database selection 163, 180, 212-215, 229, 241
database subsets 80, 84, 245-256
dBase 157, 180
defacto standards 19, 59-60
DIALOG 106, 131-132, 139, 145, 169, 173-176, 181, 208, 210-211, 214-215, 262-263, 272
Dialoglink 174-179
DB-25 48-49
DCE 45
dialing 61-63
dibits 53
digital communication 50-51
DIP switches 65-66
directories 93
Disclosure II 221-223
display 29-32
DOS 91-96
dot matrix printers 33-35
Dow Jones 143
downloading 103-106, 125, 158-160, 192-199, 261-264
DTE 45
duplex 46-47
Dynabook 21

EasyNet 211-212
echoplex 46-47
Electronic Scroll 241
ELHILL 157, 223-224
end-users 203-212
ERIC 84, 188, 245, 257
ERIC MicroSearch 245-249
expanded memory 76-77
expansion cards 75-77
expert systems 235-242
external modems 63-64

field labels 158, 187-189
Filelok 205
files 91, 95-96, 119, 125
filtering 126
FINDER 199
fixed disks 80-81
floppy disks 79-80
flow control 117-118
Flugelman, Andrew 122
FRED 238
freeware 122
frequency modulation 53
front-ends 165-191
full duplex 46-47
full-text databases 239, 241, 252, 256, 272-273
fuzzy sets 240

gateways 207-216
generic micros 19-20
GENIUS monitor 30-31
Grateful Med 228-232, 236, 239

half duplex 46-47
handshaking 49-50
hard disks 80-81
hardware, general considerations 17-21
Hayes 19, 51, 59-63, 126-134
Hayes commands 60-63
help screens 106, 123, 225, 230
Hepatitis Knowledge Base 239
heuristics 235-236
hybrids 252, 257

IAC 252-255
IBM 19-20, 90, 239
IIDA 237-238
indicator lights 64-65
information retrieval 6-7
InfoTrac 252-256
ink jet printers 35-36
input/output 7-11
In-Search 173
installation 120
intelligent terminals 10-13
interrupts 119
ISI (Inst. for Scientific Information) 168-172, 192-198
IT 191

jukeboxes 83-84

KAware 250
Kay, Alan 5-6, 21
Kaypro 19-20
keyboards 28-29
Knowledge Index 210-211

Laserlock 205
laser printers 38
LCDs 32
Leading Edge 20
learn mode 143
letter-quality printers 36-38
Licklider, J.C.R. 5
linefeed 129, 153-154

Macintosh 94
macros 100-107, 124-125, 130-133
magnetic memory 73
mark and move 155
Medline 106, 132-133, 145, 154, 181-186, 228-232, 239, 269-270
medium 6-7, 7-13
memex 4-5, 193-197, 266-267, 272-273
memory, adding 74-75
Menlo Corporation 173-174
menu-driven software 127-128, 141-143, 172, 177, 224-225, 230
MicroDisclosure 221-223
micros as terminals 13-15
Microsoft 76, 90, 94
Microsoft Access 140-145
Mirror 121
modems 41-67
modems, choosing 58-60
modulation 50-55
monitors 29-32
MS-DOS 91-96

National Air and Space Museum 270-272
NLM 145, 157, 169, 181-186, 228-232, 256, 263, 239, 269-270
NLQ printers 33
noise 53-54
numeric databases 160, 222-223, 241, 272-273

OASIS 191
Ol' SAM 238
operating systems 87-89

optical disk drives 83
optical memory 73, 82-84
optical publishing 251-259

packet switching 56-58
PaperChase 269-270
parallel 26-28
PARC 5, 21
passwords 136, 143, 176, 204
path managers 108
PATSEARCH 252
PC/Net-Link 180-181
PC-Talk 121-126
phase modulation 53, 55
pins 49-50
plasma display 32
portables 20-21
post-processing 151-162, 187-191, 192-199
power supply 23-24
printers 32-38
Professional Bibliographic Software 198-199
programming 109, 137-139, 143-145
Prokey 102-107
Prolok 205
Pro-Search 173-174
PsycINFO 84, 105, 188, 257

query translation 170-171, 212, 236-237
question answering systems 239

RAM 74-79
RAM disks 78-79
RAM-resident software 77-78
reformatting 152-157, 265-266
registers, modem 61-62
reports 178, 186, 193-196
resident commands 92
RS-232 47-50

Sci-Mate Manager 192-198, 267
Sci-Mate Searcher 168-172, 235-236
scripts 137-145
SCSI (Small Computer Systems Interface) 83
SDC 169, 179-180, 181

SDI (Selective Dissemination of Information) 105-106, 143-144, 171, 188

Search Helper 220-221
search languages 143-145, 163-164, 236-237
SearchMaster 179-180
search process 163-165
SearchWare 213-214
SearchWorks 181-191, 235, 240
security 204-207
semiconductor memory 73
serial 26-28
shells 107-109
signals 49-52
Silver Platter inc. 257
Smalltalk 94, 240
Smart Cable 48
Smartcom 49, 59-63, 126-134
Smithsonian 270-272
Social SciSearch 193-197
software selection 111-115
speed, modem 53-55, 58-59
spreadsheets 160-161
standards 19, 42, 47-53, 59-60, 76, 83
start bit 27
stop bit 27
subdirectories 93
Superkey 103-107
symbols 41-44
synchronous 27-28

telecommunications 42-59
telecommuting 21, 227
templates 187, 192
terminal mode 119-120
terminals 7-13
term selection 239-240
thermal printers 36
thesauri 77, 214
tone signaling 51-53
training 206-207, 237-238, 268
transient commands 92
truncation 171, 280
TSW 240-241
tutorials 169, 183-185, 206-207, 228-229, 237-238

UART 28
UNIX 90
uploading 100, 103-106, 125, 169, 177
user interface 93-94, 118-120, 240-241, 257-258, 269-270

Userlink 191
utilities 99-109

V.22bis 52
value added 261-273
videodiscs 252-253, 258, 270-272
video PATSEARCH 252, 257

weighting terms 240
Wells, H.G. 3
Wilsearch 223-228, 235
Wilsonline 223-224
World Brain 3-4
World Encyclopedia 3-4

Xerox 5, 21
XON/XOFF protocol 117

Zenith 20-21